Free Bonus $499 V

I0008639

12 Online Compliance Coaching
& First Year Membership In the
Business Technology Consumer Network.
See Details Inside.

Buy the book—Read the book—Get the free bonus offer!

I am so certain that you will benefit from the materials presented in this book that I am offering you a bonus valued at more than $499. Here is how it works: Check the BizTechNet.org website and complete the Modern Pirates login form using your company email address—your password will be the dollar amount listed on page 207. You will gain immediate access to the strategic software, compliance, and technology asset management strategies available only to members who have read the book. In addition to this free one year international membership, you will receive 12 issues of the exclusive "Modern Pirates Coaching Newsletter". This unique resource provides direct software compliance and life cycle management coaching strategies that you can use to save money on software assets as well as significantly reduce compliance risk.

Would you like a sample? At press time the United Kingdom announced the creation of a new, and massively powerful enforcement group—this time funded by British taxpayers: "A police unit dedicated to combating movie piracy and those responsible for the manufacture and distribution of pirated films has launched in London..." See the BizTechNet web site for a link to the BBC article. In a further quote, the unit will operate: "...In partnership with the Federation Against Copyright Theft (Fact), the new unit will pursue individuals and groups profiting from the sale of fake DVDs." Think this kind of strategy will not come to the States? Think again.

So? Come on! Join up with other corporate software and technology consumers from around the world—and down the block. Become part of the solution, instead of remaining a helpless victim. Help us change the industry.

This offer is subject to change without notice.
Please check the biztechnet.org web site for details and updates.

$50,000 Reward

MODERN PIRATES

Protect Your Company
From The Software Police

Alan L. Plastow

MODERN PIRATES

Protect Your Company
From The Software Police

Alan L. Plastow

Cover design and book layout by Bonnie Bushman
bbushman@bresnan.net

Morgan James Publishing, LLC
1225 Franklin Ave. Ste 325
Garden City, NY 11530-1693
800-485-4943
www.MorganJamesPublishing.com
info@MorganJamesPublishing.com

Habitat for Humanity®
Peninsula
Building Partner

Plastow, Alan L. 1953-
Modern Pirates/ Alan L. Plastow
ISBN 1-933596-39-2

DEDICATIONS

This book is dedicated to the memory of:

Lynn and Peg Plastow – You are always with us.

Also in memory of:

Garry Schwichtenberg – I'll miss you, my friend.

ACKNOWLEDGEMENTS

To the people who kept the faith and helped this project come together: My sincere thanks for all the hours of review, corrections, and insightful commentary. Any errors or omissions in the text have been, and will always be, mine.

Thanks to the following professional software asset managers for your advice on the manuscript, your excellent anti piracy insights, and your incredible confidence in my vision for this profession & industry.

Tom Wills – Software Asset Management Professional, Compliance Professional, Technology Asset Management Professional.

Rita Bowman of SoftwareManagers.org – Software Asset Management Professional, Compliance Professional, Technology Asset Management Professional.

Carolyn Hall – Certified Software Asset Manager, Certified Technology Asset Management Professional.

Mary Darren – Certified Software Asset Manager, Certified Technology Asset Management Professional

As well...

Ron Finklestein – Akris.net – Your personal & professional coaching and advice helped me move this project forward beyond the boundaries of the naysayers.

Todd Williams – Graduate Student of English, Kent State University – Thanks for time you spent editing and commenting on the initial manuscript.

Terry Shockling, Esq. – Thanks for your perspectives on piracy litigation events.

Robert Shockling, Esq. – Thanks for your unwavering confidence in my credibility.

Seth Breskin, Esq., of Meyers, Roman, Friedberg & Lewis – Thanks for your insightful commentary, advice, & editing skills.

Larry Bollough - Avid reader, reviewer, friend, & supporter of my many projects.

Lynn & Mike Lyons – Thanks for finding the invisible slip-ups in the text.

Alex Yu – Thanks to my technical guru and, more importantly, my friend.

Bryan & Kathy Corban for all the reading and for over thirty years of support and confidence.

Dan McMullen, Esq. for your advice, support, and encouragement through the strangest of times.

Chris & Sarah Pfendler – Thank you both for the support & friendship you have given me for over two decades.

And, finally, to my family – Alice, Thomas, Colleen, Alexis, & Nikki – Thank you for having the patience to realize that my consuming focus on researching and writing have, indeed, culminated in a tangible result.

If I have missed anyone, please accept my apologies and sincere thanks!

TABLE OF CONTENTS

If you own a business with two, or two million, computers it is critical that you understand your exposure to piracy litigation. If your company uses, or employees have access to, operating systems, software, graphics, fonts, music, games, or video, you are exposed to potential litigation. What should you look for to begin a proactive compliance assurance process? How do companies commit software suicide?

In the United States, there are over twenty-six distinct copyright enforcement entities monitoring copyrighted products that you use every day. Globally, the number reaches nearly ninety-four enforcement groups—watching your business. Who are they? Where are they? What do they do? Do they represent the government? Which ones should you consider a threat to your revenue stream?

What are the laws and regulations that guide and control your use of copyrighted products? Is a given law applicable on the local, national, or global level? How do the copyright holders and enforcement entities use legislation to further their goals? What penalties will you face when you are confronted for copyright violations or software non compliance? What can you do to lower your risks?

Chapter 4 - What Are The Software Police Looking For?

When you are confronted for piracy or software license non compliance, what are the auditors searching for? What is a forced compliance audit? What is a forced voluntary audit? What is the process for a vendor audit? What is a proactive compliance assurance audit and how can it prevent you from losing hundreds of thousands of dollars along with your business credibility?

Chapter 5 - Costly Communications Mistakes

What mistakes do companies tend to make when communicating with copyright holders or enforcement entities? How will these mistakes impact your company? What can you do to control communications and reduce the costs of a confrontation?

Chapter 6 - How Do I Conduct The Compliance Audit?

What are the steps in conducting a compliance audit? What are the differences between a reactive and proactive audit? What should you look for? What should you document? How do you maintain control of the process? What is a discovery tool? How can this process enable you to maintain control over your environment? How can you pay for all of this without impacting your bottom line?

Chapter 7 - What Is My Best Defense Against Piracy?

When is the best piracy or non compliance defense a good offense? What is an audit review team and how can they cut your exposure and costs? What is a wall of due diligence and how will one significantly reduce both piracy exposure and ongoing costs? What are the bricks in the wall of due diligence and how do you gain and retain control over them? How do you gain control over the ongoing compliance assurance process?

Chapter 8 - Paperwork And Peoplework

What do we mean by paperwork and peoplework? What makes each a critical concept in ongoing compliance assurance processes? How does dirty data impact piracy and compliance assurance? What is the difference between format and formutt? Precisely why is it so critical that you understand and practice the process of human change management? Why do policies tend to fail and how can you reverse the trend?

Chapter 9 - What Are My Reactive & Proactive Cost Savings Opportunities?

How can you convert piracy and compliance monitoring processes into ongoing cost savings opportunities? How do you initiate a low cost pilot study to determine your needs? How do you collect, process, and deliver data to justify your need for changing the way your company manages copyrighted products? What are some of the precise steps you can take to begin cutting costs—right away?

How can you make use of the information provided in this book to expand cost avoidance, ongoing savings, and cost reductions across the entire life cycle of your technology assets? How can standardizing the technology environment give you more control while significantly cutting your costs? Why is managing by exception so important? What mistakes does your company make in establishing and monitoring criteria? How would you use a half dozen more significant savings options?

Free Excerpt from Follow-up Book:

Second in the Real World Solutions Series, Agreements will give you a front line review of a wide range of license and agreement terms and conditions. Next, Agreements will discuss the meaning of each clause along with its impact on your company. Finally, Agreements will provide suggestions for modifying or eliminating strategic clauses to lower the negative impact or enhance the benefits of each.

Author's Introductory Note:

What are the differences in impact between piracy (non compliance) and un-managed software:

1. You will pay a significant amount of money in any piracy or non compliance event but, generally, you may only pay this amount once.
2. You will pay significantly more through not managing the life cycle of your software and technology assets, and you will pay this amount every single day until you bring the software asset management process under control.
3. The size of your company doesn't matter. You will lose the same basic proportion of your technology budget.

Are you controlling your software or is it controlling you?

For nearly a decade, technology asset managers have been asking me to write about my experiences in the fields of software licensing, piracy, and compliance. It seems like every time I step in front of a group of business professionals my questions and observations cause astonishment and reactions of acute frustration.

*   How can seemingly knowledgeable business people be so blind in terms of their business use and misuse of copyrighted products?
*   How can the copyright enforcement and software industries sue their own clients for literally millions of dollars and with such frequency, yet remain in business?

- Why is it that the vast majority of explanatory documentation regarding software licensing, piracy, compliance enforcement, and life cycle management is produced by the very companies that stand to gain the most from our collective errors?

- If the compliance enforcement and copyrighted products industries have been delivering so much anti piracy education, why is the very generation they've been targeting with all of that education apparently violating copyright with the most frequency?

- Why do companies continue to acquire over-priced software and other technology products that are bloated with overly complex and unnecessary features?

- What motivates companies to bind themselves to unfavorable software-related agreements with little or no attention to the terms and conditions of the documents?

- Why doesn't executive management realize how much money is being wasted on unnecessary technologies? More importantly, why don't they listen when asset managers point out purchasing or licensing alternatives?

I don't think any of us would deny that the computer and software industries have changed our world more dramatically than a vast majority of historical cultural and scientific evolutions. However, I believe that today we are at a significant, and apparently invisible, crossroads.

Through aggressive interpretations and use of local, national, and international copyright and intellectual property laws, a limited number of multinational corporations appears to be placing a noose on future technological growth and innovation.

Global corporate consumers of copyrighted technology products are caught up in an aggressive web of unnecessarily complex licensing as well as compliance and piracy litigation that is severely limiting their potential growth and development. Is all this controversy about intellectual property rights? Or is it about the sheer power to limit and control the future of that intellectual property?

This book will discuss, at length, the subjects of software and copyright piracy. You will gain knowledge of the enforcement entities that examine your companies on a regular basis. Discover how their systems of rewards and punishments ensure that companies of every size, in every country, will eventually become audit targets. Consider the legislation that the IP special interest groups have sponsored to give them the litigation power they wield with near draconian zeal. Review numerous industry-proven methodologies that you can use to protect your company from these nearly 100 global copyright enforcement entities. Learn how to implement a proactive wall of due diligence that will not only mitigate your risk but will actually contribute significantly to lowering your corporate technology life cycle costs.

You may not think that your company is involved in piracy or copyright violations but the chances are incredibly high that there are literally dozens of incorrectly licensed products on your company computers, PDAs, and cell phones. If your employees use, or have access to, operating systems, software, graphics, fonts, music, video, or games, you are exposed. If personnel access the Internet or utilize company owned notebook computers outside the office, you are exposed. Traditionally, the questions have vastly outnumbered the answers — until now. The answers are here, in *Modern Pirates*. I can virtually guarantee that you will find savings or cost avoidance concepts in these pages that, if implemented correctly, will enable you to save your company at least $30,000 and, in many cases, in excess of $250,000.

Not sure if you have incorrectly licensed
copyrighted products?

How much do you want to lose today?

Are you interested in reducing technology life cycle costs?

Are you interested in taking control of your
technology environment?

How much do you want to save today, tomorrow,
and every other day?

Chapter 1

What Is Piracy And What Are My Chances Of Being Accused?

Chapter Goals: First, we all absolutely have to know...

What is piracy?

How do we find ourselves labeled as pirates?

How do our computers, PDAs, and cell phones expose us to litigation?

What are the invisible piracy threats in every company?

How do our companies commit software suicide?

Pirates!

"People who have been stealing our movies believe they are anonymous on the Internet...They are wrong. We know who they are, and we will go after them..."

> Quote from Motion Picture Association of America
> President and CEO, Dan Glickman

Do you think you're safe from copyright piracy? Maybe *you* aren't a pirate, but would you know if someone in your company was using copyrighted products illegally? Your business is an easy target for the copyright enforcement industry. The sooner you come to grips with the risks and realities, the sooner you can plug the potential piracy holes. The hidden savings are impressive. The costs of failure are massive.

Pirates! To some the name breathes adventure and excitement. To others a pirate represents the ultimate violation of freedom and personal space. Like thieves in the night, pirates glide silently into our most fearsome dreams, taking what they want and leaving us with shattered lives—if we're lucky. On the high seas of the 16th century it was difficult to tell which crews were the pirates and which were the honest sailors. Rules changed as quickly as the rulers. The lines of ethical behavior often blurred, and one day's honest sailor could easily become the next day's pirate. Our world hasn't evolved much since the days of the buccaneers. The people who make the rules continue to change. The rules continue to change and the people who have ethics and who have worked hard for their money continue to pay the penalties for the actions of those who don't.

You may not be a pirate but you will *still* continuously pay the price for piracy.

Is this piracy?

Real World – A 2005 television commercial for an Internet music delivery service depicted a corporate employee who reacted to any question or confrontation by playing a burst of music on his desktop computer.

Is this piracy? Most likely. In fact, this *is* probably a form of piracy that's occurring in your company right this minute. Did the employee in the commercial clip above use the Internet to download the music in question or did he copy it from the original media of his own CDs? There are two basic problems here: While, technically, the music belongs to the employee, the computer where it is loaded belongs to the company.

According to the rules, only products that are legally acquired and licensed to the company may be placed on the system. Technically, the copyrights were violated the instant the employee placed the music on the corporate computer. What's more, copyrights, even for the most insignificant product, are strictly governed by federal and global laws. Let's take a look at the potential impact of this single employee's copyright violations.

A simple count of the number of tunes played by the employee during the commercial (5 of them), multiplied by a potential civil penalty of up to $150,000 per copyright will suggest a fraction of the probable financial risk of this single piracy incident. Do you suppose this company has an extra $750,000 to pay the copyright violation fines? But, wait: there's more! The average song consists of *two* copyrights—one for the music and one for the lyrics. Guess we'll have to multiply the number above by an additional factor of two. For those of us who are math-challenged (like me), the potential fine for five illegal music titles on a corporate computing device could easily total around $1,500,000.

Are you certain that there are no unlicensed music files, graphics, or software on any of your corporate computing devices? Using the figures above, could you estimate your possible financial exposure to incorrectly licensed copyrighted products on corporate computers? Try this potential measuring rule: the copyright enforcement industry informs us that a potential one in four computers will contain at least one violation. How many systems do you own? Divide by four. Multiply by $150,000.

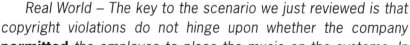

Real World – The key to the scenario we just reviewed is that copyright violations do not hinge upon whether the company **permitted** *the employee to place the music on the systems. In*

reality, that music is usually present **despite** those permissions. The majority of companies, even if they have any policies covering piracy usually do not enforce those policies.

Are you a pirate?

Simple Answer - You became a potential pirate the day you purchased your first computing device.

Complex Answer - Operating systems, software, music, graphics, games, fonts, and the complex copyright licensing agendas that control the way these products are used have drawn you into a vortex of potential piracy litigation. A vortex that continues to gain speed—propelling your company toward piracy violations, fines, and penalties.

There is an incredible disconnect occurring in the technology marketplace between the software consumers and the software publishers to the extent that many of those same publishers now regularly sue their own customers. The *forces of global justice* have gathered together a massive and powerful copyright police force tasked with protecting the world from the evils of intellectual property theft—piracy. Sounds like something out of Marvel Comics™, doesn't it? Lucky for us they don't wander around wearing purple tights. Unfortunately, their impact on our companies is all too real.

You may have heard of counterfeit designer consumer goods: jeans, perfumes, toys; the list is endless. Huge tonnages of pirated counterfeit goods are produced around the globe and distributed every day as genuine products. Real world pirates still board ships at sea, bent on stealing cargos and making substantial profits at our expense.

Who pays for piracy? We all do—consumers as well as suppliers—but, realistically, suppliers mostly transfer the burden to consumers through higher prices. Modern-day pirates are literally everywhere we look, stealing valid products as well as producing and distributing counterfeit goods of every description — products that we could easily purchase without realizing their origins. The concept with which we need to be concerned is that the anti piracy industry seems to have adopted an attitude assuming that *every* consumer is a pirate wanna-be.

Here's a stunning thought: you or some of your friends are probably already modern-day copyright pirates. Let me ask a question, would you know if you purchased a counterfeit product? Probably not. "Aye, matey! Bring yerself aboard the Bonne Homme Richard. Here be demons!"

Captain John Paul Jones welcomes you to *Pirates Anonymous*. Would you like a designer eye patch? Step right up to the mast and tell us your name, your company, and your chosen criminal activity. What's that you say? *I'm no pirate. I would never consider performing an illegal act.* Wrong. Here's why.

Let's forget about the guys with guns. Let's put aside the philosophical discussion of the incredibly wide range of world piracy activities or the links between piracy, organized crime, and global terrorism. What we need to consider is our real world day-to-day exposure to the potential illegal possession and use of copyrighted intellectual property products. In our case, let's limit the discussion to the primary violations of intellectual property rights — copyright piracy — that we encounter literally anywhere we find technology.

Every single day that you own computers, PDAs, cell phones, printers — even photo copiers — you are exposing yourself and your company to potential piracy litigation. Do your computers use operating systems or software? *You're exposed.* Do you or your employees listen to digital music on corporate computers? *You're exposed.* Does anyone in your company use licensed fonts or graphics? *You're exposed.* Is anyone downloading ring tones or other sound bites onto their computer, cell phone, or PDA? *You're exposed.* Is anyone copying licensed documents or images on the copy machine? *You're exposed.*

Is anyone taking advantage of the powerful corporate Internet connection to download digital movies? *You're exposed.*

---

*Real World – Corbis, a photo agency with over 3 million images, places a digital watermark in images marketed via the Internet. The watermark proved too easily defeated so the company began tracking the pixel patterns of its images. This pixel **fingerprint** enables the company to identify pirated copies of its copyrighted products.*

Does anyone in your company use graphics from the Internet (or anywhere else, for that matter) in presentations and printed materials? I'm not suggesting that you are currently guilty of violating copyrights, but it is time to understand that you are definitely exposed to significant risk. You do not have to actually *do* anything dishonest to be exposed to copyright violations. Somewhere, sometime, somebody is going to load a copyrighted product on one of your computing devices without ensuring proper licensing. Merely the presence of uncontrolled technologies in your company can be the same as living with a silently ticking litigation time bomb.

Enter the *software police*

"We have evidence that your company is engaged in the unlawful copying and use of our software in violation of the Copyright Act, Title 17 United States Code."

(First sentence of a software police audit letter.)

Congratulations! The fabled software police have just targeted your company, along with thousands of other businesses

---

of every size, for software piracy litigation. In fact, if you are the CEO or CFO, they may actually target you, personally, as the party responsible for corporate piracy. Yes, Virginia, they do exist, they rarely lose a confrontation, and you are about to receive a painful lesson in applied copyright law—a very expensive lesson that will shake your company and its public credibility to the core.

Real World

- *$564,350 – Settlement paid to the software police by an Ohio polymer products corporation for possession of incorrectly licensed software.*

- *$1,000,000 – Settlement paid to the Recording Industry Association of America by an Arizona technology company for the incorrectly licensed use of MP3 music titles.*

- *$2 Million Tuesday – Amount in piracy fines announced in the U.S. by a single software license compliance enforcement company on a single day in October, 2004.*

- *$100,000 – Fines paid by a private university in Pennsylvania for possession of incorrectly licensed software.*

- *$65 million – Total accumulated fines collected as of 4Q2004 by a single software publisher license enforcement team.*

- *$50,000 – Reward offered by an American software piracy enforcement company to whistle blowers for reporting companies for possessing and using incorrectly licensed software.*

Settlement: GA – Structural Engineering Co. - $127,327.09

(Due to hidden settlement fees, the conservative total cost of each of the audits you see throughout this book is estimated to exceed three to six times the published settlement.)

———————⌣———————

Is your company ready for a software license compliance audit? Would anyone in your company be completely familiar with the requirements of proving compliance? Do you know what documentation the enforcement entities expect you to produce? More importantly, does anyone know where all of the proper documentation is filed? Life has changed for the technology consumer since shortly before the infamous Y2K technology frenzy.

Revenue Streams – Between 1998 and 2003, software sales in developed countries significantly tapered off. Economies flexed dynamically with the changes in the century and in technology implementation growth. Corporate consumers had finally concluded building their initial technology infrastructures. Most companies were concentrating on making more effective use of the technologies they already had in place rather than blindly buying into **the next big thing***. Software industry profits, while still high, diminished and copyright holders began looking for new revenue streams. Copyright compliance enforcement activities increased while ever more complex licensing schemas began to emerge to tap into additional sources of revenue. Piracy litigation became a significant recognized revenue stream.*

Settlement: AZ – Civil Engineering Firm - $228,709.95

Whether you own two computers or two million computers, you and your company are exposed every day to the potential for illegal possession and use of copyrighted products. This exposure isn't a matter of corporate size. In terms of copyright violations, company size is irrelevant. Instead, piracy is a symptom of an overall lack of control—control over your technology environment—the failure to proactively manage technology assets. Do you know—absolutely know—what software or other copyrighted products your company uses? Few of us do, or far worse, many who believe they are compliant tend to base those claims merely on a technology employee giving their unfounded opinion that corporate use of copyrighted materials is perfectly legal.

Hint: Don't rely on personal opinions regarding copyright compliance. They are useless in a piracy litigation event. For the most part, the majority of our business personnel are (unfortunately) clueless when it comes to the realities of discovering, removing, or preventing copyright violations. Thousands of corporations become victims of this lack of understanding every year.

Real World –

"On average, at least one company is caught and confronted with threat of legal proceedings every business day."

Attorney for Microsoft ™ Corporation

This statement represents the experience of only one of the multitude of enforcement entities working the anti piracy landscape. Think about your environment in relation to this statistic.

Settlement: CA – Media Services Co. - $145,000

Will today be your day to become a target of the software police? The reality of this question is that it's not a matter of *if* you will be audited but of *when* you will be audited. Please remember that statement—it is critical to your company.

Let's take a quick test of how you might prepare for a software piracy audit. Try answering the following questions with only *quantifiable* answers—answers that can be clearly supported by documentation. Keep in mind that best guess figures will indicate that your process is not effective—nor will it be legally defensible.

- Can you or your company produce a clear and detailed purchase trail for every operating system, software application, licensed font, licensed graphic, copyrighted music title, game, or video title on every computer, PDA, or cell phone you possess?

- Can you produce a current automated audit that accurately documents the presence and location of every copyrighted product on every computer?

- Can you prove that the software titles you possess are not counterfeit?

- Are your receipts properly detailed and are they from valid suppliers?

- Can you produce the proper documents, stamps, seals, or certificates of authenticity for any applicable products in your possession?

- Can you produce all of your licenses and their respective terms and conditions of use?

Let's pretend that you have already been targeted for non compliance and you have less than thirty days to acquire and present this information. What are your real world chances of collecting and detailing the data for every software title on every system in your possession? Can I make a prediction? Slim to none?

Settlement: CA – HVAC Co. - $65,000

An incredible number of businesses have been where you are. Very few of us can honestly and accurately answer these questions. We never had to. See what I mean by clueless? It isn't that software consumers are ignorant. Instead, the rules for documentation and for compliance assurance have changed and we somehow weren't effectively notified. Unfortunately for the consumer, our ability to accurately answer questions such as these directly determines our chances of being targeted for—and losing—a piracy audit by the software police or copyright cops.

> In early 2002, I began advising companies to actively monitor systems for, and remove, unauthorized music or sound files. At the time there was very little overt enforcement activity for these copyrighted works but it was clear that changes were approaching. Those companies that listened to the warnings were ahead of the enforcement curve when the recording industry began its copyright crackdowns.

As of the first quarter of 2005, there is no *direct* evidence that the copyright enforcement industries are actively auditing the licenses for copyrighted products on corporate PDAs or cell phones. Yet, corporate consumers have to remember that every one of these devices contains, or could contain, copyrighted operating systems, software, music, fonts, graphics, video, and games. Violations in these two technologies represent a huge potential untapped revenue stream for the copyright holders. How long do you think it will be before the enforcement industry figures out how to cash in? Wake up and get your company proactive.

Settlement: CA – IT & Advisory Services Co. - $104,000

What is piracy?

Simple Answer - Piracy is the illegal duplication, distribution, possession, and/or use of copyrighted products such as operating systems, software applications, graphics, licensed fonts, music, games, or video titles.

Complex Answer - In general, there are two distinct arenas of piracy: intentional (criminal offenses) and unintentional (civil offenses). Nearly every business is guilty at some level of unintentional piracy (*don't panic, yet*). Many others are guilty of intentional piracy. Here's how it generally works.

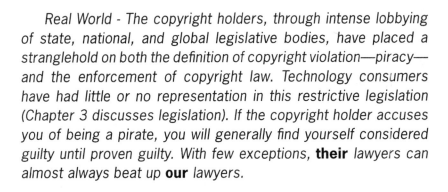

*Real World - The copyright holders, through intense lobbying of state, national, and global legislative bodies, have placed a stranglehold on both the definition of copyright violation—piracy— and the enforcement of copyright law. Technology consumers have had little or no representation in this restrictive legislation (Chapter 3 discusses legislation). If the copyright holder accuses you of being a pirate, you will generally find yourself considered guilty until proven guilty. With few exceptions, **their** lawyers can almost always beat up **our** lawyers.*

Lobbying in the Federal Government - FY2003

Computer Software Industry - $30.5 million

(Including)

Microsoft - $8.7 million

Oracle - $1.7 million

(Source: USA Today)

(Ongoing stats are available at: www.opensecrets.org)

Settlement: CA – Wholesale Distributor - $205,791.70

Intentional Piracy

When an individual or group reproduces, uses, and/or distributes as genuine, unauthorized duplicates of copyrighted products for financial gain and with intent to defraud, the act is considered intentional piracy. Technology and the Internet have opened highly lucrative opportunities for the true pirates of the world. It has become a relatively simple matter to illegally duplicate software master media, CDs, and DVDs. Printing technologies have enabled counterfeiters to precisely duplicate licensing documentation; complex documents, stamps, seals, or certificates of authenticity; proofs of purchase; master media labels; and packaging. Counterfeit product is readily available and, once in place, very nearly invisible.

Quite frankly, the copyright holders themselves sometimes have difficulties identifying the fake products from the genuine. If these experts can't tell the difference, how can you? (See brief in Chapter 6) Yet, if the software police or any member of the copyright enforcement industry can target your company as a consumer of counterfeit or incorrectly licensed products, they can hold you accountable for violations of state, federal, and/or global copyright laws. It is critical for you to keep in mind that even a marginally talented modern pirate can duplicate and distribute millions of dollars worth of counterfeit products in a home garage, quickly and cheaply, then disappear before law enforcement can build a case. You, the consumer, *will* be left holding the bag.

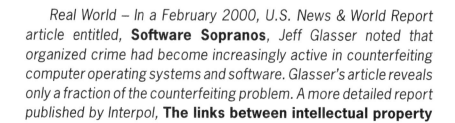

Real World – In a February 2000, U.S. News & World Report article entitled, **Software Sopranos***, Jeff Glasser noted that organized crime had become increasingly active in counterfeiting computer operating systems and software. Glasser's article reveals only a fraction of the counterfeiting problem. A more detailed report published by Interpol,* **The links between intellectual property**

Settlement: CA – Auto Parts Co. - $70,000

crime and terrorist financing, *highlights the enormous global scope of counterfeiting operations. In reality, counterfeiting is often considered much more lucrative than selling drugs because enforcement activities are not as rigid and counterfeiters face no significant jail time if caught.*

We'll assume that if you are engaged in any of the previous activities you are well aware that you are violating the law and you are reading these pages to make yourself more proficient at your chosen trade. A bit of advice: quit it. You're making life difficult for the rest of us. (*Sure* — that'll *slow those nasty pirates down!*)

A significant number of companies and individuals allow themselves to fall into the realm of intentional piracy when they knowingly make, acquire, or use illegal copies of operating systems, software, fonts, graphics, music, games, or video titles. In their efforts to save money, or merely through an inappropriate personal conviction that what they are doing is acceptable, consumers entrap themselves and become guilty of piracy.

As the users of technology, we have virtually no control over the people who actually generate and distribute pirated products. However, simply because we can't control these individuals doesn't mean we're not directly affected by them.

Real World – In 2005, the U.S. Department of Justice, the FBI's Cyber Division, and law enforcement entities from 10 countries participated in Operation Site Down, conducting over 90 searches in the 10 countries and multiple states, and investigating over 120 individuals involved in an enormous online piracy, and counterfeit distribution ring. This ring was responsible for making and selling

illegal copies of software, music, and video titles valued at over
$50 million.

(Link: http://www.cybercrime.gov/OperationSiteDown.htm)

The question we each need to ask, here, is: who purchased the counterfeit copies that these pirates produced? The answer: any of us can easily acquire these products without knowing they are counterfeit. Even if we purchase these products from a legitimate dealer we can still easily find ourselves guilty of receiving and possessing counterfeit goods. If we can't prove that we didn't know the goods were counterfeit we expose ourselves to charges of criminal piracy.

Unintentional Piracy

Unintentional piracy is more subtle. This form of copyright violation is usually accidental or occurs without our knowledge. In my experience, unintentional piracy (or the appearance of it) is one of the most frequently recurring forms of copyright violation in businesses of all sizes. A distinct lack of background knowledge on the parts of those personnel who manage software and related products exposes companies to dozens of accidental copyright violations. This lack of knowledge and understanding is complicated even more by a consistent failure of executive management to provide the tools and *active* empowerment necessary to effectively manage the most commonly pirated products.

*While performing training programs in over forty cities in multiple countries I have found that a distressing majority of companies very carefully **appear** to monitor compliance with copyright regulations. In reality, this appearance is frequently a sham. The actual efforts are thin veneers of false due diligence. Does*

Settlement: CA – Educational Software Co. - $56,479.12

*your company merely **appear** to be monitoring systems? Are you committed to protecting your respective assets or are you seriously monitoring copyright compliance?*

Keep in mind that in our day-to-day world unintentional piracy is only a symptom of a more complex enterprise technology life cycle management problem. Quite simply, we become victims of piracy because we fail to control our software, our computing devices, and the actions of the people using those devices. This unfortunate lack of control contributes directly to our easy target status in the vast majority of piracy enforcement activities. The best way to prevent piracy litigation is by proactively gaining and retaining control over your technology environment.

*Receipts can kill. If your purchase receipts do not comply with the standards of the individual copyright holder, you can be guilty of non compliance—even though you legally purchased genuine products. The majority of settlements I have encountered frequently hinged upon the existence and quality of the purchase receipts. The secret? Every entity of the software police looks at receipts in a slightly different way; **you** have to cover **all** potential forms of receipt, documents, stamps, seals, or certificates of authenticity, and proofs of purchase because you will never know which entity is going to audit you. (More on this problem, as well as ways to correct it, in Chapter 6.)*

Is my company exposed?

All right, I'll cut you a break. Maybe you aren't a pirate. Maybe you, like millions of others, have absolutely no idea how you should be managing soft technology assets such as computer operating systems, software applications, licensed graphics, licensed fonts, music, games, or video titles. Maybe you, like millions of others, never realized how the technology and entertainment industries' copyright enforcement activities have accelerated in recent years. The bottom line—incorrect licensing practices and uncontrolled use of copyrighted materials have spawned a lucrative anti piracy enforcement industry. There is plenty of essentially easy money to be made confronting clueless corporate consumers for license non compliance, copyright violations, and piracy.

If nearly one in four corporate computers contains at least a single incorrectly licensed product, it is altogether too easy for corporate consumers to slip up. How are we going to lock all of these systems down to prevent mistakes yet still function as a corporate entity? Now, I'm sure we all agree it's a no-brainer that we can't operate our businesses without giving people access to technologies, right? Absolutely. So, if we are going to permit people to use these technologies, our only realistic option for avoiding piracy issues is to focus more closely on controlling the technologies themselves—not so much the people.

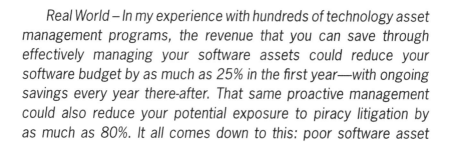

Real World – In my experience with hundreds of technology asset management programs, the revenue that you can save through effectively managing your software assets could reduce your software budget by as much as 25% in the first year—with ongoing savings every year there-after. That same proactive management could also reduce your potential exposure to piracy litigation by as much as 80%. It all comes down to this: poor software asset

Settlement: CA – Specialty Retailer - $60,000

management doesn't merely make your company an easy target. Poor software and technology management contribute to huge unnecessary costs that repeat on virtually a daily basis until you gain control over the entire life cycle of the assets.

Famous last words

"My computer people have it covered. This company has no problems with copyright." I have heard this statement from executive management in hundreds of businesses. The assumption is that the technology experts of your company are effectively monitoring the use of licensed products. The reality is that you are inadvertently placing huge faith in the wrong hands. In doing so, you significantly risk your corporate credibility along with generous sums of money every day that this simple misconception continues. Technical people understand technology. Their job is to get technologies installed, get them operational, and keep them that way.

News Flash: Most technical people have very little clue regarding the complex ways in which license terms and conditions work. What's more, technical people change jobs with distressing regularity, usually leaving behind minimal data describing the systems they maintained. Consultants and other outside technical experts often have uncontrolled access to computing systems. These outsiders could place virtually anything on your computers and you would have no record of the action. In a piracy event, the owner of the computer is liable, not the technician nomad—not the system users. Technical people also tend to be a bit on the ineffective side when it comes to keeping paperwork. Keep in mind that these are the folks who are assuring you that every copyrighted product is being used according to the license terms. I have massive respect for technical personnel—I used to be one. But, when it comes to piracy litigation, reliance on undocumented assurances

---

Settlement: CA – eBusiness Consulting Co. $77,580

is like living in a house of cards — when the winds of copyright enforcement blow, you won't like the results. Keep the techies doing techie things. What you need is, pardon the phrase, a *Software Nazi*.

The Software Nazi

Software Nazi. Isn't this a scary concept? Think for a moment of all the negative connotations that this second word calls to mind. Are you hearing the *Jaws* theme, yet? In corporations across the United States the resident Software Nazi (SWN) is frequently the only person in-house who remotely understands the company exposure to piracy litigation. This phrase came about because, once upon a time, many companies were at least partially emphatic about monitoring the copyrighted products under their control and they appointed some poor defenseless human being to monitor software use.

The SWN is generally an overworked, underpaid, undertrained, unsupported, and definitely under-appreciated female who was literally drafted into the job. (*Sorry, ladies, but in my experience you* are *usually the ones who get stuck with this one.*) The vital roles these unfortunates play include those of being aware of, and internally enforcing, copyright. When they perform their duties well, fellow employees begrudgingly and semi-humorously refer to them as Software Nazis. In reality, the majority of these enforcers spend much of their time in futile argument with other employees, management, and, frequently, the many techies who chose to ignore copyright.

———⌣———

Real World – Have you heard this one? "We absolutely had to have that software package today so we went ahead and loaded it using another department's master CD. When we have time, we'll buy the extra license." Most frequently, the technicians never

find that time; the additional license is never purchased; and the
company is exposed to yet another piracy violation.

Another phrase used in referring to the corporate SWN is
scapegoat. Thanks to some of our more emphatic friends in
the legal profession, companies have been led to believe that
the mere existence of a resident SWN will protect them from
litigation for copyright violations. The thinking goes something like this: "If we are audited, we can point to our due
diligence efforts and claim that we are performing the necessary actions." Or, a more common attitude is, "We can blame
the SWN for not doing their job." Wrong. In reality, since you
are ignoring the reports of these internal sentinels, you could
actually be expanding your copyright infringement instances
from civil offenses — unintentional — to criminal offenses — intentional.

Real World – In the US, criminal violation of copyright—
willful violation with intent to defraud—carries a penalty of up
to $250,000 and up to five years incarceration. Civil copyright
violations—unintentional—carry a fine of up to $150,000. Both
penalties are **per copyrighted title infringed.** *(There is some*
minor good news regarding the actual application of penalties
but, for now, we'll limit our discussion to the potential maximum
fines.)

Are we the good guys, or the bad guys?

There is another Software Nazi mentality that we need to
consider. The external SWNs work for the industries that produce copyrighted works. Their job is to locate and confront

Settlement: MA – Public School System - $78,927.90

companies as well as individuals that violate copyright. Virtually every major software publisher has a license enforcement group, as do the music, licensed font, graphics, gaming, and film industries. The software industry, alone, has more than twenty-six investigative groups operating in the United States. They are aggressively looking for and confronting copyright violators and, in many cases, leveraging *any* license violations. These software police invest tens of millions of dollars in advertising actively encouraging your own employees to report your company via toll free confidential telephone lines — complete with substantial rewards for information (*Up to $50,000*). Many consumers suggest that this "report your boss" concept has directly likened these anti piracy operations to another special interest group in Europe in the 1940s that aggressively used the same basic tactic of setting people up to report the activities of their friends and neighbors. Scary, and somewhat distasteful, isn't it?

Your risks of direct exposure for illegal possession and use are based on the investigative practices and tactics of this controversial and often confrontational copyright enforcement industry. These folks are very active and they enforce their copyrights with near-microscopic focus. If you incorrectly use their products, you easily become an audit target. If you violate their copyright willfully, they have every right to challenge you with criminal charges — and they should.

Phrases and terms can be frustratingly interchangeable.

<u>Compliance</u> – Should mean that you are following the terms and conditions of the license agreement. It should also apply to both parties in the contract. Unfortunately, in practice, neither is quite true.

<u>Non Compliance</u> – Almost always means that the

> consumer is failing to follow the terms and conditions of the license.
>
> _Piracy_ – Another form of the consumer failing to follow the terms and conditions of the license. Unfortunately, this term seems to be being applied rather indiscriminately to nearly every license violation.
>
> _Counterfeiting_ – Technically, as noted previously, this should be the intentional duplication and/or distribution with intent to defraud. Unfortunately, it has become a bit of a catch phrase.
>
> _Copyright Violation_ – Yet one more form of consumers failing to follow the terms and conditions of the license.

The most effective way to estimate your exposure to a potential piracy confrontation is to honestly survey your environment. Commonly pirated products include commercial operating systems, software, music, licensed fonts, graphics, games, and video. (_I'll keep listing these until you remember them in your sleep. It's_ that _important._) In the enforcement industry, a user is generally said to be in violation of copyright if they are out of compliance, or non compliant, with the terms and conditions of their license. An individual or company found to be non compliant is very frequently referred to by the copyright enforcement industry as being guilty of piracy.

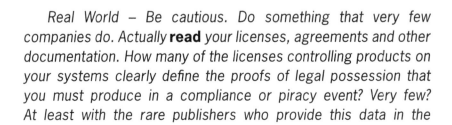

Real World – Be cautious. Do something that very few companies do. Actually **read** your licenses, agreements and other documentation. How many of the licenses controlling products on your systems clearly define the proofs of legal possession that you must produce in a compliance or piracy event? Very few? At least with the rare publishers who provide this data in the

---

Settlement: MA – Fund Raising Firm - $175,000

license agreement, you know where you stand. The remaining publishers—the ones that do not detail compliance assurance requirements—can change their compliance requirements at will—and they do. (We'll cover this topic much more extensively in Chapter 6.)

Think about your environment in relation to this lack of licensing clarity. Will today be your day to be challenged to produce compliance documentation you weren't aware you needed to retain—maybe even never received?

Real World – In an audit event, a software publisher has been known to demand only documents proving authenticity when confronting a company. Then, in another audit event, the same publisher might demand to see receipts, or maybe they'll just ask for the licenses and install baseline. Another tactic used by some copyright holders is to include a clause in the license permitting the publisher to change licensing terms & conditions at any time, provided the changes are posted **out there somewhere** *on a web site. Unless you* **lock in the expectations**—*in writing—during license negotiations—before you pay the invoice—the compliance assurance rules can, and do, change at any time.* **You** *will be the loser.*

Piracy risks in your company

To get an idea of your own piracy risks, try determining how many of the following conditions are present in your company. These very basic potential licensing issues can directly expose you to piracy litigation. They include, but are not limited to:

- *External Hard Disk Loading* – This practice occurs when a hardware supplier places illegal software on a computer then delivers the system to the user. I've seen hundreds of instances of undocumented–pirated?–products placed on systems by providers. Sometimes these are blatantly illegal copies placed to increase profits. Systems providers caught performing this practice are regularly confronted by software publishers and heavily fined, as they should be. However, the usually unsuspecting computer consumer suffers when copyright holders use the hardware provider's own customer list to confront users with additional litigation for possessing illegal software titles. Any chance that you have this problem?

- *Internal Hard Disk Loading* – Internal loading occurs when your own (or external) personnel mass-configure systems with a master image containing incorrectly licensed titles. Remember the techies who had no clue how licensing actually works? They could very easily place illegal software on systems without realizing the error. Sometimes, however, these instances become more deadly still when they consist of perfectly legal copies of fully functional, but time limited, trial products. Could this happen in your company?

- *Shareware* – Shareware is a great deal but its illegal use is one example of the practices above. With shareware, the consumer has license to try the product for a limited time period. At the end of that period, the consumer must *either purchase* the product *or remove* it from the computer. If you do not fully uninstall the product from the computer when the period expires, you could very easily find yourself in violation of the license. There is no question in my mind—you *will* find unlicensed shareware on systems. Hint: check for zip/unzip products such as WinZip. These are some of the more frequently violated licensed products. In mid-2005, WinZip changed ownership. The new company issued a statement that they would be tightening up on licensing. What are the chances that you have WinZip on your systems? Look again.

- *Soft Disk Loading* – Soft disk loading occurs when a hardware provider includes legal copies of shareware, or trial software, on a buyer's computers. Often these products are provided as bonuses or special deals. Unfortunately for most companies, the titles tend to quickly become invisible. After all, we're not using it so why should we take the time to uninstall it, right? Wrong. This simple mistake is widespread and results in direct exposure to potential piracy accusations when the trial period expires and the hidden product illegally remains on systems. Do you have shareware-style products on your systems?

- *Upgrade Licenses* – You may recall seeing upgrade licensed products on store shelves. These licenses are significantly less expensive to acquire. This makes them prime targets for incorrect licensing—piracy. There are generally two types of upgrades. Version upgrades are used to urge the customer to stay with a given product line as it changes over time. The provider wants you to buy this latest improved release of a product you already have. Competitive upgrades are used to encourage users of competitive products to switch their allegiance. In both cases, the license terms and conditions are very strict regarding both how the purchase may be made and the precise documentation that the buyer must have in place before and after the purchase. Very few companies understand the rules behind upgrade li-

Settlement: OH – Computer Sales Co. - $984,000

censing and frequently fall victim to this violation. In addition, very few retailers will ensure that the consumer is legally entitled to an upgrade license prior to permitting the purchase. Although this makes sense because it isn't a task they are suited to monitor, these retailers significantly contribute to your real world risks of possessing illegally licensed products. Do you have any upgrade licenses in-house?

- *Academic Licensing* – These licenses, generally offered to college students, faculty, or staff, are significantly less expensive than general licenses. However, they cannot be used privately or for commercial purposes. In early 2003, I conducted a license review for a major research corporation and discovered that a very scary number of licenses were academic versions. It seems the CEO was also a professor and bought the products from the campus bookstore. We repurchased the proper licenses, but this could have represented a massive negative compliance event. (*Be careful, though, I have also seen* multiple *instances of resellers delivering Academic licenses—in error, I hope—to corporations that do not qualify—instant invisible violation.*)

- *Softlifting* – A so-called softlifting or sneaker net violation occurs when a company purchases a single legal copy of a product and then loads the product on more than one computer. This intentional practice is common in, but by no means limited to, small to medium size businesses. In my experience, architects, engineers and academics tend to make this serious mistake because they frequently see no problem with sharing software. (*Don't rush out and accuse these folks on your staff without checking to see if your corporate culture matches my experiences.*) Softlifting violations are some of the most frequent reasons behind a piracy audit because many personnel do not understand, or don't care, that

---

Settlement: OH – Computer Sales Co. - $60,000

they are violating federal law by sharing copyrighted materials (*Unless, of course* they *are the holder of the copyright.*). Do your personnel share software?

- *Bundle Breaking* – Bundle breaking is another of the more frequent piracy violations. Many corporations do not realize that it is illegal to break up and redistribute the individual software titles that come bundled in a suite. It is perfectly legal to load only a single application from a bundle onto a computer provided the user shelves all the other titles, retaining them for use only on that same computer. Loading the separate titles from a single bundle onto different computers is not merely a single copyright violation. Bundle breaking represents a separate violation for each individual copyrighted product in the suite—plus an additional violation for the overall suite copyright. Is anyone manipulating bundled software on your systems?

- *Internet Piracy* – Internet piracy occurs when a consumer downloads illegal software from the Internet. Keep in mind that there are perfectly legal download sites, but it is very easy to fall victim to illegal sites masquerading as valid distributors. Unlicensed or incorrectly licensed downloads represent a serious threat to ethical software consumption and should be very closely restricted in a corporate environment. Do you permit—or do you control—Internet downloads?

- *Shrink Wrap* – The shrink wrap license is the license included inside the box of software and related products when purchased in small license counts – most commonly a single license. The licenses in these plastic-wrapped boxes are considered the most unfavorable license agreements a company can acquire. As a result, the consumer is rarely aware of the full range of usage limitations that are put in place once the license is activated by opening the box. Shrink wrap licenses represent very common softlifting violations. Do you purchase shrink wrap software? If so, I would strongly recommend that you stop. Shrink wrap is considered the least cost-effective and least favorable software license purchase you can make. Negotiate every license to ensure you have rights under the contract.

- *Click Wrap* – With the growth of the Internet came the interesting license format of click wrap. Quite simply, a click wrap takes effect in two potential ways. First, when the person performing an Internet download is asked to agree to the license before completing the download. Second, when a technician installing a software application or product is asked to click a license box to continue the install. Both of these licenses carry substantial risk to the consumer, the most significant being that these licenses are rarely read by qualified personnel (or, for that matter, anyone at all). As well, click wrap licenses are frequently difficult or impossible to print. As a result, an employee has no clue that the license they are electronically signing binds the company to the terms and conditions of an undocumented mystery license. How would you identify click wrap licensed products?

- *Client Access Licenses* – The famous CAL can represent a not so subtle way to increase revenue by requiring users to purchase a client license for any computer that accesses a given networked application or server. In discussions with hundreds of qualified software asset managers and technical licensing specialists I have yet to find more than a handful who actually understood CALs. Makes you wonder if someone once commented, *"Let's see: if we can devise a licensing schema that is so complicated that no one can understand it, we can virtually guarantee additional copyright violation revenue."* Do your people understand CALs? How much are you willing to bet? CAL violations occur with incredible frequency in licensing disputes.

- *Network License* – Network violations generally occur when a company breaches the license by distributing a non-network application over a network. An additional instance of network license violation occurs when a company distributes more copies of a network software title than it has license to use. Are your network license counts correct?

- *Concurrent Use* – Concurrent use licenses permit the consumer to access a clearly defined set number of active users all at one time. For example, under a concurrent agreement a company with one hundred computers can purchase only twenty licenses for concurrent use by any twenty people. The twenty-first person wanting to use the software must wait until one of the existing users closes the program and frees up a license. Consumers violate this licensing process by allowing more users to access the product at one time than the license permits. Are concurrent limitations in place?

- *Licensed Fonts* – Some font packages are licensed—copyrighted—by their developers. Licensed fonts are frequently licensed to a specific individual computer or printer. Many are tied directly to a particular software application. Do you know where every licensed font is located in your company and are they carefully tracked? These products also tend to become invisible and are easily overlooked—until you are audited.

- *Graphics* – Many graphics are copyrighted and can only be used in a narrow range of operations before the user must pay a royalty. Review all graphics—especially those used by personnel developing their own presentations. Eliminate unnecessary graphics and carefully license any graphics that are deemed necessary to the operation of your company. Additional hint: Licensing

Settlement: CA – Landscape Architect Firm - $63,222

for royalty free graphics can change at any time and a formerly free graphic can become licensed. Are you monitoring graphics?

- *Music* – The recording industry has stepped up its piracy enforcement activities across the globe. If an employee downloads music from the Internet, or copies music from personal CDs, your company is liable for every title found on company computers. Remember the commercial?

- *Video* – Thanks to the considerable power of a corporate Internet connection, illegal movie downloads have soared since 2000. In the average company there should be very few legitimate videos present on corporate systems. What is your method of identifying those that are properly licensed and eliminating all others?

Do you have complete control over every one of these licensed products? Are you in the group of consumers that permits license compliance to slip to the back burner? It's easy to find out. Try another quick litmus test. Ask yourself:

- Do we acquire software from non-standard dealers or on-line auction sites? Do we buy operating systems, or any other copyrighted products, from a guy named Vinnie over at the auto parking lot? (*No kidding. This type of purchase happens very frequently.*)

- Are the computing devices we purchase delivered with preloaded software? Are other copyrighted products present? Do we clearly license and document all of these titles? Show me the paperwork.

- Do we have a standard corporate image for specific computing devices? Is every product present on that image fully licensed and documented?

- Do we maintain and follow clear summaries of the terms and conditions of every license for every copyrighted product on our business computing devices? Show me.

Settlement: FL – Architecture Firm - $150,000

- Can we document precisely how many computing devices the company owns that can contain potentially illegal copyrighted products? Do we know where each device is located, who uses it, and which products are present on each device? Let me see the report.

- Do our employees or technicians bring software from home? Screen savers? Games? Greeting card creators? Utilities?

- Are there shareware products still on our company computers beyond the grace period? Show me the audit report.

- Has anyone downloaded music or sound clips from the Internet or copied music CDs onto company computing devices? Video? Licensed graphics?

- Have any of our employees, consultants, temps, or their children performed any of the actions above? What controls do we have in place?

Are you are getting the picture? There are dozens of questions we could apply here. Consider the previous bulleted lists. How many of these activities apply to your company? Most of them? If you could dramatically reduce your exposure to piracy litigation by doing so, how many of these activities could you change right now? If you could cut technology life cycle costs and improve the return on your investments, would technology asset management make sense?

> *You could ignore every other recommendation in this book but, if you take only enough time to act upon the previous lists, you will still drastically reduce your company exposure to piracy litigation while increasing your software asset management efficiencies. Keep in mind that eliminating even a single*

> *incorrectly licensed copyrighted product from your environment can mitigate your exposure by as much as $150,000.*

The primary keys to preventing piracy in your environment are to ensure that the entire company is aware of the realities of piracy and to remove as many of the opportunities for error as possible. Effectively addressing these questions is a pretty good beginning. The proper use of copyrighted products is critical to the finances, credibility, and even continued existence of the company.

Real World – A Pennsylvania company permitted its employees to bring their children to work on weekends. The company set aside a room with a television, toys, and a computer for the kids. Within weeks, well-meaning parents had loaded the computer with over thirty software applications and games for their children. Since the company owned the computer but did not legally own these thirty copyrighted products, each illegally loaded title became a direct piracy risk. Let's see, thirty times $150,000... .

Kindly step up onto this chair and place your neck in this noose

Think you're not exposed? Think again. The software licenses and agreements that your personnel have bound the company to, *even when they didn't realize they were doing so*, are considered permissive legal documents. This means that the copyright holder gives you very specific permissions in the license regarding how you are allowed to use the software or other copyrighted product. If the license doesn't give you permission to use the product in the manner you are using it — you are in violation of the agreement — you have breached the contract. Technically, you could easily have become a pirate.

Real World – The majority of software licenses contain a "right to audit" clause. This means that any, or all, of the 26-94+ software publisher audit or other enforcement entities representing the copyrighted products on your computers, can audit your company at any time. Each entity can, and will, audit you repeatedly if you are found in violation—often for a period of 3 to 5 years after the initial piracy audit.

*Each enforcement entity only has to look at your environment once to punish you. You have to monitor that environment **every single day** to avoid their attentions.*

Consistently, we consumers do it to ourselves. We agree to licenses, clauses, terms, and conditions without carefully considering the limitations that these same agreements place on our environment and corporate culture. If the license doesn't fit our environment or intended use — and very few of them do — we assume that we can merely move forward with the product and the publisher won't mind our little changes. Wrong. They *will* mind, but usually not until after we have signed the license and committed the infraction. This is a hard issue to confront but maybe we should add a third type of pirate: the clueless pirate. If we do not become collectively more aware of the issues involved in acquiring, licensing, and managing copyrighted works, we will have no clue which laws

Settlement: KY – Civil Engineering Co. - $157,654

we are violating. Comfy? Good. Now, kick the chair out from under your feet. Thank you.

Software Suicide: You're guilty

Would you like to know how I can tell that you are probably a pirate? Clairvoyance aside, the solution is simple observation. I have yet to find a company that closely monitors *all* the terms and conditions of *every* licensed product on *every* computing device. If you haven't accomplished this task, you can't possibly be in compliance with the permissions granted in all of those licenses. Certain members of the software publishing, music, graphics, font, gaming, and film industries have no reservations about using highly complex licensing agreements to confront companies for non compliance — illegal use of the copyrighted product. Like it or not, the bottom line is that you or another company employee agreed to the terms of the license when you acquired the product. You gave the copyright holder permission to audit you.

Companies commit software suicide on a daily basis when they acquire copyrighted products that may, or may not, perform the functions for which they were purchased. These same products are controlled by licenses that are distinctly unfavorable to the consumer — licenses that we frequently do not negotiate. According to industry technology managers over 70% of all software licenses are not negotiated by the consumer. This statistic, combined with an almost complete lack of knowledge of existing license terms and conditions, virtually ensures that the average software consumer breaches a license contract nearly every time they blink — software suicide.

Remember that piracy litigation represents a significant revenue stream for the copyright holders — a revenue stream that is, like the true mass of an ocean-bound iceberg, virtually hidden from public view.

Settlement: NJ – Software Development Co. - $175,000

Think you understand the industry?

Each of us is a victim of our assumptions. When it comes to copyright compliance, false assumptions can very quickly destroy us. Don't get me wrong, the copyright holders have every right to enforce their copyright and I will support their rights throughout this book. Intentional piracy is a crime and should be policed very carefully. However, the single-mindedness of the copyright enforcement industry — the software police — has repeatedly reached beyond mere enforcement and deeply into our collective pockets. I am constantly astounded that many representatives of the collective software police have labeled people who question their tactics as "...*malcontents who want to get away with stealing software.*"

Real World – When I conducted a software life cycle training program in Sidney, Australia in 2004, a member of one of the compliance enforcement companies was invited to speak. When the attendees questioned the validity of the statistics this individual presented, he grew upset. It seems that no one was permitted to challenge the credibility of the statistics. As he left the room, he commented to my assistant to the effect that the attendees were: '...malcontents who want to get away with stealing software...' In fact, the people in the class were there to learn how to **prevent** *incorrect software licensing.*

Perhaps it would be wise to formally and carefully monitor your suppliers to ensure that they properly register your purchases. Include in your relationship agreement a clause requiring the supplier to provide you with timely documentation proving that they registered your licenses. If they don't comply, or if they make mistakes — you could lose a piracy confrontation. If this is a possibility with any of your providers, maybe it's time to consider finding a new supplier.

Are you a malcontent? Do you purposely steal software or other copyrighted works? I don't think so. The software police constantly bombard us with their sponsored surveys showing that more than three-quarters of all license violations are intentional. Yet, more than 90% of the hundreds of software and technology managers with whom I have discussed this topic have informed me that they do not intentionally violate their license agreements. It is unfair and confusing to those who try to be ethical to witness what appears to be an entire industry openly treating its customers as thieves. I believe it is time for a significant change.

In the industries that use technologies and copyrighted products, it is critical that we confront the disconnect between the consumer, the supplier, and the enforcement industry. Mutually beneficial relationships must become the rule, rather than the exception. Litigation must be minimized, rather than continuing to be used as a revenue generator. Who is the customer? Who pays the bills? Tell me, again, who are the real pirates?

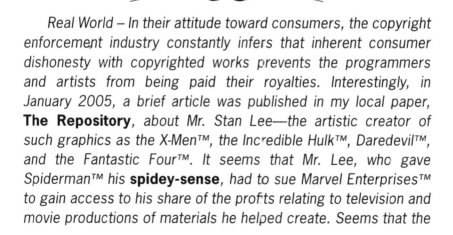

Real World – In their attitude toward consumers, the copyright enforcement industry constantly infers that inherent consumer dishonesty with copyrighted works prevents the programmers and artists from being paid their royalties. Interestingly, in January 2005, a brief article was published in my local paper, **The Repository***, about Mr. Stan Lee—the artistic creator of such graphics as the X-Men™, the Incredible Hulk™, Daredevil™, and the Fantastic Four™. It seems that Mr. Lee, who gave Spiderman™ his* **spidey-sense***, had to sue Marvel Enterprises™ to gain access to his share of the profits relating to television and movie productions of materials he helped create. Seems that the*

Settlement: ME – Boat Manufacturer - $33,000

movie industry might not mind depriving those same artists that they accuse their consumers of abusing if it means bigger profits. Tell me, again, who is the pirate? Marvel Enterprises is appealing the U.S. District Court of Manhattan ruling.

Core knowledge: What have we learned?

- You do not have to be guilty of piracy to be accused. You will eventually become a target merely because you possess computing devices.

- The copyright holder, based on the terms and conditions (Ts & Cs) of the license or possession documentation, very loosely defines piracy. To ensure that you do not become a target, you must not only know and follow the Ts & Cs for every copyrighted product in your possession, but you must understand what the software police are looking for.

- Don't commit software suicide. Negotiate every license agreement to ensure that the Ts & Cs are mutually beneficial. Ensure that expectations are mutually and clearly defined, and then follow them closely. You have the right, and the fiscal responsibility, to negotiate beneficial contracts.

- Counterfeit and incorrectly licensed products tend to become invisible. Search them out and eliminate or license them.

- Take managerial control of each computer system and the copyrighted products it contains. Closely monitor the way people use technologies. Prevent as many piracy actions as possible.

- Pay close attention to the activities of the software police. Minimize your exposure by knowing who they are and what they are permitted, by contract, to look for in your environment.

Settlement: FL – Deco Co. - $120,000

• Remember: The business software consumer will always be a target for non compliance and piracy litigation. It is our responsibility to ensure that the bulls eye is as small as we can possibly make it.

Questions to help you become aware of your needs and encourage changes:

1. How will your company address each of the issues listed in this chapter and in the list on the previous page?

2. Make a brief list of your observations and ideas to solve any internal problems you may have found in reading this chapter.

3. Did you answer all of the questions about license types? Keep a record of these questions, your risks, and the ways you might modify current conditions.

4. What about your list addressing your control over licenses and systems? What are some of the methods you could use to increase control?

Coming in Chapter Two: Time for a quick look. Who *are* the software police and copyright cops?

Chapter 2
WHO ARE THE DREADED SOFTWARE POLICE & COPYRIGHT COPS?

Chapter Goals: First, who *are* these people?

Who is targeting my company for copyright violations?

Do they work together & share information?

How do they influence copyright laws?

—————⌒—————

Real World – The owner of a computing system is legally responsible for copyrighted products loaded or installed on that system. It doesn't matter how the products got there. It doesn't matter if you knew they were there. You—the system owner—are the one who will be targeted in the audit litigation. Here are the organizations, entities, and government agencies that will use you for target practice.

—————⌒—————

Call them what you will: the software police, the copyright cops, the good guys, or the bad guys. The copyright enforcement industry is a significant force that every responsible business owner and software manager must recognize and thoroughly understand. In all honesty, these folks have a thankless job made more difficult by consumers, pirates, and the software publishing and other copyrighted product developers along with the complex technologies that have given them birth.

Since the first monk re-crafted the first manuscript, copy-righted product use and enforcement have nearly always rep-resented a disagreeable battlefield between providers and con-sumers. On the enforcement side of the equation are over two dozen American and more than ninety global investigative en-tities representing the software publishers, copyrighted prod-uct producers, and enforcement associations. They establish and enforce the rules by which we all dance with one another. After all—their products are copyrighted, so they definitely have the right to define our use. Thanks to numerous and high-ly complex local, national, and global copyright legislative guidelines, the copyright dance is incredibly disjointed. We, the consumers of copyrighted products, twist and turn to the contractual tempo in a sort of benign confusion—until we are audited for copyright violations. Then, we tend to throw up our hands and lament our bad luck—just prior to paying the fines.

Copyright violations are not a matter of bad luck; they are direct results of a lack of accurate knowledge coupled with ineffective corporate asset management processes. Let's come back to our piracy scenario. It is critical for executive man-agement to recognize that if the company does not possess the capabilities to succeed in a confrontational battle with this op-ponent, they should not initiate that battle. In fact, if the oppo-sition has superior numbers, knowledge, authority, equipment, and commitment, any sane captain of industry would do well to keep a low profile and be sure to take all possible defensive and evasive measures. (*This particular enactment of the David and Goliath scenario definitely lacks stones and a sling.*) An effective leader will also gain maximum proactive intelligence of opposition tactics and carefully consider all aspects of the possible levels of corporate risk. If we fail to take significant defensive action, then sailing the high seas of technological commerce can grow progressively more hazardous.

Today, when we use technologies in our corporate opera-tions, we are clear and—frankly—easy targets for the copyright enforcement industry. Our combined knowledge of copyright management is incredibly incomplete and the opposition's capacities for confrontation practically guarantee a stormy relationship.

Who *are* these people?

The collective software police is a multitalented, multifaceted group of global companies, associations, and governmental agencies that work closely—and cooperatively—to monitor and enforce copyright laws. In the United States, there are more than twenty-six separate entities aggressively searching out and confronting companies and people guilty of piracy and copyright infringement. Globally, this number swells to over ninety-four copyright enforcement entities that are constantly watching for your company to make a mistake in licensing or to incorrectly use copyrighted products.

Whether you are purposely stealing software or other licensed products—or if you have merely made an honest licensing mistake—your chances of being located and punished by these groups are very high. When as many as half of all small to medium sized businesses could easily be audited in a given eighteen month period, it's only a matter of time before you are approached and you get your chance to play the role of target.

Another serious and previously invisible issue that confronts the technology consumer is that you could very easily be audited by more than one of the groups we are about to discuss. Being targeted for an audit by one enforcement group does not cancel any other enforcement group interest in your company—nor will your audit frequency stop at a single audit. Once targeted, you could easily be subjected to repeated audits for three to five years. Is this beginning to sound like a serious problem?

Settlement: CT – Investment Management Co. - $275,000

Real World – In 2002, a CEO informed me that he did not fear an audit. While he admitted that he was aware of some incorrectly licensed products in his environment, he wasn't concerned because he kept an extra hundred thousand dollars in his budget, "**just in case**." He honestly believed that this was an ethical and realistic method of preparing the corporation for compliance. On review of his systems, we located over $300k in potential fines coupled with approximately five times that amount in potential piracy related costs. However, legally, since he was aware of the problem and had taken no corrective action, this individual could easily have been charged with willful violation of Federal Copyright Law—a criminal act punishable by fines of up to $250,000 per copyright violated and up to five years imprisonment. That $100k bank balance doesn't sound like such a brilliant idea after all, does it?

In the minds of the average consumer, noncompliance with copyright is generally considered an error in software or technology asset management. In effect, most consumers that I encounter consider the multitude of potential copyright and licensing mistakes to be—well—mistakes. Unfortunately, the copyright enforcement industry appears to have adopted the perception that virtually any violation of copyright law is an instance of piracy. These respective attitudes are important to keep in mind as you consider possible real world strategies for managing software life cycles within your organization's technology environment.

Solving the incredibly complex issues and difficulties relating to the legal use of copyrighted products and infringement enforcement is definitely a thankless task. The people and organizations listed in this chapter are actively and honestly trying to make a difference. Are they performing their roles effectively? That represents an interesting question when we consider that some copyright holders and enforcement teams appear to be laying down conflicting rules and standards as they go along. (More on this license management confusion in Chapter 6.)

It's unfortunate that many of the enforcement industry players are considered by consumers to be overly aggressive, unnecessarily confrontational, and inconsistent in their collective due diligence activities. The bottom line is that they *are* opening the doors of piracy awareness around the globe. Let's take a look at who these people are.

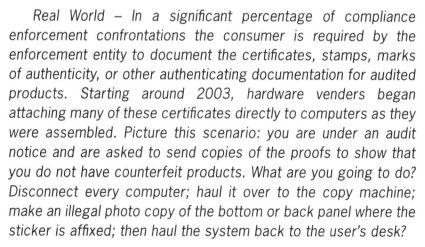

Real World – In a significant percentage of compliance enforcement confrontations the consumer is required by the enforcement entity to document the certificates, stamps, marks of authenticity, or other authenticating documentation for audited products. Starting around 2003, hardware venders began attaching many of these certificates directly to computers as they were assembled. Picture this scenario: you are under an audit notice and are asked to send copies of the proofs to show that you do not have counterfeit products. What are you going to do? Disconnect every computer; haul it over to the copy machine; make an illegal photo copy of the bottom or back panel where the sticker is affixed; then haul the system back to the user's desk?

The hardware provider will tell you that the software publisher demanded they affix the stickers to the systems. The software publisher will state that this process is a necessary portion of

---

Settlement: OH – Fixture Provider - $36,250

its ongoing anti piracy program. The enforcement entity doesn't particularly care about your problems, as long as you submit copies of the authenticity proofs. You will be scratching your head trying to figure out how all this will work. And, finally, I'll point out to you that we have yet another very expensive disconnect between the consumer and the copyright holder. Bottom line? The authenticity issue will create such havoc that you'll wind up conducting a messy audit and paying heftier dollars in fines. Great customer relations concept, isn't it?

What member associations are active in copyright enforcement?

Member associations of software publishers and technology industry leaders have been cropping up like dandelions on a golf course. Their focus is to protect the interests of their respective industries and member companies. Included are associations that represent the software industries, recording industries, movie industries, graphics industries, gaming industries, and font foundries. The associations take a membership fee from industry players and may provide networking opportunities; industry-wide strategic planning and education opportunities; legislation monitoring and lobbying; copyright infringement investigative actions; and other cooperative services.

Referring to themselves as *industry watchdogs*, the enforcement associations are mostly controlled by their own and their industries' definitions of ethics and operational necessity. Their actions and procedures are often contradictory and do not appear to be regulated by any governmental oversight agency. Interestingly, many global software management professionals have noted that these enforcement groups appear to consider their copyright violations targets guilty until proven guilty. Could it be time for some enlightened government, somewhere, to implement an *animal control agency* to reign in potential *watchdog abuse* by the copyright enforcement industry? When we consider the sheer power that these folks have over businesses around the world, this lack of vendor-neutral oversight is incredibly scary.

Let's take a look at some of the characteristics these clubs have in common:

- Contrary to popular misconception, one that seems to be encouraged by many of the enforcement companies, they are not agencies of any government—they are generally non-profit corporations.

- They invest a great deal of their time and money in monitoring and supporting local, national, and global legislation favorable to the industries they represent.

- A piracy event or investigation can be launched by a report from a knowledgeable disgruntled current and/or former employee, ethical employee, competitor, or vendor (*an unhappy spouse?*) by dialing a series of highly published toll free confidential phone numbers.

- In general, the software enforcement associations retain the fine portion of the settlements they bring to fruition while the publishers retain software reimbursement penalties ranging from 1.5 to 4 times the list price of each instance of each copyrighted product violated.

- A confrontation with one enforcement group does not guarantee that you will not be re-audited. Nor does it eliminate your exposure to any of the other enforcement entities. Theoretically, each individual enforcement entity could audit you at any given time. (*Yes, you should be nervous.*)

- Keep in mind that the majority of copyright enforcement entities discussed in this text are predominantly concerned with products being used in distributed environments and on personal computers (*Later, I'll discuss why we are going to quit using that term.*).

Settlement: CA – Health & Wellness Co. - $100,000

- Mainframe copyright holders tend to police their own clients.

How does all this work?

Real World – Consider this scenario: you locate software on your systems that you do not believe is correctly licensed. You contact the software publisher and ask for advice. Representatives from the software publisher check the products and discover that they are counterfeit. Within a week you receive a notice from a compliance enforcement entity that a **confidential source** *has reported that you have illegal software. The enforcement entity orders you to freeze all configuration activity on your computer systems and to cease all communications with software publishers until your piracy issues are resolved. You receive a letter informing you that, even though you were proactively working to resolve the pirated license issues, you were still operating in violation of Federal Copyright Law, Title 17 of the U.S. Code, and were subject to a fine.*

Before we start: The information contained in this section is general information and not intended to be an exhaustive or definitive explanation or depiction of the existence or functionality of any of the entities listed. In a sincere effort to avoid misrepresenting these folks I have specifically quoted their own descriptions from their web sites. For additional, more complete, and up-to-date information, refer to the web sites listed for each group. In addition, we will be looking at numerous monitoring and enforcement entities. Don't let this data bog your reading down. If your mind becomes numb and

---

Settlement: TX – Residential Builder - $50,000

your eyes start to glaze, skip over the list and move on. This information is provided so that you have a non-threatening place to start becoming more aware of the sheer numbers of forces arrayed to monitor the copyrighted products consumer.

The Business Software Alliance (BSA)

(United States & Global) (Offers Rewards)

www.bsa.org

Who are these folks?

Members include, but are not limited to: Adobe, Apple, AutoDesk, Avid, Bentley Systems, Borland, CNC Software/ Mastercam, Internet Security Systems, Macromedia, McAfee, Microsoft, PTC, Solidworks, Sybase, Symantec, The Mathworks, UGS Corp, and Veritas.

How does the BSA view itself?

According to its web site, the Business Software Alliance (BSA) is the "foremost organization dedicated to promoting a safe and legal digital world." BSA also considers itself the "voice of the world's commercial software industry before governments and in the international marketplace." BSA "educates consumers on software management and copyright protection, cyber security, trade, e-commerce, and other Internet-related issues."

What do consumers see?

The BSA is arguably the most aggressive and pervasive enforcement company. With operational units in over 60 countries, this group represents a very real threat to virtually any business using technology.

Settlement: TX – Workforce Mgt. Co. - $53,500

- BSA is a member association of some of the major desktop, network, and PC/Mac software publishers as well as many hardware technology industry movers and shakers.

- BSA is one of the few enforcement entities with a policy of issuing press releases announcing many of its settlements. In my opinion, these releases represent the most potent piracy awareness process in the industry because they clearly reveal the offenses, frequency, and basic costs of piracy violations. (It's hard to deny facts like these.)

- The organization conducts special educational license review events (such as its "Grace," "Truce," and "$2 Million Dollar Tuesday" events) and has announced settlements totaling more than $3 million during a single week in the US (Example: June, 2003).

- Many of the global BSA units (operating in 60+ countries) offer significant rewards (up to $50,000 in the US at press time) to individuals who report copyright violations or piracy.

- The BSA works directly with targeted companies or often appears to hire independent legal firms to confront suspected pirates.

- According to BSA, a high percentage of its targets are reported via toll free confidential telephone numbers with additional reports via Internet-based forms.

- The BSA has been known to use Internet-based web crawlers to automatically troll the Internet for key words, phrases, offers, and discussions that allude to piracy activities.

- Investigating and stopping the producers of pirated and counterfeited products are two additional, very positive, actions being taken by the BSA to reduce the volume of illegal software on the market.

Settlement: TX – Life Science Research Co. - $89,440

The Recording Industry Association of America (RIAA)

(United States & Global) (Offers Rewards)

www.riaa.org

Who are these folks?

The member list posted on the RIAA web site includes, among others: BMG, Sony, Universal Music, and Warner Brothers. A more comprehensive listing of active members is available at:

http://www.riaa.com/about/members/default.asp

How does the RIAA view itself?

Right off the web site: "The Recording Industry Association of America (RIAA) is the trade group that represents the U.S. recording industry. Its mission is to foster a business and legal climate that supports and promotes our members' creative and financial vitality. Its members are the record companies that comprise the most vibrant national music industry in the world. RIAA members create, manufacture and/or distribute approximately 90% of all legitimate sound recordings produced and sold in the United States."

Further:

"In support of this mission, the RIAA works to protect intellectual property rights worldwide and the First Amendment rights of artists; conduct consumer industry and technical research; and monitor and review state and federal laws, regulations and policies."

- RIAA is a member association of recording industry professionals, producers, and distributors.
- The RIAA is not a governmental agency.

- The RIAA offers rewards of up to $10,000 for reporting piracy production operations.
- The RIAA appears to be very active in the efforts to restrict and/or eliminate peer-to-peer — file sharing — activities over the Internet.

What do consumers see?

Unless you have spent the last two years imprisoned in the brig of a dismasted merchant seaman off the coast of Norway you have more than likely heard about the activities of the Recording Industry Association of America as it sends thousands of cease and desist letters while filing hundreds of lawsuits against Internet music-sharing pirates (*Such as the honor student next door?*). With allied associations in most developed countries, the RIAA has become a global threat to consumers of questionably licensed copyrighted audio products such as MP3s.

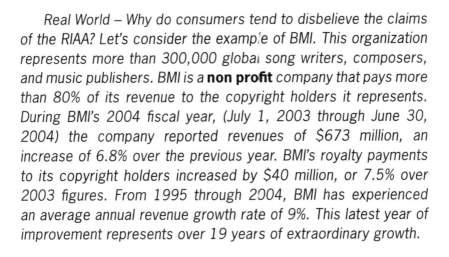

*Real World – Why do consumers tend to disbelieve the claims of the RIAA? Let's consider the example of BMI. This organization represents more than 300,000 global song writers, composers, and music publishers. BMI is a **non profit** company that pays more than 80% of its revenue to the copyright holders it represents. During BMI's 2004 fiscal year, (July 1, 2003 through June 30, 2004) the company reported revenues of $673 million, an increase of 6.8% over the previous year. BMI's royalty payments to its copyright holders increased by $40 million, or 7.5% over 2003 figures. From 1995 through 2004, BMI has experienced an average annual revenue growth rate of 9%. This latest year of improvement represents over 19 years of extraordinary growth.*

Settlement: AZ – Architecture Firm - $200,000

Long ago, I heard a phrase that I honestly believe applies to a significant percentage of the reported copyright industry issues with piracy. It went something like this: "If your statistics do not support your point of view, you obviously need more statistics." (*What was that old sixties phrase? Who's zooming who?*)

Real World – In late September, 2005, Apple Computer was still resisting intense pressures from the music industry to raise download prices for its iTunes Music Store Web. Apple co-founder Steve Jobs is quoted as saying: "The labels make more money from selling tracks on iTunes than when they sell a CD. There are no marketing costs for them...if they want to raise the prices it just means they're getting a little greedy." (Associated Press report printed in the Wall Street Journal 9/21/05.) For over a year, many of the five top music labels have been pushing to raise the price for each downloaded song from 99 cents to an amount between $1.25 and $2.99. This from an industry that is "recording" "record" profits.

No wonder people tend to justify piracy. While it's a criminal act for an individual, piracy seems to be acceptable when accomplished on the multinational corporate level.

The Motion Picture Association of America (MPAA)

(United States & Global) (Offers Rewards)

www.mpaa.org

Who are these folks?

On its board of directors are the Chairmen and Presidents of the seven major producers and distributors of motion picture and television programs in the United States. These members include:

Buena Vista Pictures Distribution (The Walt Disney Company), Sony Pictures Entertainment Inc., Metro-Goldwyn-Mayer Studios Inc., Paramount Pictures Corporation, Twentieth Century Fox Film Corporation, Universal City Studios LLLP, and Warner Bros. Entertainment Inc.

How does the MPAA view itself?

Right off the web site: "The Motion Picture Association of America (MPAA) and its international counterpart, the Motion Picture Association (MPA) serve as the voice and advocate of the American motion picture, home video and television industries, domestically through the MPAA and internationally through the MPA."

- MPAA is a member association of film industry professionals, producers, and distributors.
- MPAA is not a governmental entity.
- This organization invests time and money monitoring, drafting, and supporting favorable legislation at the state, national, and global levels.
- The MPAA offers rewards of up to $10,000 for reporting video piracy production operations.
- The MPAA has influenced, and in some cases drafted templates for, such legislative acts as the US state-by-state Super DMCA laws in an effort to reduce the impact of illegal video distribution on the movie industry.

What do consumers see?

Are these the people who want to make it illegal for us to fast forward through the commercials on our rented video and DVD movies? Are they the folks who developed the templates for some of the state-to-state Super DMCAs?

*Real World – Is the movie industry truly losing money on piracy? I don't for a minute believe any of us would doubt that piracy is certainly taking its toll on many industry players. However, interestingly enough, the Hollywood Reporter.com published an article May 23, 2005 noting that the MPAA companies reported record revenues in 2004 of $44.8 Billion—an increase of 9% over 2003 figures. Check "***Studios spell income D-V-D****" on the Hollywood Reporter.com web site.*

Maybe it's time someone clarified a couple questions. Could there be a distinct probability that many of the reported industry losses due to piracy tend to reflect a percentage loss of *projected* profits—not necessarily losses of actual profits? Could the figures used to quantify all of these losses have been slightly skewed because they were provided by the movie industry itself? (*Or are these unnecessary questions?*)

The Software & Information Industry Association (SIIA)

Formerly the Software Publishers Association (SPA)

(Mostly United States) (Offers Rewards)

www.siia.net

Who are these folks?

Although membership numbers vary, the SIIA considers itself the physically largest software industry association with approximately 750 reported members.

A detailed up-to-date list of members should be available at this link:

http://www.siia.net/membership/memberlist.asp

How does the SIIA view itself?

According to its web site, "The Software & Information Industry Association is the principal trade association for the software and digital content industry. SIIA provides global services in government relations, business development, corporate education and intellectual property protection to the leading companies that are setting the pace for the digital age.

PRINCIPAL MISSION:

- **Promote the Industry:** SIIA promotes the common interests of the software and digital content industry as a whole, as well as its component parts.

- **Protect the Industry:** SIIA protects the intellectual property of member companies, and advocates a legal and regulatory environment that benefits the entire industry.

- **Inform the Industry:** SIIA informs the industry and the broader public by serving as a resource on trends, technologies, policies and related issues that affect member firms and demonstrate the contribution of the industry to the broader economy."

What do consumers see?

The SIIA—you may remember their operations under the name of Software Publishers Association—is arguably the point of origin for the copyright compliance enforcement investigation industry.

- SIIA is not a government agency.
- SIIA offers rewards to individuals who report acts of piracy that result in successful settlements. In its own words:
  - » "SIIA offers rewards of up to $50,000 to individuals who report verifiable corporate end-user piracy cases to our Anti-Piracy team."
  - » See: http://www.siia.net/piracy/report.asp
- SIIA has not historically announced its settlements. While this is a dubious benefit to companies involved in the illegal use of products, many working software managers find it difficult to understand how the lack of reported settlements contributes to increasing public awareness as to the real world threat of piracy.
- SIIA reports that it relies on toll-free confidential phone lines for most of its tips.
- The SIIA has developed a compliance training program entitled Certified Software Manager (CSM) which trains corporate software managers in managing compliance.
- A confrontation with the SIIA does not guarantee that you will not be re-audited. You can face repetitive audits up until, and after, you get licensing right.
- An SIIA audit also does not eliminate your exposure to all the other enforcement entities. Theoretically, every one of them could independently audit you at any given time. *(Yes, once again, you should be nervous.)*

Settlement: IL – Electronic Games Co. - $35,000

Are any of the software publishers active in enforcement?

Major Software Publishers

(United States & Global)

Some of the software publishers that have been known to conduct audits include, but are definitely not limited to: Adobe, AutoDesk, Macromedia, Microsoft, Network Associates, Oracle, and Symantec

A significant number of the major software publishers have fielded their own copyright enforcement teams across the globe. For clear and frequently updated information check the individual software publisher's web site and perform a search for "anti piracy." If your search of an individual software publisher does not yield any results, don't get complacent. That particular publisher might be very active in enforcing its copyrights but does not release the information.

Issues to consider include:

- Many copyright holders that operate their own investigative teams are also members of one *or more* of the enforcement associations and thus represent a multiple threat.

- Publishers also gain a significant percentage of their leads from their own toll free confidential telephone lines. Remember, however, that these groups can also gain strategic information from the vendors you use to acquire software and systems.

- Publishers place "permission to audit" clauses in the majority of significant software license agreements. These clauses give the publisher—or its representatives—the right to audit your company and check on your product utilization and documentation.

- In general, once a membership-based compliance enforcement group such as BSA contacts you with an audit letter, you are no longer permitted to pursue the matter with the individual publishers.

ARE THERE OTHER GLOBAL ENFORCEMENT GROUPS?

The Federation Against Software Theft (FAST)

(United Kingdom)

www.fast.org.uk

Who are these people?

In the United Kingdom, the Federation Against Software Theft (FAST) maintains over 150 software industry members along with more than 2,300 end user members in a separate Corporate Member group.

How does the FAST view itself?

According to its web site, "The Federation Against Software Theft (FAST) was set up in 1984 by the British Computer Society's Copyright Committee. It was the first software copyright organisation [*UK spellings, don't blame me...*].

Its first action was to raise the awareness of software piracy and to lobby Parliament for changes in the Copyright Act 1956 to reflect the needs of software authors and publishers. This campaign was successful and it has since been able to influence other legislation that impacts on the proper safeguarding of software.

The work of FAST in this area has directly influenced the way that software copyright law and investigations are carried out in many other countries.

It (FAST) is also unique in that it is the only association in the world that represents both software publishers and end users. All the other associations concerned with software management generally represent software publishers only and therefore have an approach that is not directly geared to helping organisations and end users who are actually responsible for managing software.

Clearly, with a long history of working with both sides, FAST has built up a high degree of expertise and knowledge that can be drawn upon by members to help in the day-to-day management of software and any issues that may arise. In addition, any work undertaken by third parties on behalf of FAST is subject to a quality control process."

FAST delivers the following services to its industry members:

- Copyright enforcement
- Lobbying and legislative liaison,
- Working alongside corporate members,
- Information, education, and public relations

FAST also operates an end user education program focused on proactive license compliance assurance.

WHAT GOVERNMENTAL PLAYERS ARE KNOWN TO PARTICIPATE IN COPYRIGHT ENFORCEMENT ACTIONS?

Department of Justice (DOJ)

(United States & Global)

http://www.usdoj.gov/criminal/cybercrime/

What are the roles played by the DOJ?

From the DOJ web site: "The Computer Crime and Intellectual Property Section (CCIPS) is responsible for implementing the Department's national strategies in combating computer and intellectual property crimes worldwide. The Computer Crime Initiative is a comprehensive program designed to combat electronic penetrations, data thefts, and cyberattacks on critical information systems.

CCIPS prevents, investigates, and prosecutes computer crimes by working with other government agencies, the private sector, academic institutions, and foreign counterparts. Section attorneys work to improve the domestic and international infrastructure-legal, technological, and operational-to pursue network criminals most effectively.

The Section's enforcement responsibilities against intellectual property crimes are similarly multi-faceted. Intellectual Property (IP) has become one of the principal U.S. economic engines, and the nation is a target of choice for thieves of material protected by copyright, trademark, or trade-secret designation.

In pursuing all these goals, CCIPS attorneys regularly run complex investigations, resolve unique legal and investigative issues raised by emerging computer and telecommunications technologies; litigate cases; provide litigation support to other prosecutors; train federal, state, and local law enforcement personnel; comment on and propose legislation; and initiate and participate in international efforts to combat computer and intellectual property crime."

Case history:

An excellent chart of actual cybercrime cases can be found at:

http://www.usdoj.gov/criminal/cybercrime/ipcases.htm

The data included in this chart can be used to document

Settlement: MI – Engineering Firm - $30,435

historical events and justify initiating a copyright assurance program in your organization.

Federal Bureau of Investigation (FBI)

(United States & Global)

http://www.fbi.gov/ipr/

http://www.fbi.gov/cyberinvest/cyberhome.htm

What are the roles the FBI plays?

Take a look at the FBI Cybercrime home pages listed above. An excerpt from FBI information on these pages includes: "The FBI also works to prevent criminals, sexual predators, and others intent on malicious destruction from using the Internet and on-line services to steal from, defraud, and otherwise victimize citizens, businesses, and communities."

As you read more about piracy activities, don't be surprised when you encounter the word terrorism. As of 2005, multiple studies have shown that organized crime and terrorist organizations have been directly involved in significant counterfeiting and distribution of copyrighted works. The FBI is very prominent in coordinating, investigating, and participating in a wide variety of anti piracy initiatives both in the U.S. and around the globe.

Also, note that the definition of "pirate" will shift between differing enforcement entities. Pirates can range from gun-toting hooded figures boarding and hijacking ships at sea; to the 80+ year old grandmother whose grandkids download illegal music on her computer; to you, because your personal desktop system was loaded with illegal software by your hardware provider. The word also applies to people who make illegal copies of shoes, handbags, jeans, and pretty much any other product that can be registered and sold as unique.

Settlement: MN – Manufacturing Firm - $199,174

Further note on the FBI web site: "The mission of the Cyber Division is to:

- coordinate, supervise and facilitate the FBI's investigation of those federal violations in which the Internet, computer systems, or networks are exploited as the principal instruments or targets of terrorist organizations, foreign government sponsored intelligence operations, or criminal activity and for which the use of such systems is essential to that activity;

- form and maintain public/private alliances in conjunction with enhanced education and training to maximize counterterrorism, counter-intelligence, and law enforcement cyber response capabilities; and

- until such time as a final decision is made regarding the future role and location of the National Infrastructure Protection Center (NIPC), the FBI will direct and coordinate the Center's mission to protect the Nation's critical information infrastructure and other key assets."

Federal Marshal Service

http://www.usdoj.gov/marshals/

From the web site: "The marshals of the Federal Marshal Service, as the enforcement arm of the federal court..." *have the dubious task of serving the federal warrants for forced audits* (words in italics added by author).

So, when you ignore the advice in this book, you'll know precisely what the Federal Marshals want when you find them waiting in your lobby.

GROUPS INVOLVED BUT NOT NECESSARILY A PRIMARY THREAT TO YOUR ORGANIZATION.

The Internet Fraud Complaint Center (IFCC)

http://www.ifccfbi.gov/index.asp

From the web site: "The Internet Fraud Complaint Center (IFCC) is a partnership between the Federal Bureau of Investigation (FBI) and the National White Collar Crime Center (NW3C)."

Take a look at their IC3 Annual Internet Fraud Report online at:

http://www.ifccfbi.gov/strategy/statistics.asp

United States Secret Service

www.secretservice.gov

Although not particularly overt in their involvement, agents of the Secret Service have been mentioned as participating in a wide range of takedowns involving piracy and counterfeit software. Just be aware that this is simply one more group you need to consider in communicating the seriousness of acquiring or using illegal software or copyrighted products.

United States Customs Service

http://www.cbp.gov/xp/cgov/home.xml

What roles do members of the Customs Service play?

Customs agents are generally among the first on the scene when counterfeit products are shipped, received, or brought into the United States. They participate with other law enforcement agencies in investigations and sting operations that interdict illegal copyrighted products.

STOP Program

From the web site: "STOP: stands for Strategy Targeting Organized Piracy. This is actually a starting point—an aggressive multi-agency initiative to tackle intellectual property right (IPR) violations. In October 2004, the Secretary of Commerce, the Attorney General, and the United States Trade Representative joined the Under Secretary for Border and Transportation Security to announce the new STOP initiative. STOP's goal is to combat international trade in counterfeit and pirated goods and to remove them from international shipping lanes.

Using law enforcement and investigative techniques to dismantle criminal enterprises that steal intellectual property, CBP will stop fraudulent merchandise from entering our borders, and we will bring violators to justice.

For more information on STOP, please visit:

www.StopFakes.gov or call 1-866-999-HALT,

the U.S. government's "one-stop-shopping center" for protecting intellectual property rights at home and abroad."

Operation Buccaneer targets software piracy

U.S. Customs agents executed 49 search warrants in 27 cities and seized more than 140 computers in Operation Buccaneer, a 15-month undercover investigation into software piracy over the Internet.

Take a look:

http://www.cbp.gov/xp/CustomsToday/2002/January/custoday_buccaneer.xml

Settlement: NJ – Trade Show Exhibits Co. - $45,000

Interpol

The International Police Association

www.interpol.int

(Global)

Also at: http://www.interpol.int/Public/TechnologyCrime/default.asp

What are some of the roles Interpol plays?

From its web site: Interpol strives "To be the world's pre-eminent police organisation in support of all organisations, authorities and services whose mission is preventing, detecting, and suppressing crime.

Interpol has actively been involved for a number of years in combating Information Technology Crime. Rather than 're-inventing the wheel', the Interpol General Secretariat has harnessed the expertise of its members in the field of Information Technology Crime (ITC) through the vehicle of a 'working party' or a group of experts. In this instance, the working party consists of the heads or experienced members of national computer crime units. These working parties have been designed to reflect regional expertise and exist in Europe, Asia, the Americas and in Africa. All working parties are in different stages of development. It should be noted that the work done by the working parties is not Interpol's only contribution to combating ITC, but it certainly represents the most noteworthy contribution to date."

What other groups are involved in monitoring copyrighted products?

Font Foundries

Font Software Group (FSG) of the Federation Against Software Theft (FAST)

Settlement: PA – Business Sales Co. - $50,000

(UK & US)

www.fast.uk.org

Members include, but are not limited to: AGFA Monotype, Compliant (UK), Creative Publishing Solutions, Dalton Maag, Device, The Font Bureau, Fontsmith, Fontware, International Typeface Corporation, Jeremy Tankard Typography, and Neufille, SI.

Real World - In a life cycle training session for advanced software license managers, I brought up the issues covering licensed fonts. As usual, attendees were stunned: "You mean we have to manage fonts, too?" Absolutely. Although I have been presenting the need to monitor licensed fonts since 2001, it never ceases to amaze me how few companies have even considered tracking these copyrighted products.

Font foundries are the companies that design, develop and license type face fonts. There are a lot more of these licensed products on the market than you might notice. There are also a lot more licensed fonts circulating around the corporate environment than you would expect. Foundries are quietly active in monitoring and enforcing the use of their property. Fines are the same as any violation of copyright, including criminal penalties for intentional violations.

Review your environment immediately for licensed fonts. Track down acquisition and licensing information and document precisely how you are permitted to use licensed fonts. Keep in mind that it is altogether possible for an unlicensed specialized font to suddenly become licensed, so it is wise to track all specialized fonts, regardless of their copyright status. Fonts can be licensed to a computer system, program, printer, or as defined in the actual license. Adobe, for instance, licenses and sternly tracks many of its fonts. Do you have Adobe products in house?

Real World - In September of 2003, the Federation against Software Theft launched its Font Software Group (FSG). Intent? To monitor the use of licensed fonts generated by members of FAST in the UK and United States. Wait... A United Kingdom enforcement entity operating in the US? Absolutely. After all, US enforcement entities operate freely in the UK.

(Are you still by any chance thinking that you aren't a wide open target?)

Licensed Graphics

Does your company use licensed graphics in presentations, publications, or in corporate documents? Would you be aware if anyone was using these products or are you an easy target? Licensed graphics, like licensed fonts, come from a significant industry of image foundries and graphics supply houses—including photographic providers. Whether they are hand drawn, computer generated, or photographic, licensed images are pervasive in our visually oriented world.

Also keep in mind that graphics, like fonts, can change and evolve—today the graphic may be unrestricted and royalty free—tomorrow it may become fee based for corporate use but free for private use. Then the same image could shift to full royalty-based use.

Review your environment immediately for licensed graphics. Track down acquisition & licensing information and docu-

---

Settlement: PA – Private University - $100,000

ment precisely how you are permitted to use these licensed products.

*Real World – Do you purchase those inexpensive graphics collections from the local office supply store? You know, the ones that imply that the graphics can be used in presentations or newsletters? In four out of four separate brands that I researched, the user would violate copyright if they used the products for commercial purposes. The fine print clearly states, "**Not for commercial use.**"*

Gaming Industry

Gaming? Does this mean that we also need to be concerned with licensed games? Do you think I'm crazy bringing this up? Absolutely not. Although the majority of companies I have worked with over the years do not permit games on corporate systems, virtually every one of those companies still had games present—on corporate computers. You may not have put them there, or may not be aware of them, but they are loaded and operational—which means you are liable.

I personally have seen dozens of software publisher audit letters that include game titles on their list of items to be audited. Even more critically, remember that the software industry isn't the only industry monitoring the use of computer games.

Note that many of the governmental agency guidelines include monitoring copyright of gaming products.

Canadian Alliance Against Software Theft (CAAST)

www.caast.org
(Canada)

Settlement: MI – Engineering / Architecture Firm - $284,000

Who are these people?

Members include, but are not limited to:

Adobe, Apple Canada, AutoDesk Canada, Avid, Bentley Systems, Borland, CNC Software/Mastercam, Internet Security Systems, Macromedia, McAfee, Microsoft Canada, PTC, Solidworks, Sybase, Symantec, UGS Corp, Veritas.

Additional member information can be found at:

http://caast.org/about/default.asp?load=members

How does CAAST see itself?

From the web site, "CAAST provides educational information to corporations, consumers and resellers about software piracy and its implications. This non-profit organization also protects the rights of its member companies against the unauthorized sale or reproduction of software through the support of the legal prosecution of individuals or groups involved in this unlawful activity."

International Intellectual Property Alliance

www.iipa.com

(Global)

Who are these people?

IIPA members include, but are not limited to:

Association of American Publishers, Business Software Alliance, Entertainment Software Association, Motion Picture Association of America, Recording Industry Association of America.

How does the IIPA see itself?

From the web site, "The International Intellectual Property Alliance is a private sector coalition formed in 1984 to represent the U.S. copyright-based industries in bilateral and multilateral efforts to improve international protection of copyrighted materials. IIPA is comprised of six trade associations, each representing a significant segment of the U.S. copyright community. These member associations represent 1,300 U.S. companies producing and distributing materials protected by copyright laws throughout the world – all types of computer software including business applications software and entertainment software (such as videogame CDs and cartridges, personal computer CD-ROMs and multimedia products); theatrical films, television programs, home videos and digital representations of audiovisual works; music, records, CDs, and audiocassettes; and textbooks, tradebooks, reference and professional publications and journals (in both electronic and print media)."

IIPA provides copyright piracy and market impact information to 65 countries via its Special 301 report.

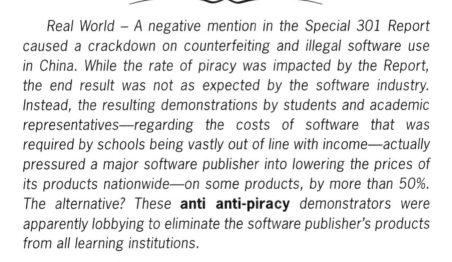

Real World – A negative mention in the Special 301 Report caused a crackdown on counterfeiting and illegal software use in China. While the rate of piracy was impacted by the Report, the end result was not as expected by the software industry. Instead, the resulting demonstrations by students and academic representatives—regarding the costs of software that was required by schools being vastly out of line with income—actually pressured a major software publisher into lowering the prices of its products nationwide—on some products, by more than 50%. The alternative? These **anti anti-piracy** *demonstrators were apparently lobbying to eliminate the software publisher's products from all learning institutions.*

Settlement: AL – Manufacturing Co. - $189,000

Entertainment Software Association (ESA)

www.theesa.com

(Global)

Who are these people?

At press time, members included such companies as:

Activision, Inc.   Atari
Buena Vista Games   Capcom USA, Inc.
Crave Entertainment   Eidos Interactive
Electronic Arts   Her Interactive
id Software   LucasArts
Square Enix, Inc.   Microsoft Corporation
THQ, Inc.   NovaLogic, Inc.
SEGA of America, Inc.   Wild Tangent
Nintendo of America Inc.   Midway Games, Inc.
Konami Digital Entertainment-America
Sony Computer Entertainment America
Namco Hometek, Inc.
Take-Two Interactive Software, Inc.
Ubisoft Entertainment
Warner Bros. Interactive Entertainment Inc.
Vivendi Universal Games

ESA's Worldwide Anti-Piracy Program

From the web site: "The primary objective of ESA's Anti-Piracy Program is to attack and reduce global entertainment software piracy, estimated to cost the U.S. entertainment software industry billions of dollars every year. The program's primary components are enforcement, training, including education and enforcement programs in the U.S. and abroad. ESA members actively participate to shape the industry's anti-piracy priorities and ensure that available resources are properly allocated for the enforcement of their intellectual property rights. ESA's anti-piracy efforts on the Internet and in the U.S. and select foreign markets are directed towards the active protection of members' game products through online enforcement, criminal raids and prosecutions and civil litigation. ESA's training programs help to elevate the protection of interactive game product as a priority for law enforcement officials, as well as enhance their knowledge of the entertainment software industry and its products. In addition, ESA's IP education and outreach efforts help to foster respect among members of the general public for the intellectual property rights of game software publishers."

Internet Piracy

"The ESA Online Monitoring and Enforcement Program monitors the Internet (websites, FTP sites, newsgroups, IRC channels, auction sites, chat rooms, forums, etc.) for instances of piracy of ESA members' products and requests ISPs to take down sites or accounts featuring infringing game product. Since the program's inception in 1998, the ESA has obtained the takedown of more than 150,000 sites dealing in pirated entertainment software.

The ESA aggressively pursues enforcement against individuals on the Internet who are involved in the illegal online distribution of our members' software, whether through criminal investigation and prosecution or civil litigation. In addition to providing support to several ongoing investigations of Internet pirate groups, ESA has also pursued civil remedies against individuals that have been identified as engaging in infringing activity via the Internet."

Entertainment & Leisure Software Publishers Association (ELSPA)

www.elspa.com

Settlement: MN – Design Engineering Co. - $150,000

(Mostly United Kingdom)

In UK call 0870-5133405 Confidential Hotline

ELSPA's Focus?

According to its web site, the ELSPA was "...founded in 1989 to establish a specific and collective identity for the British computer and video games industry. Membership includes over 100 companies involved in the publishing and distribution of interactive leisure and entertainment software. ELSPA works to protect, promote and provide for the interests of all its members, as well as addressing issues that affect the industry as a whole.

The ELSPA anti-piracy unit was established in 1994 to safeguard the intellectual property rights of members' products. The unit:

- Responds to information about illegal software received from members, the retail trade and other enforcement entities,
- Conducts investigations against alleged offenders,
- Routinely makes test purchases from alleged offenders,
- Regularly visits "car boot sales" (That would be car trunk sales for us Yanks!) and markets to monitor product being sold,
- Assists in execution of warrants at offenders' premises,
- Seizes infringing product,
- Maintains close liaison with UK Customs and Excise over importation of illegal software,
- Takes legal action against those found copying and selling illegal software,
- Attends trade shows and conferences to speak to consumer and traders,

Settlement: NY – Publishing Co. - $44,516

- Operates a 24-hour confidential hotline for anyone wishing to give information about software pirates."

International Federation of Phonographic Industry (IFPI),

www.ifpi.org

Who are these people?

"IFPI represents the recording industry worldwide with over 1450 members in 75 countries and affiliated industry associations in 48 countries. IFPI's international Secretariat is based in London and is linked to regional offices in Brussels, Hong Kong, Miami and Moscow."

IFPI's priorities

- Fighting music piracy
- Promoting fair market access and adequate copyright laws
- Helping develop the legal conditions and the technologies for the recording industry to prosper in the digital era
- Promoting the value of music in the development of economies, as well as in social and cultural life

Anti-piracy enforcement

- Central co-ordination of the international piracy effort
- Support from international investigators
- Training: Techniques for liaison with police, customs and security agencies
- How to put cases together: raids and seizures
- International CD Plant education programme

- Databases: International Intelligence and Pirate Product
- Technical assistance: surveillance techniques, security

Litigation & regulatory affairs

- Anti-piracy litigation
- Anti-piracy legal and lobbying strategies, in particular for CD plant regulations
- CD plant education and liaison
- Regulatory compliance, including competition law and data protection
- Authors' rights issues
- Monitoring the Source Identification (SID) Code, the industry's anti-piracy identifier

Internet Enforcement Group (IEG)

www.ieg-uk.org

Who are these people?

From the web site: "The Internet Enforcement Group (IEG) is a cross industry body of Internet investigators representing the book publishing, music, games, software, merchandising and film industries. The IEG was established in 2001 to work co-operatively in fighting on-line piracy on behalf of its members.

The members of the IEG are all experts in the field of internet investigations. The purpose of this group is first and foremost to protect their members' product by actively pursuing persons that contravene the above legislation."

And the list goes on...

Settlement: NY – Hotel - $147,500

International Recording Media Association

www.recordingmedia.org

REACT, European Anti-Counterfeiting Network

www.snbreact.nl

WCOIPR, Customs and industry partnership against intellectual property crimes

www.wcoipr.org

International Anti Counterfeiting Coalition

www.iacc.org

World Customs Organization

www.wcoomd.org

Central Intelligence Agency (CIA)

www.cia.gov

(Global)

Okay, I lied. The CIA isn't really involved in copyright enforcement. I'm just checking to see if you're still paying attention. Then again, since a high percentage of international piracy is apparently being conducted by terrorists and organized crime, maybe our friends at CIA *are* playing in this space after all. This could certainly make me nervous. How about you? Besides, after reading this list of hunters, those of us who are aware of being the hunted could use a little humor.

By the way, the list above is only a beginning. There must be a great deal of profit in this enforcement business because these companies are cropping up all over the world. (*Anyone surprised?*)

Where do all these people gain their authority?

You will enjoy this. The enforcement entities gain their authority from (*drum roll here*)...

You — the consumer.

It's true. You see, when you initialized the license for the copyrighted product, you agreed to permit the copyright holder or its designated representative to audit you for compliance. Honestly. The clause is present in virtually every significant software or operating system license agreement. (*I'll explain how to drastically reduce this threat in Chapter 6.*)

This audit clause not only permits the actual copyright holder to monitor your use of their products, it also permits those delegated representatives of the copyright holders to monitor and enforce your use. These would include the membership based compliance enforcement companies such as BSA, SIIA, FAST, CAAST, and others. Governmental agencies, naturally, do not need anyone's permission to monitor possible violations of state, national, or international law.

What are my liabilities?

The executive management of the corporation being audited is technically liable for any illegal activities conducted on corporate computing devices. Period. The company owns the system, the company is responsible for it — not Billy-Bob down at the tech center — the company. This means that you, the executive management of the target company, will be at ground zero in any audit event. Don't walk into this trap without thoroughly understanding where you are headed.

Consider these nicely developed legal concepts that will definitely apply when your company is confronted with a license or copyright violation:

Settlement: AL – Headware Manufacturer - $60,000

Contributory infringement: A person, with knowledge of the infringing activity, induces, causes, or materially contributes to the infringing conduct of another. If you knowingly and purposefully link to another web site that provides infringing files you could be guilty of contributory infringement. If your corporate systems are hijacked by a hacker and used to serve illegal copyrighted products, you'll be on deck again.

Vicarious liability: If you or your company have the right and ability to control the activities of the direct infringer and if you receive financial benefit from the infringing activities, this one applies to you—even if you are not aware of the violation. If your employees are loading and using illegal software on corporate systems, you could be liable under this legal definition. If you could have taken steps to prevent the crimes, and you didn't, once again, you are at ground zero. Consider this concept the next time you create a corporate policy that you do not enforce. (*This empty policy issue happens with frightening frequency.*)

How do they target companies like mine?

As we noted previously, you are targeted primarily through toll free confidential telephone reporting programs. The copyright enforcement companies also offer substantial rewards for reporting illegal use of copyrighted materials. These rewards can begin at $2,000USD and range to $10,000USD—(up to $50,000 in the case of BSA & SIIA).

In addition to your own employees, former employees, ethical employees, product vendors and third party suppliers regularly report suspected licensing issues to copyright holders. Consultants have been known to report piracy after they leave a client. Your competitors can report you, too. Here's an even more chilling thought: you do not even have to *be* reported. Remember that right to audit clause? You could discover illegal products and turn pirate during a standard copyright holder compliance check-up. Or you could find yourself under the audit microscope simply because your company name or IP address appears on the wrong client list. Are you getting the impression that you are surrounded by potential spies ready and waiting to turn you in for a little personal profit? You should be.

The reality is that virtually anyone who has a credible knowledge of your environment can report you for illegal use of copyrighted products. As I will constantly remind you, once targeted, you are essentially considered guilty until proven guilty. Rarely are the courts involved in settling these confrontations. By far, the vast majority of license violation confrontations find initial closure when companies like yours simply write a check—usually in the six figure range. Again: you will do so on the advice of your legal expert because paying up is considered (erroneously) the most effective method of making these people and these problems go away. Remember: they won't go away.

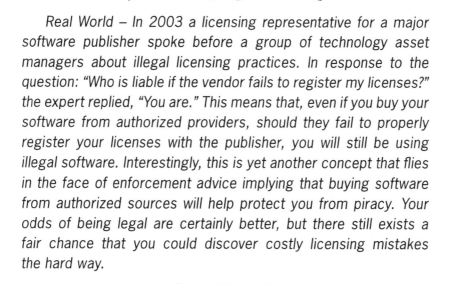

Real World – In 2003 a licensing representative for a major software publisher spoke before a group of technology asset managers about illegal licensing practices. In response to the question: "Who is liable if the vendor fails to register my licenses?" the expert replied, "You are." This means that, even if you buy your software from authorized providers, should they fail to properly register your licenses with the publisher, you will still be using illegal software. Interestingly, this is yet another concept that flies in the face of enforcement advice implying that buying software from authorized sources will help protect you from piracy. Your odds of being legal are certainly better, but there still exists a fair chance that you could discover costly licensing mistakes the hard way.

Settlement: GA – Internet Security Firm - $120,000

> *Ultimately, the responsibility for registering your licenses falls upon your shoulders. It is in your best interests to confirm that all product registrations are correctly documented by the copyright holder.*

Yes, I'm quite aware of all the "what ifs" associated with the previous story as well as many of the other scenarios discussed in the text. The bottom line is that if your software is illegal *you* will be the one held liable—not the supplier who was authorized by the software publisher to provide you with product and register your license. One only has to review the Microsoft® press release site to discover the numbers of software resellers that are being sued by this publisher (for, among other matters, the illegal distribution of Certificates of Authenticity) to get a feel for the complexity of the copyright violation and piracy risk events. It is to your advantage to set in place a very thorough and controlled process for registering and monitoring licensed products. Failure to do so will result in a very unpleasant compliance confrontation somewhere down the road.

Like the famous whistling past the graveyard concept, we now have the phrase: "My people assure me that the company is just fine with licensing." That assurance might even be true. At least, it will until you read a press release on an enforcement web site noting that your favorite discount supplier of software has just been taken down. (*Are you concerned, yet?*)

Maybe, instead, you're just a bit confused by all the rules. We each have to make individual decisions in regards to our potential exposure to piracy-related issues. Our personal ethics and perspectives can only guide us so far. Then we have to look toward some outside force for advice and assurance that we are doing the right thing—as well as doing the right thing right! Where is that outside force? Am I lost or does it appear that the vast majority of effective (read: well-funded) copyright awareness operations are those that represent or work in some close manner with the copyright holders? Is this like putting the cat in charge of the canary?

Is any government agency working directly with the consumer of copyrighted products to balance the power behind the incredible number of initiatives being brought by these special interest copyright enforcement groups? Personally, I haven't seen it. Have you? In my experience, the few organizations that represent consumer interest in technology issues have nothing remotely close to the reach and effectiveness of the tech industries. I have yet to see a government-sponsored agency that looks out for tech consumer interests and that does not work directly with at least one of these tech enforcement or product development groups. Have I missed it?

As I mentioned earlier, I firmly believe that national governments must initiate a coordinated series of strict oversight programs that monitor and regulate the actions and reach of the copyright enforcement industry.

Politically correct addendum: Those of you who are enforcement players — please keep this in mind — I believe in what you are doing, to a point. I believe that the impact of criminal piracy is significant and that it must be curtailed. However, as I have personally told many of your executives, I do not agree with your tactics. They simply too often appear to lean toward a vigilante mind set — one that, should any other industry attempt it — would lead to counter-litigation. Nor do I agree with the perspective I have witnessed for over many years: that anyone who disagrees with your methods is the enemy.

I'm not. We're not. We are your customers. We purchase the products you are suing us for purchasing. If you keep up the hard ball tactics, you might find that many of us are moving on to other products represented by companies that do not regularly threaten their customers.

Settlement: AZ – Semiconductor Services Co. - $124,575

What have we learned?

- The threat of confrontation and litigation for possessing incorrectly licensed copyrighted products is real.
- Enforcement groups are plentiful at all levels—local, national, and international.
- Unless the enforcement group is clearly part of the government, it is generally only another company—charged with copyright enforcement by the copyright holder.
- Groups can offer your employees rewards ranging up to $50,000 for information leading to a successful piracy settlement against your company.

Questions you should be asking yourself.

1. Which enforcement entities are active in locations where my company has facilities?
2. Does my company use products represented by members of a group or any single enforcement group?
3. Could an enforcement group in another country audit my facilities there then arrange to follow up with my facilities in other countries or in the States?
4. How closely do we monitor these products?
5. Are we exposed?

Okay. We've seen the scope of the problem. We've briefly discussed the enforcement activities. Now let's take a look at the laws that are being used to form the enforcement net.

Chapter 3

COPYRIGHT & INTELLECTUAL PROPERTY RIGHTS LEGISLATION

Chapter Goals: What legislation should I consider?

What laws impact my company?

How do they impact my company?

How should I prepare to counter this impact?

Hey, Buddy. Got a quarter million for a new law?

In 2005, the following funds were reported as being invested in contributions to federal candidates' 2004 election campaigns as reported by the Federal Election Commission:

Software Industry	$11,235,750
Computers/Internet Industries	$28,648,119
Movie Production Industry	$8,204,048
Recorded Music Industry	$2,872,451

Source: www.opensecrets.org

They say you can't buy happiness, but we have to wonder what levels of legislative good will can be obtained by industries with deep enough pockets. Protecting the intellectual property rights of individuals who create — be it software, music, fonts, graphics, video, games, or the written word — should be the ultimate goal of any society that values knowledge and improvement. Seems reasonable, right? But what happens when corporations, or entire industries of corporate entities, absorb the creations of those individuals, then package and market those creations as corporate assets? Has the intellectual property story changed from protecting the rights and talents of creative or visionary individuals to protecting the abilities of industries to consume, control, and limit access to that intellectual property — or innovation opportunities?

Is all of this piracy fervor really about consumers stealing intellectual property or is it about assuring corporate profit margins and locking down control of future development opportunities? Does modern legislation foster and protect the vision and creative growth of the people who make an industry work or does it protect the interests of the industries for which those people work?

Real World – An article in **BusinessWeek** *noted that, in 2004/2005, the Microsoft Corporation distributed more than $3 billion in regular stock dividends to investors, along with $8 billion in stock buy-backs. At press time, the company also planned to release an additional $33 billion to shareholders—the largest one time dividend in history.*

(Source: **Please, Sir, I Want More***, August 8, 2005)*

Author's Note *– I'm sorry, but I have to point out that, with profits like this, there is little wonder that the average person on the street in South Africa or China is not particularly concerned with the impact of piracy on this corporate bottom line. If the copyrighted products industries want to seriously curb the piracy rate, perhaps they should lower their prices and make products more affordable.*

Settlement: GA – Auto Restoration Co. - $75,631

If creative people are forced to labor under limited "work for hire" contracts, who is the beneficiary of their genius: themselves, society, or corporate executives? Do the creative artists and musicians gain maximum benefit from their works, or does the entertainment industry consume the majority of the profits while dolling out a tiny fraction of the proceeds to the people who provide the products on which the industry is based?

What is fair and reasonable? More importantly, is *anything* fair and reasonable? The average corporate executive is generally not concerned with the restrictions of legislation—up until those restrictions reach the point where the legislation directly and forcefully impacts the enterprise bottom line. When this happens—say, in the form of a software or media piracy audit—executive reactions are generally twofold: "Make it go away," and "Who can we use as a scapegoat?" As a result, companies across the globe find themselves constantly embroiled in copyright violation litigation threats.

We've seen some examples of the groups that make up the collective "software police" and "copyright cops." Now let's take a quick look at where these people gain the power to confront you and your company. If you plan on avoiding these enforcement groups, you absolutely must gain a basic understanding of the legislation and regulations that have been put in place to ensure that these watchdogs have bite behind their bark. If you understand, or are at least aware of the legal expectations, you will be more capable of proactively managing copyrighted materials according to the laws that apply.

How big is your company? Is it a local mom and pop with one, two, or more computers, a cell phone, copier, and a couple PDAs? These laws apply to you. Are you a small to medium-sized enterprise with 47 to 500+ computing devices in two or three disparate locations? These laws apply to you. Do you represent a multi-national enterprise with thousands (tens of thousands?) of systems? These laws apply to you just as well. Your exposure and the need to comply with copyright law are the same — no matter what the size of your computing environment. We all have to play by the rules as they have been set down. Unfortunately, most of us were not even aware that the game *had* some of these rules. Moreover, the rules do not generally (*ever?*) favor the consumer. The reality for the modern technology consumer is that, if you are not aware of these rules, you have already begun to lose the game by violating them. Let's look at some examples of the way that colorful piracy target came to be painted on your forehead.

As with Chapter 2, this chapter may also be tough for you to read. It contains a great deal of legalese that I think we all agree pretty much trashes our abilities to understand a given item of legislation. However, as I mentioned before, if you do not choose to *fully* read the material, at least scan the highlights. After all, these are the rules of the game we're all playing. If we don't at least marginally understand these rules, we've already lost.

Legislation:
Uniform Computer Information Transaction Act (UCITA)

(State Legislation: Maryland & Virginia)

Let's start with what is arguably the most interesting "consumer unfriendly" law we have yet to encounter. UCITA began as a modification to Article 2B of the United States Code. Fortunately for the national software consumer, and unfortunately for consumers in Maryland and Virginia, the committee charged with accepting or rejecting the 2B modification rejected it. However, the plot immediately began to thicken.

Once Article 2B failed at the national level, the software publishing industry and its representatives immediately redesigned the proposed regulations into the Uniform Computer Information Transactions Act, or UCITA. The industry then proceeded to lobby for passage of this Act in individual state

---

Settlement: CO – Steel Building Co. - $65,956.80

legislatures. UCITA passed in both Maryland and Virginia before consumer representative organizations could effectively ramp up a counter lobbying initiative. Fortunately, UCITA was brought to a halt before it moved beyond those first two states. However, as technology consumers, we absolutely must consider the seriousness of both the intellectual property industry lobbying tactics and their agendas.

Consider the following potential industry tactics:

- Quietly slip legislation into place in less sophisticated local legislatures to establish a precedent that can be cited to encourage similar legislation,
- Aggressively lobby technologically clueless legislators to pass laws that can be used or interpreted in ways they never considered,
- Ensure that many of the votes for these legislative acts are conducted on a voice vote basis so that there is no way to trace who voted for or against the legislation,
- Encourage legislative action (*stealth legislation?*) during times of social turmoil to ensure that public attention is focused elsewhere.

Is this what is happening? I'm not sure. Maybe you should decide after considering the legislation. And, what about these possible agendas:

- Aggressively lobby for favorable legislation on a nearly invisible local level to avoid potential opposition in more closely monitored national legislative arenas,
- Gain legislation that supports the rights of corporate copyright holders over those of a consuming society,
- Use the local legislation to encourage national legislation and follow that with global legislation—all modeled on the local precedent that was slipped through when nobody was watching.

Settlement: MD – Wireless Infrastructure Co. - $100,000

The legislation we are discussing can impact virtually every corporate technology consumer in the world. As well, these methods are being replicated in legislative activities across the globe to enable passage of laws that might otherwise be met with stiff resistance. Divide and conquer is still an applicable concept when special interest groups want to manage a larger or potentially disagreeable audience.

Coincidence, you say? Consider the Super Digital Millennium Copyright Laws that were being slipped into place on a state by state basis in 2003 and 2004. The copyrighted products industry didn't appear willing to risk taking on a revision of the controversial Digital Millennium Copyright Act so they developed template legislation and attempted to slip new laws through the state legislatures. (*Note to self: I will not be paranoid. I* will not *be paranoid...*)

In terms of UCITA, once consumer groups found out about the state by state strategies, many anti-UCITA laws were passed refusing to permit UCITA-like legislation in various states.

Fear Me

Think legislation is representative of collective need? Depends on which side of the collective collection you happen to live on. For instance, the Uniform Computer Information Transactions Act (UCITA) legalizes the following software industry practices:

- Software containing known bugs (defects) can be sold to consumers.

  » *Isn't the potential for bugs one of the core reasons the software enforcement industry uses to convince us not to buy pirated or counterfeit software?*

- Software can be sold even though it may contain viruses.

Settlement: OH – Marketing solutions Co. - $65,000

» *Isn't this another of the core reasons the software enforcement industry uses to convince us not to buy counterfeit software?*

- Shrink wrap licenses are binding.

» *A document can be legally binding even though you were not permitted to read it before becoming bound by it?*

- Software publishers can remotely turn off software.

» *Is it just me, or do these folks seem to be saying that it is legally permissible for the software publisher to include a back door in the software?*

- Software does not have to fulfill the specific function it was purchased to serve.

» *Does this really mean that the software doesn't have to work the way they told you it would work?*

- Publishers can use blind consumer notification of critical information.

» *Essentially, the copyright holder could post a licensing change on any public forum and you would be bound to it?*

- It is illegal to publish a negative review of the software.

» *You mean it's a federal crime for us to tell anyone that the product is defective?*

How could UCITA affect your company?

If you live in Maryland or Virginia, you are already at risk from the problems listed here for UCITA. We'll discuss options in a moment. For every other consumer:

- What would be the impact on your company if you were forced to buy software containing known bugs or viruses?

- Also, in order to remotely turn off the software you are using, the publisher must first have a back door concealed within the code. Does this impact your use of that software?

- Further, if the software you purchased does not function as you expected it to function, did you make a cost-effective purchase?

- Let's see: shrink wrap? You mean that I am completely bound by the terms and conditions of a license that I cannot read prior to being bound by its terms?

- Wait. Are you saying that a back door in the software I am using also enables the copyright holder to essentially peer over my shoulder?

- And this blind notification thing? Essentially, the publisher is permitted to post a blanket notification on any public forum, notifying me as a customer of a problem, change in the product, or change in the license and I am bound by that notification? Even though I never saw the notice?

- Oh, and I can't ever publish a negative review of the software because I will be committing a criminal act?

As a consumer of software and operating systems, does this legislation disturb you in any way? You bet your bottom line, it does. Well...it should.

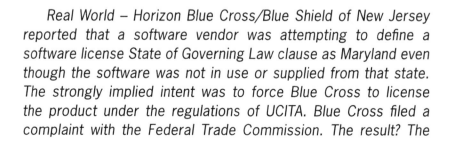

Real World – Horizon Blue Cross/Blue Shield of New Jersey reported that a software vendor was attempting to define a software license State of Governing Law clause as Maryland even though the software was not in use or supplied from that state. The strongly implied intent was to force Blue Cross to license the product under the regulations of UCITA. Blue Cross filed a complaint with the Federal Trade Commission. The result? The

Settlement: NM – Telecommunications Co. - $145,000

software publisher has the right to name the state of governing law. It is up to the consumer to negotiate the clause.

How many of your existing software licenses have declared that the state of governing law is Maryland or Virginia? If any do, you could be bound by UCITA, even though you are not located within one of those states.

Push Back

There is, however, hope for countering this threat—for all of us:

- In every software license negotiation, the consumer must place a clause that no element of UCITA will apply to that license,

- Also, you should insert a clause that no subsequent license or clause will supercede the negotiated license—including shrink wrap, click wrap, or any blind notification—unless the changes are mutually agreed-upon by both parties in writing.

- While you are considering this, consider the number of licenses you already have in place that, while they probably don't mention UCITA, actually have some of these permissions concealed within the clauses. When you see how many of these potentially explosive issues you have in your environment, you might want to reconsider your acquisition and negotiations tactics.

- Make clear in your contract or license agreement with the copyright holder a formal process for addressing bugs, viruses and defects. Ensure that you are compensated for related losses.

Settlement: MI – Memorial Medical Center - $250,000

- No back doors in code—period.
- Clearly define, in writing, all notification procedures that will apply to both contractual parties,
- Doesn't this negative review thing violate Freedom of Speech? You might want to negotiate this out so you can speak up if the publisher's product does not meet your needs.

Caution—Talk with your legal professional about the precise language for these concepts as well as other potential license traps. I am not providing you with legal or accounting advice. I am only making the observation that you might want to seriously consider these issues.

I have yet to encounter a single technology consumer who wasn't astounded by the tactics reflected in UCITA. This includes corporate executives and technology asset managers from Australia, South Africa, Belgium, and the United Kingdom. UCITA wasn't the first, but it sure appeared to be the most blatant, attempt by the special interest technologies industry to acquire legislation that clearly favors its own specific needs at the expense of the consumer. People around the world are well aware that legislative events in the United States tend to presage those that will occur in their own countries. Think these folks aren't worried about what legislative tactics are in use in the United States? Think again.

Real World – Throughout 2005, I encountered frequent informal discussions suggesting that lawyers could easily cite UCITA in an effort to show a level of precedence in cases where no other legislation may be applicable. Could UCITA come back at us through this courtroom back door?

Settlement: CA – Medical Manufacturing Co. - $117,000

As technology consumers we need to become aware of the trend to gain favorable legislation, be it local, national or global. We need to be prepared to make emphatic contact with our respective legislators and demand that they not fall prey to special interest pressure. Of equal importance, we need to follow up with those legislators to ensure that they follow up on our expectations. It all may appear to be rather simplistic and juvenile for me to even point out the obvious, but I have found that businesses are standing idle while industry sponsored legislation is creating a litigation black hole—and we are being sucked in.

Legislation:
Title 17 & 18 of the United States Code: Federal Copyright Law

http://www.gpoaccess.gov/uscode/

(US Government Printing Office)

http://www4.law.cornell.edu/uscode/html/uscode17/usc_sup_01_17.html

(Legal Information Institute – Coverage you can actually understand.)

Let's keep this simple, okay? Just an overview. You probably aren't a lawyer and neither am I, yet we both must establish some basic level of understanding of these laws. You can go to the web pages mentioned with each law we are going to discuss to review specifics if you want to learn more. As noted throughout this book: *always* consult with legal professionals before you follow up on the ideas represented in this or any other book.

The Big Kahuna

Federal Copyright Law (As outlined in Titles 17 & 18 USC) protects the creators of works eligible for copyright from unauthorized reproduction, adaptation, performance, display, or

---

Settlement: NJ – Engineering Firm - $75,000

distribution of the copyrighted works from the time that they are written. Technically, the works do not have to be formally registered to be covered.

Most other legislative Acts that we will consider tend to serve as modifications of the United States Code. What we need to be concerned with are the definitions of copyright infringement and the penalties for civil versus criminal copyright violations. Sometimes, I honestly believe that these regulations can change in sequence with the phases of the moon, but my legal folks assure me that it just isn't so. Well, I *think* that's what they keep telling me. Which of us really understands lawyers, anyway.

Civil Violations – "Oops, I messed up."

Civil violations of copyright regulations are generally considered of a more minor nature or occur where the violation was essentially unintentional. Civil violations of copyright carry penalties of up to $150,000 per copyright violated.

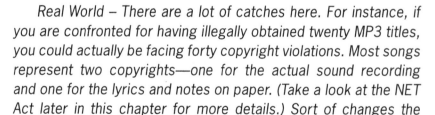

Real World – There are a lot of catches here. For instance, if you are confronted for having illegally obtained twenty MP3 titles, you could actually be facing forty copyright violations. Most songs represent two copyrights—one for the actual sound recording and one for the lyrics and notes on paper. (Take a look at the NET Act later in this chapter for more details.) Sort of changes the perspective, doesn't it?

Criminal Violations – "You'll never take me alive!"

One of the major criteria that shifts a civil offense over to the criminal arena is the concept of intent. Did you commit

---

Settlement: CA – Carpet Service Co. - $110,000

the offense on purpose with the willful intent to defraud the copyright holder? Were your actions motivated by, or resultant in, commercial advantage or private financial gain? Did the copyright holder incur a financial loss due to your actions? If you choose to play in this arena, welcome to the world of criminal records.

Criminal violations of Federal Copyright Law are punishable by fines of up to $250,000 per copyright and up to five years in prison. You can also be further charged with civil liability for actual financial damages including lost profits and statutory damages incurred by the copyright holder. Repeat offenders can spend an additional five years as guests of the Feds.

Forced Voluntary Audits? – "Oh, by the way!"

In many cases, we are seeing settlements that clearly do not reflect the penalties just mentioned. Here is why: Out-of-court or negotiated settlements tend to be governed by the lower fine rates of $750-$30,000 per copyrighted work. Usually, this occurs because the company or person violating the copyright "comes clean" and admits that they made an honest mistake. Here is how it works.

According to Title17 Section 504 c.2:

"Except as provided by clause (2) of this subsection, the copyright owner may elect, at any time before final judgment is rendered, to recover, instead of actual damages and profits, an award of statutory damages for all infringements involved in the action, with respect to any one work, for which any one infringer is liable individually, or for which any two or more infringers are liable jointly and severally, in a sum of not less than $750 or more than $30,000 as the court considers just. For the purposes of this subsection, all the parts of a compilation or derivative work constitute one work."

Settlement: CA – HVAC Co. - $50,625

This section is one of the key strategic reasons why most piracy confrontations are paid off without resulting to that rather expensive day in court. You see, if a company knows that penalties and costs can be cut significantly merely by quietly admitting to the mistake and correcting the problem voluntarily, the odds of non-judicial closure in favor of the enforcement entity increase dramatically. When one of the hallmarks of a successful corporate attorney is the ability to keep the client out of court, this little option virtually guarantees that the copyright holder will win any serious confrontation it initiates.

What do they call that, again?

Let's see. What do they call it if all I have to do is mention that I will perform some dastardly deed (like take you to Federal Court and make your supposed crimes a matter of public record) unless you write me a check?

Now, what are the chances that, even if you don't believe you did anything wrong, you will go ahead and write the check just to get me off your back and eliminate the potential negative publicity?

Push Back

There is no particular push back on Federal Copyright Law. You need to know what the expectations are and follow them to the best of your abilities. However, you should monitor legislative activities to ensure that special interest groups are not tweaking amendments or acts of modification. Once again, only through remaining aware of legislative activities and following up with our legislators will we be able to take more control over what laws are being passed.

Settlement: CA – Law Firm - $170,000

Legislation:
Fair Use Doctrine {USC Title 17, Sec 107}

The "fair use doctrine" of federal law is a complicated area. Basically, it limits the extent of property interest granted to the copyright holder. For example, this might allow citizens to cite a quotation from copyrighted material when the excerpt is used for teaching, research, news reporting, comment, criticism, or parody.

There are some limitations. Whether the court allows you to reproduce, distribute, adapt, display and/or perform copyrighted works depends upon the nature of the use (commercial purposes, non-profit, educational), the length of the excerpt, how distinctive the original work is, and how the use will impact the market for the original work.

Generally speaking, one is not allowed to take the "value" of a song without permission, and sometimes that value is found even in a three-second clip. When in doubt, it is always wise to check with the copyright owner, because in many cases even a small clip of a song may not be "fair use."

Real World – An excellent example of the potential violation of the Fair Use Doctrine could easily be represented by yet another commercial being aired in 2005. In this particular clip, a high speed ISP is touting its download capabilities. The fictional user has used his Internet connection to record an Eric Clapton performance and has further isolated sound bites from two versions of the song Layla. He has loaded those sound bites, including the very prominent song introduction, onto his cell phone as a ring tone. This action could easily represent a violation of copyright as well as the Fair Use Doctrine. If the cell phone belongs to this person's employer, significant penalties or litigation could be in that company's near future.

Settlement: OR – Fresh Food Prep. Co. - $54,151.25

Legislation:

Audio Home Recording Act of 1992

Public Law Number 102-563

Addresses the rights of consumers to make recordings of audio for use at home.

What's it do?

Copyright holders waive the right to claim copyright infringement against consumers who use digital audio recording devices in their homes for non commercial use.

Provided?

This Act includes the proviso that manufacturers or importers of these devices and related media must comply with the following:

- Register each product with the Copyright Office,

- Must pay a royalty tax on the devices to compensate for potential use by consumer to copy copyrighted audio,

- Devices must contain a system preventing the consumer from making copies of copies

And this Act applies to?

The Audio Home Recording Act applies to audio cassette recorders, minidisk players, and DAT players as well as all future digital recording technologies. However, this Act does not apply to multipurpose devices such as a general computer or CD-ROM drive.

Real World – The citizens of Australia currently do not have a law permitting them to make recordings for personal use. This

means that, **technically***, anyone in Australia who makes a copy of an audio or video work is at risk of violating Australian Copyright Law.*

Legislation:
No Electronic Theft Act (NET Act)

Public Law No: 105-147

(Federal Law)

http://www.eff.org/IP/NET_Act_sentencing/

Site contains an overview of Net Act by the Electronic Frontier Foundation

Amends Section 101 of Title 17 of U.S. Code:

Permits the Recording Industry to criminally prosecute sound recording infringements (including digital) even where no monetary profit or commercial gain is derived from the activity. The definition of financial gain to include the receipt (or expectation of receiving) anything of value, including receipt of other copyrighted works (as in MP3 trading). Extends the statute of limitations for copyright infringement from three to five years.

Penalties?

Penalties for violation include up to $250,000 in fines and as many as five years in prison. Individuals may also be liable for civil damages, regardless of whether the activity is for profit, for actual damages, lost profits, or statutory damages of up to $150,000 per work infringed. Repeat offenders can be imprisoned for six to ten years.

Settlement: AL – Mortgage Co. - $65,575

How do I qualify as a NET Act violator?

"NET Act violations occur by the reproduction or distribution, including by electronic means, during any 180-day period, of 1 or more copies or phonorecords of 1 or more copyrighted works, which have a total retail value of more than $1,000, shall be punished as provided under section 2319 of title 18, United States Code." (*See what I mean by legalese?*)

Summary?

Here is my interpretation—not necessarily the same one a Federal Judge might give but it is the interpretation of the average technology consumer. Does this make it more clear? If,

- during any 180 day period,
- you make 1 or more copies or recordings of one or more copyrighted works,
- with a total retail value of more than $1,000,
- you can be confronted under the NET Act.

Remember, as noted above, you do not have to actually receive payment for these pirated products—you need only expect receipt of anything of value (including other copyrighted products).

How could the NET Act affect me?

Real World – According to this legislation, all I have to do is share music with others. I don't have to sell the titles or trade them; I could be just giving them away. If I reach the threshold, I qualify for a no expense paid visit from the Recording Industry.

Corporate? – Of course, if this is one of my employees who is using corporate computers for violating copyright law, I could

Settlement: CA – Financial Services Co. - $115,000

wind up like the Arizona company that paid over $1,000,000 for sharing illegal music files on its internal network.

Okay, Rocky. Where were you on the night of the fifth? Tell us the truth. Precisely how many music files are secreted on your corporate systems? Are you already of criminal caliber? Is your day in court over-due? My advice is that you should clean up your systems right away. Get the sound bytes licensed or deleted. Set in place effective policies and procedures regarding copyrighted sound use and ensure that they have bite. (That's bite—not byte!)

Legislation:
Digital Millennium Copyright Act (DMCA)

Federal Law 105-304

http://www.copyright.gov/legislation/dmca.pdf

Site contains an overview of DMCA.

http://www.anti-dmca.org/faq.html

Site contains frequently asked questions covering DMCA issues.

What does it do?

The DMCA modifies Title 17 Section 1201 of the US Code to address the unauthorized access to a copyrighted work or unauthorized copying. DMCA also addresses the making or selling of devices or services that circumvent the Copyright Management Information (CMI) on a protected product.

DMCA formalizes a notice and takedown procedure between Internet service providers and copyright owners. When an ISP is aware of infringing activity on its systems, it must

Settlement: CA – Financial Services Co. - $300,000

take steps to remove the materials or it may be held liable for any resulting damages.

What are the penalties?

It is a criminal offense to violate Section 1201 or 1202 willfully or for purposes of commercial advantage or private financial gain. Penalties range up to a $500,000 fine or up to five years imprisonment for the first offense and up to a $1,000,000 fine or up to ten years imprisonment for subsequent offenses.

How could DMCA affect your company:

DMCA could significantly damage independent research into the quality or defects of software and other copyrighted products by punishing researchers that bypass security. Although DMCA has since been modified to protect certain types of research, it remains a potential example of industry controlled legislation. Coupled with license clauses that forbid publication of negative information or negative reviews, the DMCA can be used to suppress the dissemination of consumer warnings regarding software defects.

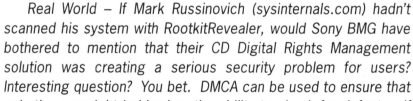

Real World – If Mark Russinovich (sysinternals.com) hadn't scanned his system with RootkitRevealer, would Sony BMG have bothered to mention that their CD Digital Rights Management solution was creating a serious security problem for users? Interesting question? You bet. DMCA can be used to ensure that only the copyright holder has the ability to check for defects. If they chose not to release that information, who would know?

Settlement: OH – Maintenance & Repair Co. - $81,500

DMCA can also be used to prevent consumers of videos from fast forwarding through commercials on rented or owned media. How can they enforce this? Simple, DMCA makes it illegal to circumvent the protection systems within the video. The only way to bypass the commercials on some DVDs is through modifying this code.

DMCA has already been used in litigation to establish precedent in monitoring competitive activities in the remanufacturing of printer toner cartridges.

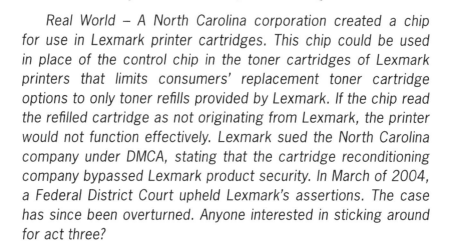

Real World – A North Carolina corporation created a chip for use in Lexmark printer cartridges. This chip could be used in place of the control chip in the toner cartridges of Lexmark printers that limits consumers' replacement toner cartridge options to only toner refills provided by Lexmark. If the chip read the refilled cartridge as not originating from Lexmark, the printer would not function effectively. Lexmark sued the North Carolina company under DMCA, stating that the cartridge reconditioning company bypassed Lexmark product security. In March of 2004, a Federal District Court upheld Lexmark's assertions. The case has since been overturned. Anyone interested in sticking around for act three?

What will happen when other printer companies begin to file similar law suits against independent companies that refurbish cartridges. Do you suppose that a significant shift to sole source replacement options could just possibly increase the costs of replacement cartridges?

DMCA is dangerous and bears close observation by the technology consumer.

Settlement: AZ – Technology Co. - $1,000,000

Legislation:
Federal Anti-Bootleg Statute

Applies to Title 18 U.S. Code Section 2319A

http://www.grayzone.com/faqindex.htm

Grayzone site discusses both this statute and others of interest.

What's it do?

Prohibits the unauthorized recording, manufacture, distribution, or trafficking in sound recordings or videos of artists' live musical performances. Signed into law as part of the General Agreement on Tariffs and Trade (GATT) in December 1994, this Federal Statute not only applies to illegal recordings made in the United States but also provides for seizure by U.S. Customs of bootleg recordings or music videos manufactured outside the United States at the point of importation. Through this statute, bootleg recordings are subject to seizure and forfeiture like any other property that violates U.S. laws.

What are the penalties?

The penalties for violation of the Anti-Bootleg statute include a fine of up to $250,000 and/or imprisonment of up to 10 years.

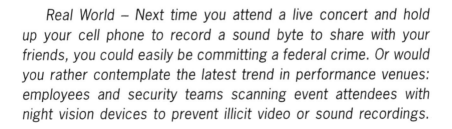

Real World – Next time you attend a live concert and hold up your cell phone to record a sound byte to share with your friends, you could easily be committing a federal crime. Or would you rather contemplate the latest trend in performance venues: employees and security teams scanning event attendees with night vision devices to prevent illicit video or sound recordings.

Settlement: TX – Software Development Co. - $80,000

Is somebody watching you? (I will not be paranoid. I will not be paranoid...)

Legislation:
Sarbanes-Oxley Act (SOX)

Public Law Number 107-204

http://www.sec.gov/divisions/corpfin/faqs/soxact2002.htm

Securities and Exchange Commission SOX site.

http://www.aicpa.org/sarbanes/index.asp

The American Institute of Certified Public Accountants

What is it?

The Sarbanes-Oxley Act was originally designed to address corporate executive responsibilities and accountability in terms of Federal Trade Commission rules and regulations. Among other expectations, the Act requires publicly traded companies to put in place and maintain clearly defined formal processes and procedures for tracking and monitoring expenditures and significant financial transactions. It also requires that whistle blowers be provided with a non-retaliatory method of reporting violations of Federal Trade Commission regulations.

How could SOX impact your company?

SOX can directly impact your software compliance management and technology environment in several interesting and essentially significant ways:

- First, SOX is all about developing and maintaining fiscal accountability, controls & formal financial oversight processes. Since most IT projects and purchases represent very significant investments for the average company, close monitoring of project costs and controls should be mandatory.

- Second, the CEO and CFO must annually sign off on the accuracy of corporate financial control records. Those records may easily include revealing any software piracy settlement because such a settlement represents a significant unbudgeted expense. As a result, shareholders (and the public?) may now become aware of an audit—something that has been traditionally kept behind the scenes.

- Third, publicly held companies must provide a confidential, non retaliatory process for whistle blowers to report violations of Federal Trade Commission regulations. Although this process does not directly address reports of violations of Federal Copyright Law, the Act does include a clause that requires the same basic protections for anyone reporting *any* violation of Federal Law.

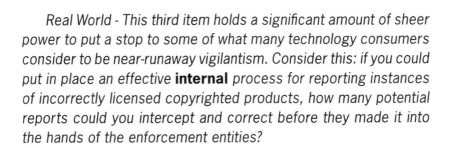

*Real World - This third item holds a significant amount of sheer power to put a stop to some of what many technology consumers consider to be near-runaway vigilantism. Consider this: if you could put in place an effective **internal** process for reporting instances of incorrectly licensed copyrighted products, how many potential reports could you intercept and correct before they made it into the hands of the enforcement entities?*

Want to be heroic in the eyes of your executive staff? Use SOX as the foundation for implementing an effective inter-

Settlement: NE – Marketing Services Co. - $60,534.13

nal technology asset management and compliance assurance program.

This concept is extremely interesting in its possibilities. It could also put a significant dent in the income potential of many of the enforcement industry players. By developing an internal reporting program, companies could identify and rectify illegal product situations and police themselves—without having to pay fines or penalties. Since ethical companies are already performing a process something like this, we should merely need to formalize and document the procedures to make it happen.

Remember: we aren't trying to avoid being caught violating copyright laws—we are trying to ensure that we never violate them in the first place.

Legislation:
Author, Consumer, and Computer Owner Protection and Security Act (ACCOPS) (House Resolution 2752)

Status as of date of publication: Referred to House Committee on Courts, the Internet, and Intellectual Property - 9/04/03

(Applies to Section 2319(b) of Title 18)

What's it do?

From the Library of Congress web site: "Author, Consumer, and Computer Owner Protection and Security (ACCOPS) Act of 2003 - Amends Federal law to require the National Intellectual Property Law Enforcement Coordination Council to develop guidelines to ensure that its component members share among themselves law enforcement information related to infringement of U.S. copyrighted work.

Requires the Attorney General, subject to specified limitations, to provide to a foreign authority evidence to assist it in:

Settlement: OK – Manufacturing Co. - $40,000

(1) determining whether a person has violated any of the copyright laws administered or enforced by the foreign authority; and (2) enforcing such laws.

Establishes criminal penalties for the unauthorized placing of a copyrighted work on a computer network accessible to members of the public who are able to copy the work through such access.

Establishes criminal penalties for any person who knowingly offers for download over the Internet enabling software (that, when installed on the user's computer, enables third parties to store data on that computer, or use that computer to search other computers' contents over the Internet) without warning any person downloading such software that it could create a security and privacy risk for the user's computer, and without obtaining the user's prior consent.

Establishes criminal penalties for persons who: (1) provides knowingly and intentionally fraudulent information in registering domain name; or (2) willfully infringe a copyright by the unauthorized reproduction or recording of a motion picture as it is being performed or displayed in a motion picture theater.

Declares that the knowing and intentional provision of material and misleading false contact information to a domain name registrar, domain name registry, or other domain name registration authority in registering such domain shall be considered evidence of willfulness regarding infringements committed by the domain name registrant through the use of such domain."

Penalties

ACCOPS carries a fine of up to $250,000 and as many as five years imprisonment for making copyrighted information available over a network without permission.

For purposes of section 2319(b) of title 18, the placing of a copyrighted work, without the authorization of the copyright owner, on a computer network accessible to members of the public who are able to copy the work through such access shall be considered to be the distribution, during a 180-day period, of at least 10 copies of that work with a retail value of more than $2,500...'

SEC. 304

Prevention of surreptitious recording in theaters.

Section 506(a) of title 17, United States Code, is amended--

(1) in paragraph (1), by striking `or' after the comma;

(2) in paragraph (2), by inserting `or' after `$1,000,'; and

(3) by inserting after paragraph (2) the following:

`(3) by the unauthorized reproduction or recording of a motion picture as it is being performed or displayed in a motion picture theater,'.

Interesting? Didn't we just see legislation that covers recording or video taping a live performance under the Federal Anti-Bootleg Statute? Evidently, the more laws we can put in place, the higher the chances of enforcement entities finding *just the right law* to cite in their law suits. Redundancy is good, right?

How could ACCOPS affect your company?

Technically, if ACCOPS is eventually passed, you will not be able to place any copyrighted products on your network systems. Also, based on the way various legislation is being interpreted, if an employee places copyrighted materials on your systems and makes those materials available to others, the company could be held liable—even if you didn't know about the violation.

Real World – So? What if one of your employees makes that illegal concert cell phone recording on a corporate cell phone? What if elements of the recording, or the entire recording, somehow wind up on the corporate intranet? What would be the value of that recording if it was calculated by determining the average concert ticket price multiplied by the total number of attendees, then divided by the total entertainment time? Want to bet the retail value of a simple illegally recorded ring tone sound byte could be calculated to exceed the $2,500 minimal value cited in ACCOPS? Want to guess if ten or more people may have accessed that same file on your network to download the byte in any given 180 day period?

Could we really be entrapped this easily? I'm absolutely certain that the industries that lobbied for this law will emphatically state that such was not their intended interpretation of the regulation. But, then again, what do we know about the legal system? Do courts and lawyers address the *intent* of a legislative act or do they consider the *letter of the law* itself? *I will not be paranoid. I* will not *be paranoid...*

Legislation:
The Sonny Bono Copyright Term Extension Act (1998)

Public Law 105-298

Federal

http://thomas.loc.gov/cgi-bin/bdquery/z?d105: SN00505:@@@D&summ2=m&

Library of Congress summary.

Settlement: LA – Staffing Co. - $39,757.50

What does it do?

This Act extends U.S. copyright from the life of the creator plus fifty years to the life of the creator plus seventy years. If the work was "made for hire," generally meaning a corporation holds the copyright instead of the actual work creator, the term is extended from seventy-five years to ninety-five years. Is this merely an interesting way to ensure that corporate revenue streams can be extended through legislation? Or could it be just one more way of not telling consumers: "*I got you, babe!*"

Legislation:
Super Digital Millennium Copyright Acts (SDMCA)

State by State Legislation

http://www.eff.org/IP/DMCA/states/

Electronic Frontier Foundation summary of SDMCA forms.

http://www.eff.org/IP/DMCA/states/20030408_eff_red-line_of_mpaa_model.php

EFF line-by-line analysis of MPAA template.

What are the SDMCAs?

SDMCAs, being passed on a state-by-state level by industry lobbyists, mostly working with the Motion Picture Association of America and the cable operator industry, make it a criminal act to connect or possess any device that constitutes an "unlawful communications or access device" to cable, satellite, or Internet lines.

SDMCAs each have somewhat different language but all are based upon a legislative template series developed by the MPAA. Essentially, the thrust of these acts is to reduce the capacity of individuals involved in the illegal exchange of video or other copyrighted materials to communicate anonymously over the Internet. Unfortunately, the latter of these acts could potentially be interpreted to make it a federal crime for individuals or corporations to use security processes such as a firewall, encrypted email, or virtual private network. After all, each of these common business practices could enable anonymous Internet communications.

While the sponsors and lobbyists assure anyone who will listen that they will not interpret the Acts in such simplistic ways, once again we find ourselves wondering about the odds of those assurances holding up after the Acts have been passed into law. Will industry legal teams enforce the *letter* of these laws or their *intent*? (*I'm sorry. Did I just ask yet another foolish question?*)

How could Super DMCA impact your company?

As noted, if passed in your state, SDMCA could directly affect your ability to send and receive information anonymously over the Internet. This limitation could make it illegal for companies to operate virtual private networks, send encrypted emails, or maintain secure firewalls. (*Are you beginning to see a pattern, here?*)

Is this another example of a special interest industry spending money lobbying individual state legislatures for favorable legislation? In a process many are calling *stealth legislation* the Motion Picture Association of America and other industry lobbying groups have ensured that many of these state laws were pushed through while consumers and legislative oversight groups were *distracted* watching the global events of post-911.

States where SDMCA is currently active:

Arkansas, Delaware, Florida, Illinois, Maryland, Michigan, Pennsylvania, Virginia, Wyoming, and still counting.

Settlement: IL – Equipment Rental Co. - $150,000

Family Entertainment and Copyright Act of 2004

(Also entitled Artists' Rights and Theft Protection – ART Act)

Public Law Number 109-9

Passed April 27, 2005

"(Section 102) Amends Federal criminal code to prohibit the unauthorized, knowing use or attempted use of a video camera or similar device to transmit or make a copy of a motion picture or other copyrighted audiovisual work from a performance of such a work in a movie theater. Sets forth penalties for such violations, which may include imprisonment for not more than three years for a first offense. *Considers the possession of a recording device in a movie theater as evidence in any proceeding to determine whether that person committed such an offense, but shall not, by itself, be sufficient to support a conviction for such offense.*" The italics were added by this author so you would be able to understand that, technically, all one of your employees has to do is carry a camera phone into the theater to be in violation of this law. You might be even more concerned when you realize that, according to this law, the owner, operator, or employee of the movie theater has the right to detain and hold for questioning any person they consider to be committing such an offense. (*No offense to these folks, but I'll take my chances with the Feds.*)

"(Section 103) Establishes criminal penalties for willful copyright infringement by the distribution of a computer program, musical work, motion picture or other audiovisual work, or sound recording being prepared for commercial distribution by making it available on a computer network accessible to members of the public, if the person knew or should have known that the work was intended for commercial distribution."

Settlement: CA – Restaurant Co. - $50,000

Legislation:
Trade Related Aspects of Intellectual Property Rights (The TRIPS Agreement) 1998

World Trade Organization

http://en.wikipedia.org/wiki/Agreement_on_Trade-Related_Aspects_of_Intellectual_Property_Rights

(I know the link above is confusing, but it is a direct link to the free on-line Wikipedia.)

"The TRIPS Agreement applies to all works, including computer programs, compilations of data, cinematographic works, and sound recordings.

Performers' Rights – Performers have the right to prevent fixation of their unfixed performance, the reproduction of that fixation, and the wireless broadcasting of their live performance when done without their authorization.

Producers' Rights – Producers have the right to authorize or prohibit the direct or indirect reproduction of their sound recordings and the rental of their recordings.

Broadcasters' Rights – Broadcasting organizations have the right to prohibit the fixation, reproduction, or broadcasting by wireless means any of their broadcasts.

Limitations – Through incorporation of relevant provisions of the Rome Convention, signatory countries are free to define any personal use as non-infringing activity, regardless of the impact on the copyright owner, and therefore impose limitations on the articles of this Agreement.

Enforcement – Allows countries to bring action against another country if it is found to be in violation of the TRIPS agreement. Countries must protect all recordings released within the past 50 years."

(Did I miss the part about consumers' rights? Must have. At the very least, put those cell phones back in your pocket during live performances.)

Settlement: CA – Bankcard Processing Co. - $90,000

The World Intellectual Property Organization Copyright Treaty (WCT) and the WIPO Performances and Phonograms Treaty (WPPT)

Held in 1996 to address digital issues and to further clarify Berne and TRIPS.

From the web site: "World Intellectual Property Organization Copyright Treaty (WCT) clarifies and extends protection offered under Berne and TRIPS, established to address digital concerns. Applies to computer programs, compilations of data (databases, though not the data itself), cinematographic works, and sound recordings.

Right of Distribution – Provides copyright owners with the exclusive right to authorize the making available to the public of the original and copies of their work through sale or other transfer or ownership. Refers to fixed copies as tangible objects only.

Right of Rental – Like TRIPS, owners of sound recordings and computer programs have the right to authorize or prohibit the commercial rental to the public of originals or copies of their works. Refers to fixed copies as tangible objects only.

Right of Communication – Grants authors the exclusive right to make their works available to the public in a manner in which the public may access them through on demand services (such as with the Internet). It also provides that such availability is to be considered a communication to the public, as opposed to an individual communication.

Technological Measures – Requires that countries prohibit the circumvention of technological measures used by copyright holders to protect their works.

Rights Management Information – Requires that member countries must provide adequate and effective legal remedies against persons who remove or alter electronic rights management information without authority, distribute, import for distribution, or broadcast works knowing that electronic rights management information has been removed without authority. Rights management information identifies the work, the author, the owner of any right of the work, the conditions of use, and any numbers that represent this information.

Other Legislation or Legislative Trends You May Want to Consider

Special 301

Congress created "Special 301" when it passed the Omnibus Trade and Competitive Act of 1988, which amended the Trade Act of 1974.

Special 301 requires the U.S. Trade Representative to identify those countries that deny adequate and effective protection for intellectual property rights or deny fair and equitable market access for persons that rely on intellectual property protection. Countries which have the most onerous or egregious acts, policies or practices and which have the greatest adverse impact on relevant U.S. products are designated "Priority Foreign Countries," and at the end of an ensuing investigation, risk having trade sanctions levied against them.

Countries can also be placed on other lists which do not result in immediate trade sanctions, such as "Priority Watch List" and "Watch List."

To take a look at a Special 301 Report, go to:

http://usinfo.state.gov/products/pubs/intelprp/301.htm

Refer, also, to the affects on China of being cited in a Special 301 Report as noted in Chapter 2 under IIPA.

Canadian Copyright Law

The Canadian Copyright Act (the "Copyright Act") is a federal statute.

The Copyright Act is the principle statutory protector of computer programs.

Settlement: CA – Health Enterprise Co. - $175,000

Bill C-32, which includes the statutory damages regime, was proclaimed into force on October 1, 1999.

In practice, Industry Canada Minister (John Manley) and Canadian Heritage Minister (Sheila Copps), are jointly responsible for the Copyright Act.

From the web site: "The Copyright Act does not protect ideas, but rather the 'expression of ideas.'

For copyright law purposes, the 'expression' of an idea may be in the form of a literary, dramatic, musical or artistic work. Computer programs are considered 'literary works.'

Civil versus Criminal

- Under the Copyright Act, authors are entitled to certain remedies when their rights are infringed.
- Remedies for infringement of copyright can be divided into two broad categories: civil and criminal.
- Civil remedies allow the copyright holder to take direct action against a person or company who infringes his/her/its copyright.
- There are a number of civil remedies, including: an injunction, damages and an account of profits. In addition, where a copyright holder is successful in suing an individual or company for infringement of copyright, the copyright holder may be awarded a portion of his/her/its legal costs.

Separate provisions of the Copyright Act provide for criminal remedies.

- Where criminal remedies are pursued, typically it is the Crown (i.e. the government) who instigates proceedings against the infringer.
- The Crown has the choice of proceeding by way of summary of conviction or by way of indictment.

Settlement: CA – Electrical Construction Co. - $100,000

- In the case of a summary conviction, the accused may be subject to a maximum fine of $25,000 or to imprisonment for a term up to six months, or to both. In the case of a conviction on indictment, the accused may be subject to a fine of up to $1,000,000 or to imprisonment for a term not exceeding five years, or to both.

- It is improper to use the word "charges" to describe civil allegations made against a defendant.

Statutory Damages Provision

- Statutory damages are fixed amounts awarded per work infringed. They are an alternative to actual damages.

- Generally, statutory damages range from $500 to $20,000 per work infringed. Judges will consider a number of factors before deciding what sort of penalty is appropriate, including: the conduct of the parties before and after the event, as well as the good or bad faith demonstrated by the defendant.

- Statutory damages have been available for some time in the United States where it is believed that they have been instrumental in reducing piracy rates."

Interestingly enough, the Canadian Legislature refused to pass a Canadian version of the Digital Millennium Copyright Act. They must have been reading up on the problems with this legislation in the States.

Just a Little More Legislation We Might Want to Monitor:

Intellectual Property Protection and Courts Amendments Act of 2004

Public Law Number 108-482

United States

Settlement: NC – Software Development Co. - $49,308

Covers counterfeit packaging and labels. (*As in Certificates of Authenticity*)

Computer Owners Bill of Rights

Senate Bill Number S563

United States

Referred to Senate Committee on Commerce, Science, and Transportation on March 6, 2003.

"Requires the Federal Trade Commission (FTC) to establish standards for the provision of technical support for computer and computer-related products by computer hardware and software manufacturers, as well as consultants and resellers that provide technical support."

National Computer Recycling Act

House Resolution 1165

United States

Referred to Subcommittee on Environment and Hazardous Materials on February 25, 2005.

Get ready. This one will probably include a disposal "fee on the sale to an end-user of any computer, monitor, or other designated electronic devices" containing "waste materials in used computers that may be hazardous to human health or the environment ..."

Many of the technology asset managers I communicate with are of the opinion that this particular bill is being held up because the hardware producers do not want to be saddled with providing the service themselves. Instead, the story goes, the hardware industry would like to modify this Act to place the burden for disposal on the consumer.

At this time, the Environmental Protection Agency has the ability to investigate illegal disposal of technology hardware and fine violators up to $10,000 per chemical found in the systems. For our purposes, hardware could be composed of systems units, monitors, cell phones, pagers, and anything with a circuit board—possibly even batteries. If the hardware can be traced back to your company, you *could* be in for a significant financial surprise. (More on this in Chapter 10)

Finally!

Are you confused? Overwhelmed? Who wouldn't be? Each of these regulations, when considered from an independent perspective, could be viewed as perfectly reasonable (*well, except for UCITA which is just plain inexplicable*). However, when we look at an overview of all the various legislative activities placed side by side, a pretty scary picture seems to want to form in our beleaguered brains. When all of the restrictions of the global legislative acts are linked with current trends in software licensing and technology product legal agreements, conscientious systems asset managers begin to glance around for the nearest Kevlar™ vest and bomb-proof underground shelter.

Let's play a quick game of *What if?*.

- What if a given industry or series of industries could directly influence local, national, and international laws to give itself, or themselves, a complete lock on innovation in their given trade?

  » A key to growth and development is our ability to begin with a given product or technology and then improve upon it. Much of the legislation denies virtually anyone outside of the originator of the product the ability to do so.

- What if an entire industry utilized its powerful financial clout to make strategic political contributions that virtually guaranteed passage of favorable legislation?

  » Stealth legislation anyone?

Settlement: KY – Horse Show Group - $175,000

- What if an entire industry could fund apparently independent market research that will be used as the definitive justification for enacting protective global legislation?

  » Is it just me or have free speech and independent research started taking on the qualities of poorly produced infomercials?

- What if a group of corporations could creatively interpret statistical evidence so that entire governments would act to ensure that those special interest corporations' assets were protected by government law enforcement agencies?

  » Legislators are constantly basing legislation on special interest industry-funded surveys, citing research that is occasionally composed of significant percentages of estimated data reported as pure fact.

- What if a group of corporations could arrange it so that creative people were virtually required to sign over all of the intellectual property rights for their creations to the company?

  » If the only job you can obtain to support your family is a work for hire contract that deprives you of the benefits of your innovations, you might eventually become less creative.

- What if a group of corporations could prevent any access, use, derivation, or application of processes or works they own by anyone other than their own designated creative employees?

  » If only the software publishers are permitted to unlock software security to search for and communicate defects, who will provide independent third party oversight?

- What if corporations could ensure that their ownership of intellectual property rights extended well into the distant future?

> *Maybe Sonny & Cher were right: I got you, babe!*

Is this a valid analogy?

Would you be willing to pay for a car designed in such a way that, once the tires wore out, you would be required to purchase an entirely new vehicle? What if the vehicle was not compatible with 50% of the roads you needed to travel? What if you were forced to pay for dozens of specialized options you would never use? What if the same automobile manufacturer also controlled the quality and production of tires to ensure that any tire you placed on that car would magically wear out every 21 months? Should we ponder the analogy and get with the program (*so to speak*) or make certain that our collective heads are buried firmly in the sand?

Careful... From that position your defenseless assets will be fully exposed. You could easily lose them.

What shall we do?

The major legislative acts that impact corporations using copyrighted products include Federal Copyright Law – Title 17 US Code, The Digital Millennium Copyright Act, The No Electronic Theft Act, and UCITA. You need a basic under-standing of each of these to ensure that your environment does not inadvertently stray into non compliance.

Monitor Legislative Activity — Primarily, you do not need to be an expert in international law to understand the main thrust of proposed legislation. Begin monitoring the legisla-tive oversight web sites and keep yourself and your staff up to speed on developing activities.

How do various laws impact your company? Unfortunately, with the advent of stealth legislation and huge investments on the part of the technologies industries, the majority of mod-ern copyright-related legislation does not favor the consumer.

Violation definitions often do not reflect the realistic flow of technology usage. Fines and penalties are significant and they are being enforced—in near vigilante style—by industry groups with virtually no governmental oversight or control.

How should you prepare to counter this impact? Become an active part of a professional networking organization. Communicate with others in your field to share perspectives and legislative trends. These trends should include any questionable licensing or contractual activities that the industry introduces.

Communicate your pleasure or displeasure to your legislative representatives. Pile on the pressure to resist big money special interest lobbyists.

If you do not take time to monitor what is being done, you may find yourself waking up some day discovering that what has been done, has been done to you!

Real World – Are we discouraging innovation? - In the late seventies, (yes, I'm dating myself) I worked for a Fortune 500 multinational marketing corporation. As a dedicated employee, I submitted half a dozen suggested marketing campaigns for use in promoting the company's products. Nearly every idea was used. In fact, one of my ideas was picked up as one of the most successful marketing campaigns in the company's history. My reward for thinking outside the box and helping the company make millions more dollars? Nothing. In fact, when I asked if the campaign was based on my idea, I was threatened with termination for asking the question. My future innovative contributions to that company? Zero.

Settlement: CA – Energy Conservation Co. - $147,206.09

Questions you may want to consider

1. Is your company in a UCITA state? If so, how could you control its impact?

2. Is the company under any licenses or contracts that cite UCITA-style requirements?

3. Does the company have summaries of legislative requirements that can be utilized in negotiating licensing terms and conditions?

4. Does anyone in the company monitor industry trends and share risk analysis with key personnel?

Now let's discuss the various auditing methods used by industry watchdog groups to enforce their rights under these laws.

Chapter 4

WHAT ARE THE SOFTWARE
POLICE LOOKING FOR?

Chapter Goals: First, we need to know what we need to know...

What are the significant general audit facts?

What is a forced audit?

What is a forced voluntary audit?

What is a proactive voluntary audit?

What are the software police doing?

Simply put? They are looking for you! If you are violating copyright, then you become their number one target. Unfortunately, even if your violations are inadvertent, you will most likely be treated the same as the criminal side of the equation. In general, the collective enforcement players don't appear to differentiate much between the civil and criminal intent of consumers in their initial confrontational audit attitudes and methods.

One of the key indicators of confrontation success appears to be how easily you will back down. Essentially, if the enforcement industry lawyers can beat up your lawyers (*In court. Not out in the parking lot.*), you will quickly find yourself paying whatever fines or penalties they choose to apply to your offenses. Since the vast majority of consumer corporations do not retain crack legal teams with unlimited discretionary funds, many enforcement entities are well aware that they play the winning hand in virtually any confrontation. You'll pay because you can't afford to play.

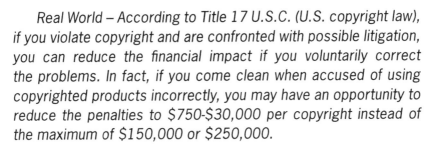

Real World – According to Title 17 U.S.C. (U.S. copyright law), if you violate copyright and are confronted with possible litigation, you can reduce the financial impact if you voluntarily correct the problems. In fact, if you come clean when accused of using copyrighted products incorrectly, you may have an opportunity to reduce the penalties to $750-$30,000 per copyright instead of the maximum of $150,000 or $250,000.

(Guess why the majority of companies don't fight the piracy accusations.)

Are the audit activities monitored or regulated?

While some basic guidelines are in place within the U.S. Code, they mostly apply to governmental agency activities and judicial actions, not necessarily out-of-court confrontations. If the policing entity is a governmental group, they must follow their respective agency guidelines in their investigations. If they represent a software publisher, group of publishers, the music industry, the film industry, graphics industry, font industry, or gaming industry there are no formal guidelines or controls in place as to how they may or may not operate. You, the consumer, are quite simply fair game for whatever tactics they choose to employ. Again, if you can afford the costs of fighting a massive international enforcement group with nearly bottomless litigation pockets you might have an even chance of winning. If you can't—you won't.

Settlement: NC – Manufacturing Co. - $75,000

Real World – While virtually every significant software license has a clause permitting the copyright holder to audit for compliance, very few have clauses that define compliance or provide clear expectations and procedures for proving compliance. (Have you ever shadow-boxed? The same basic principles apply here.)

Unfortunately, governments do not appear to be overly concerned with the actions of the private copyright enforcement industry. As noted, the copyright holders definitely have every right to manage the consumption of their products—we should all consider this a perfectly credible option. However, outside of legislation (local, national, and global) that is quite often built upon templates designed by the copyright holders themselves, or their lobbyists, there appears to be a significant blind spot on the part of governments in terms of regulating enforcement actions. While most of us support these actions when they apply to criminal infringement, we might be wise to also become very concerned with the seemingly blanket enforcement processes coupled with highly diverse and constantly changing compliance assurance requirements that are being applied to every infringement, however unintentional or inadvertent.

What are these people looking for?

For the most part, an auditing group is searching for multiple items of strategic information. The short version reads like this:

> *They want you to be able to prove that you are using the products you are legally entitled to use, in the numbers and manner in which you are entitled to use them,*

Settlement: IA – Plastics Co. - $90,000

that your documentation is accurate and clearly covers
every purchase and license count, and that the products
you are using are not counterfeit.

The keys to the average audit are:

- The copyright holder wants to accurately document precisely how many computing systems you have at the location mentioned in the audit request or warrant.
  - » These will include every computing device or media storage resource that could hold or deliver copyrighted products. Yes. Your servers, too.
- They will want to detail precisely which of their company's, or member companies', products are present on each computer.
  - » In general, an enforcement group is only permitted to review systems for the products of its members — and only when those members approve the specific audit in question. Software publishers may only review compliance issues for their own products. Government agencies are essentially guided by their charters and applicable laws and may be capable of reviewing piracy levels for any copyright violations under their individual jurisdictions.
- The audit entity will minutely examine your paperwork documenting where you purchased each product, what you paid and how you paid, the details on each and every receipt, actual license documents, any certificates or proofs of authenticity that apply, and any other related items they might wish to request.
  - » These items appear to be the core focus of most audits. Do your receipts cover each and every specific product present on your computers? Are the receipts correctly and completely filled out? Watch this one. Receipts are ticking bombs because so many are not correctly completed by the supplier — yet you will

be the one to suffer the consequences if the information is not correct.

» Certificates, or proofs, of authenticity and license documents are often counterfeited. Even though you will not be able to identify counterfeit documentation, you are still going to be held accountable if you possess it. This is essentially the same concept as receiving stolen goods. You still lose your investment and, if you were aware the product was illegal, you knowingly acquired stolen goods.

» If you have purchased upgrade licenses, you will be expected to document the upgrade paths in accordance with the upgrade agreement. This is another significant process companies traditionally have not followed. You could easily be heavily fined for not being capable of producing the entire paper trail of upgrades—all the way back to the original purchase.

(See Chapter 6 for more details.)

• Auditors will compare the numbers, versions, and releases of every product you have on your systems against the numbers, versions, and releases you are legally entitled to have. They will then produce a document that clearly details your licensed product shortfall. *(And trust me—you will be short.)*

» If all the numbers match, you are in good shape. If they don't match, then "let the negotiations begin!"

• They'll most likely "suggest" that you remit the following fines and penalties for an out-of-court closure. Some of the costs you will face will most likely include:

» Fines for each violated copyright. Based on copyright law *(See Chapter 3.)*, these fines could meet or exceed $250,000 per copyright violated,

---

Settlement: PA – Technology Outsourcing Co. - $115,000

» You will pay a penalty of 1.5 to 4 times the publisher's list price for every instance of incorrectly licensed copyrighted products,

» You will pay the costs for all legal teams and audit personnel involved with the audit as well as all costs for copyright holder representatives involved in the audit,

» You will pay the cost of the automated audit tool used in the audit,

» You will pay the cost of corporate down time,

» You will pay the costs for technicians to remove incorrectly licensed products,

» You will pay the costs to acquire and reconfigure correctly licensed products,

» You will pay the costs of implementing an approved life cycle compliance program,

» You will pay the costs of exposing the corporate reputation to negative global publicity,

» You will pay the costs of exposure to damaged vendor relations.

» *Pay us now. Pay us later. Pay us again. Pay us more. Pay our friends. (Are you sensing a pattern, here?)*

• Finally, the auditing entity will expect you to conduct follow-up audits. These can include, but aren't necessarily limited to:

» The costs of additional follow up audits by the same enforcement entity,

» An increased exposure to subsequent audits by other enforcement entities,

» An increase in potential subsequent audits by individual copyright holders,

» Potential exposure to follow-on audits of any additional facilities your company may hold in other local, national, or international locations,

Settlement: CA – Employment Training Co. - $74,000

> » Potential exposure to audits of any of your clients or customers who might have received benefit from your piracy activities,
>
> » Once you admit guilt, you could easily become a permanent ongoing target...

Are you even remotely ready for this process? Let's take a look.

Audit Scenario One - Forced Audit

Step One – Forced Audit

In general, at least in the U.S., a forced audit is a rare event. This particular action is about as traumatic as they come and is usually either the last resort confrontation with an uncooperative corporate consumer or it is a high impact confrontation with a criminal piracy group. Forced audits function precisely the way they sound—the enforcement team conducts an audit under force of a search warrant served by (usually) United States Marshals—or, in the case of countries outside the U.S., virtually any applicable law enforcement group. Frequently, additional federal agencies will become involved, such as in the case of organized criminal activities. Also, in general, agencies like the U.S. Department of Justice do not become involved unless there has been a clearly criminal violation of Federal Law or the scope of the operation is multinational.

Real World – The copyrighted products industries are pushing hard to gain legislation enabling the Department of Justice and other governmental agencies to investigate and follow-up on any violation of Federal Copyright—criminal or civil. (Is this like having the government perform the dirty work for you, or is it my imagination?)

Settlement: MO – Mortgage Co. - $90,000

A forced audit does not usually stand alone. Most frequently, the enforcement entity or software publisher has repeatedly made efforts to bring issues to closure prior to documenting evidence and requesting that a Federal Judge issue a search warrant. These activities may range from simple "cease and desist" letters, to visits by copyright holder representatives, to requests that the target company conduct a voluntary audit, to offers by the enforcement entity to conduct a voluntary audit on behalf of the target company. If all these efforts are ignored by the target company and the offenses are considered significant enough, a forced audit may be conducted.

Step Two – Forced Audit

In general, during a forced audit, U.S. Marshals will enter the corporate facility and serve a search warrant to the most senior executive present. They will be accompanied by representatives from each software company whose products are suspected of being used illegally by the target company. If an enforcement entity is involved, representatives of that entity will also be present. Quite possibly, there may also be additional auditors present who will assist or augment the main audit team.

Step Three – Forced Audit

Once the warrant is served, the target company usually must cease all computer-related activities until the physical audit is concluded. In most modern companies that rely on computers to operate, this means you could be essentially out of business throughout a period that could last one to several days. During this period of time, auditors will conduct physical reviews of every computer system covered by the warrant. These systems will include servers, desktops and notebooks; but they frequently can also include any other systems, possibly even bare hard drives that may be in storage. Yes, com-

Settlement: MN – Consulting Co. - $58,000

puters and hard drives that are not in use may also be audited to determine the copyrighted products loaded, and you will be held liable for these licenses along with those that are actually in use.

The audit process does not usually touch upon any of your corporate electronic files so you generally do not need to be concerned with possible damage to corporate records or resources. The audit team is basically searching each computing device for a clearly defined group of executable, command, and system files that activate the copyrighted products noted on the warrant. However, (*You knew there would be a caveat, didn't you?*) consider this: if your systems contain suspicious application-related files—as in maybe one of your technical people uninstalled or deleted the evidence—your systems may be confiscated, forensic searches conducted, and materials held as evidence for court. This is called spoliation of evidence and it is a very foolish action on the parts of many soon-to-be-audited companies.

"Don't attempt to trash evidence—*vee haf vays uf makink your seestems talk!*"

While one group of auditors is reviewing the physical systems, another will be conducting a nearly microscopic review of all the acquisition and licensing documentation the target company possesses. In actuality, this phase is frequently the most time consuming. Consider—where are all of your proofs of purchase, proofs of authenticity, licenses, master media, or other forms of documentation located? If you had to do so right this minute, how long would it take you to recover these documents? How long would it take if there was an audit group, including federal agents, breathing heavily at your back or waiting for the documents in your conference room? Yes, Virginia, this type of one-on-one confrontation can, *and does*, happen right here in the good old U.S. of A.!

Step Four – Forced Audit

Next, the audit team will compare the documentation covering what you are legally permitted to possess against the audit information covering what is actually in place. These two numbers are reconciled and, as noted, if you are short on license documentation and over on your counts of products that are actually loaded on systems, your legal team will either go to court or start down a very long and expensive negotiation road.

Step Five – Forced Audit

This is important. Please keep in mind: in the average audit settlement, nearly everything is negotiable. Rarely will anyone in authority admit this, but it's true. Consider the cost, public forum, and length of a court case. Most companies and enforcement entities would much rather negotiate out-of-court settlements than face the potential damage a court case may wreak—publicly as well as financially. If your legal team is not experienced in negotiating with the compliance enforcement industry, have them gain access to additional team members who *are* experienced. Effectively managed negotiations can significantly cut your costs and penalties. Ineffectively managed negotiations will effectively cause you to cut your own...well, your... (*I think you could finish this sentence yourself.*)

Step Six – Forced Audit

Plan on this: you will be expected to maintain your compliance into the future. This may include initiating a formal software compliance assurance program and drafting copyright policies. Many settlements include a right to re-audit at any time for between three and five years. They may also require executive management to provide a yearly signed statement confirming compliance (*Does this sound anything like Sarbanes-Oxley?*). There will be plenty of hoops to jump through before you will be able to move these issues away from possible front page news releases and get your company back into normal operations.

It is very important to remember, however, that all of these hoops you will be pushed through by the threat of litigation are also the milestones you could achieve in developing your own effective — proactive — enterprise software life cycle management program. Essentially, if you accomplish all of these processes yourself, before you are audited, not only will your (eventual) audits be relatively painless but you will reap a significant level of ongoing budget savings through more effective management of the software and other copyrighted products on your systems. Let's see what this forced audit would feel like:

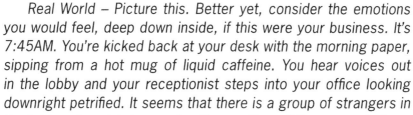

Real World – Picture this. Better yet, consider the emotions you would feel, deep down inside, if this were your business. It's 7:45AM. You're kicked back at your desk with the morning paper, sipping from a hot mug of liquid caffeine. You hear voices out in the lobby and your receptionist steps into your office looking downright petrified. It seems that there is a group of strangers in the lobby who wish to speak with you. Two of these people have identified themselves as United States Marshals. The trip from your desk to the lobby seems to take a lifetime.

As you round the corner, you note that there are, indeed, eight well-dressed and very stern-looking individuals lurking just in front of the entry doors. Two of these people approach you, introduce themselves as Federal Marshals, then request your name and position in the company. They ask to speak with you privately in your office where they present you with a search warrant issued by a Federal Judge.

Settlement: MT – Printing Co. - $40,006.50

Within minutes, this team of auditors, representing a membership organization of software publishers as well as individual representatives from several software copyright holders, fans out across the facility. They are here, escorted by Federal Marshals, to conduct a surprise software license compliance audit on corporate computers. While the majority of these investigators conduct physical audits on every computer, several accompany you to a conference room where they ask you to arrange to have an employee bring all of your software purchase and possession documentation.

While the entire staff stands back, unable to use their computers, your accounting personnel attempt to locate the correct documents. The pressure is on. People are confused and genuinely afraid. Some documents can be located—many can't. The auditors return with their results from the individual systems. Within minutes, they produce a detailed list of copyrighted products loaded on every computer you own.

Then the audit team begins trying to match the documentation to the copyrighted products you have on site. Within a couple of hours you discover that your proofs of purchase and licenses do not match the product count. Maybe there are even a few counterfeit products mixed in with the genuine ones. A significant percentage of your proofs of purchase is not acceptable due to discrepancies in details. Other critical documents are missing entirely. Your life perspective is rapidly moving from rosy to rocky.

After an eternity, the audit team leaves and the lawyers begin their discussions. Your company is fined approximately $70,000 for software piracy. The eventual primary cost of the entire process exceeds $150,000. Long term costs exceed this amount by a huge and unpredictable margin.

Settlement: NJ – Software Development Co. - $100,000

What should you do?

If you have been confronted with a forced audit situation, pay close attention to all instructions and follow them to the letter. Get your lawyer on site as quickly as possible and be certain that anything that is said or written down is very carefully monitored and edited for accuracy. The audit team has every right in the world to begin the audit immediately. If they are willing to wait for another executive or your attorney to arrive on site, they are doing you a favor. Don't plan on it happening. Let them get rolling. If possible, either remove all employees from the premises or isolate them away from the audit team.

Real World – Employee conversations around auditing team members during an on site review process can tip the team to non compliance issues of which they may not have otherwise been aware.

If possible, delegate a responsible individual—one who can keep themselves silent—to accompany each auditor within the facility and clearly document what they do. Ensure that this person's actions follow the parameters of the search warrant. Do not interfere or intrude on the auditors' activities. *Do not* allow your employee *guide* to make any unnecessary comments or provide unnecessary assistance. Their task is to merely observe, document, and remain polite. Review this concept with—and have it approved by—your legal counsel before attempting it during an actual audit. If possible, set up a formal process right now—before you are forced to do so.

A forced audit is definitely an intense experience for any normally law-abiding individual or group. The pressures on you and your employees are awesome. The audit team will literally control and guide the entire process. You will discover an entirely new feeling of helplessness within the confines of your own company. Follow orders and you will not be shot while trying to escape. (*No...no wait, I didn't mean that. To my knowledge no software compliance audit target has ever come close to becoming a real target of anything other than legal bullets. This reading was becoming too intense and you* really *needed to lighten up a bit.*)

Just do what you are asked to do and be helpful without incriminating yourself or the company. Discuss your possible actions with your legal team, now, *before* some incredibly large human being with a badge wanders into your lobby. If your company has withheld compliance action until it has been targeted for a forced audit, the odds are extremely good that you have had plenty of warning shots across your bows. Or it could very well be that you are already well aware that you are using copyrighted products illegally. In either case, you were given a chance to do the right thing. Now you get to experience the consequences of ignoring Federal Copyright Law. Good luck.

Audit Scenario Two - Forced Voluntary Audit

A forced voluntary audit is, in general, an audit that you perform on your own systems at the *request* of an enforcement entity or copyright holder. While, these groups may *appear* to be asking that you conduct this audit voluntarily, the very strong implication is that, should you decline to conduct the voluntary audit, they will be more than happy to perform the audit for you—possibly by force (see previous).

In the forced voluntary audit, the enforcement entities are searching for the same information detailed on the previous pages. This time, however, you will provide all of the information yourself. However, whereas in the forced audit you paid for the labor of skilled external compliance auditors, during the voluntary audit you will pay even more for the (*Shall I hint at unskilled?*) internal labor to conduct the entire audit.

> At the onset of a forced voluntary audit your legal team has two primary immediate tasks. First, they need to negotiate an extension to the initial thirty day time limit for conducting an audit. This will give you more time to conduct the audit correctly. Second, they need to lean on the auditing entity to clearly define and limit the specific products encompassed by the non compliance accusation. This step allows you to narrow your search down, making it more manageable.

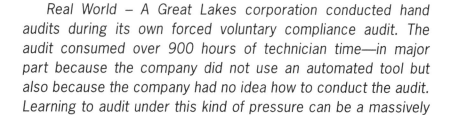

Real World – A Great Lakes corporation conducted hand audits during its own forced voluntary compliance audit. The audit consumed over 900 hours of technician time—in major part because the company did not use an automated tool but also because the company had no idea how to conduct the audit. Learning to audit under this kind of pressure can be a massively expensive mistake.

Once again, you will be conducting a system by system review and you will detail the numbers and names of individual products loaded on every computing device. You will also have to assemble and organize all the related purchase and licensing documentation. Remember that collecting and interpreting this information is easily the most intense experience in the audit process.

Settlement: PA – Manufacturing Co. - $132,000

Next, you will have to compare the numbers of installed products against the numbers of products you are legally entitled to possess and document any shortfall in the licensed product count. Then, you will have to email, snail mail, or fax copies of all requested materials to the enforcement entity for review. Much of what you send will be challenged and the telephone, email, and letter negotiations marathon will commence.

> *Big Caution*: Whoever you have designated to communicate with the enforcement entity had better be well trained in these communications or you could be in serious trouble. They used to say, "Loose lips sink ships." In a copyright compliance audit, even a single misspoken sentence can cost hundreds of thousands of additional dollars (Review *Communications* in *Chapter 5*). Carefully document and prioritize any potential negotiation issues and risks. Do not permit your representative to step into discussions cold, or without effective documentation. Do ensure that at least one other qualified person listens in on the negotiation to provide support and advice to your lead negotiator. An uninformed or unqualified negotiator will not be an asset when your assets are on the line.

It is also important to note that, while many audit entities might provide their own *free* automated audit tool, you could just as easily be charged for a short term license for that tool. Also, most free audit tools tend to be limited to a relatively small number of computers—any additional systems would require a license. If you are forced to acquire one of the free tools for the initial audit, you may have a more limited choice over which tool is used and the money you spend could be lost. Consider the cost savings and potential long term return on investment if you could review and acquire that automated configuration discovery tool after considered thought, rather than being pressed into the decision as an audit requirement.

Settlement: NH – Manufacturing Co. - $80,000

*Real World – If a high percentage of the **free** audit tools provided by the enforcement entities are limited to 50 computers, or even 100 computers, how do you suppose this (or these) numbers reflect a **favored target** size for the entities monitoring compliance?*

If you represent a small to medium sized company—the chances are very high that *you* are quite probably the preferred target for enforcement investigation and litigation. However, if your company is larger, don't get complacent—you are still a target, just a more complex and time consuming one.

The importance of the forced voluntary audit concept is that, while control of the audit process is nominally in your hands, the control of the actual outcome is most frequently in the hands of the audit entity. Again, your entire corporate operation could easily be disrupted and firmly constrained from any production by the outside audit entity throughout the process. Let's look at some examples.

Once you receive the registered "intent to audit" letter, you are usually not permitted to make any changes in the configuration of any computer at the premises noted in the letter. The systems must be frozen to prevent possible spoliation of evidence. This means that, until you receive permission from the auditing entity, you most likely will not be permitted to:

- Apply patches or fixes,
- Update anti virus signatures,
- Modify servers,
- Load or remove any copyrighted products,
- Dispose of any unused systems,

- Enter into or continue any negotiations with software vendors or publishers,
- Communicate with copyright holders about the audit,
- Configure newly purchased computing devices,
- *...and the beat goes on...*

Spoliation of evidence means that you have deleted illegal copyrighted products or in some manner modified systems to destroy evidence. If you spoil the evidence in any manner, the copyright holder may escalate the audit process by confiscating systems for forensic reconstruction.

Essentially, while the surface issue of these requirements is to deny you the option of deleting any illegal products, this tactic also serves very effectively as a not so subtle pressure on you to settle the case quickly so you can get back to work. Consider the impact to your company if you were not permitted to patch defective software during a global virus attack on those defects.

Remember, the compliance dance is defined by the copyright holder. When you agreed to the license or contract, you most likely did not require a clear and written definition of compliance, the audit process, or any one of a number of compliance and piracy-related details. If your use or misuse of the copyrighted product has progressed as far as the audit letter, you are still not in control of your environment. Again, if this is your position, the copyright holder can demand virtually anything it wishes.

If you cannot produce the required documentation or information, you could easily be considered legally out of compliance. (For more detailed information on negotiating and changing license agreements as well as gaining proactive savings while protecting your company from the software police, review the *Critical Software License Terms & Conditions* series and the *Negotiating Software Agreements* series at www. biztechnet.org.)

Audit Scenario Three - The Vendor Audit

Another audit scenario that falls within the realm of externally controlled audits is the vendor-initiated audit. In this process the copyright holder, generally a software publisher, activates the *right to audit* clause in their software license agreement. Although there is still a pronounced level of pressure during the vendor audit, this process is generally not as intense as that of an audit by a compliance enforcement company. Again, don't get complacent. Treat this as an extremely serious event.

When an enforcement company performs an audit it may do so representing as few as one or two, or as many as ten or more, software publishers or copyright holders. The enforcement company audits are correspondingly intense due to their larger scope. Conversely, though, when a copyright holder audits a customer for compliance, it is only permitted to audit for its own products—a significant reduction in scope and intensity.

An audit by the software publisher or copyright holder will require you to provide the same basic data as represented in the previously discussed audits. Again, since there are no governmental regulatory guidelines, the copyright holder may demand virtually any justifying documentation or records it wishes to review. In addition to the general data we have discussed, your closure could hinge upon your ability to produce any single one, or all, of the following:

- The copyright holder may be in the midst of investigating a global outbreak of counterfeit products and could demand a review of only your certificates, proofs, or documents of authenticity to prove your products are genuine,

- The audit team could be checking only proofs of purchase against actual utilization counts,
- The copyright holder may require you to produce only the licenses that apply to their products,
- The copyright holder may want to review your policies and procedures, or discuss your compliance assurance actions with your executive management,
- The auditors may only demand to inspect your master media,
- The copyright holder may be reviewing your upgrade licenses to ensure you legally acquired them through the proper upgrade paths,
- The copyright holder may be minutely reviewing license terms and conditions to ensure that you are using the product precisely as you are permitted (*Look at the next scenario.*),
- Again, *the beat goes on...*

Vendor audits most frequently progress with very little direct confrontation, but don't bet money on it. The vendor is generally sincerely interested in checking its products and assisting you and your company in clarifying processes of mutual interest. Some vendors will not penalize you for honest mistakes, providing you take corrective action. However, and again, if you are intentionally violating your licenses or agreements, the vendor audit team has every right—and a responsibility—to confront you for the violations and penalize you accordingly. Remember, in many cases such as this, it isn't the copyright holder who is acting contrary to good business ethics.

Real World – In every compliance assurance and software asset management course I teach, I always point out this critical fact: the vast majority of software publishers or copyrighted product developers are not your enemy. Most of these folks want to create mutually beneficial relationships and they are willing to work with you to do so. There is a very tiny—but powerful— minority of confrontational copyright holders of which you must become aware. If you are prepared for anything this minority may throw at your company, you will be in excellent shape in terms of compliance.

Let's move on. We have walked through condensed versions of the externally controlled audit processes. Now let's take a serious look at the only audit process that will reduce your company's exposure to non compliance audits and, at the same time, substantially lower your ongoing software-related costs. In fact, if you put forth the effort to make serious use of the processes and information provided in this next section, you will be capable of reducing quite a few of your hardware costs as well as software costs.

Audit Scenario Four - Proactive Voluntary Review

A proactive review is one that you perform without being backed into a corner by any copyright enforcement group. In a proactive review, you investigate your technology environment and eliminate or correct any licensing issues that you locate. Since you will be performing this review as part of your ongoing compliance and systems due diligence, you have every right—and responsibility—to remove incorrectly licensed products—without penalty. If you are not already conducting this type of systems check on a regular basis I strongly recommend that you immediately begin doing so. Scratch that. *I am telling you that this is the only sane way to manage your technology assets.* Proactive voluntary systems reviews are a significant portion of any effective software (and hardware) asset management program. The issues that you discover and correct during these checks remain internal and will significantly reduce your exposure to the potential fines and penalties that may be levied by external auditing groups. (*Please re-read this paragraph. It is really important.*)

A proactive audit can save you significant dollars in some of the following ways:

- In a proactive review process, you acquire your own tool based upon your own real world operational criteria, needs, and expectations. The configuration discovery tool can be used for *many* more purposes than merely compliance audits, thus increasing its ongoing value.

- If you are functioning proactively, your personnel will have plenty of time to become experts at gaining maximum return on this tool because it will become a critical part of their operational toolkit.

- As noted, your initial review of systems enables you to proactively eliminate *any* non compliance issues — without penalties or potential damage to your corporate reputation.

- An ongoing systems review process enables you to discover and re-license or remove products that are under-utilized or no longer in use. Big savings, here.

- You will be able to monitor product versions and releases to ensure that all company users are working with the same, or at least compatible, products.

- You can identify products on servers or mainframes that could be more economically transferred to, and licensed at, the desktop level.

Settlement: TX – Auto Shipping Co. - $100,000

- You can identify products on desktops that could be more economically transferred to, and licensed at, the server or mainframe level.
- You can locate and eliminate illegal audio, video, graphic, or gaming products. Again, without penalties.
- And *the beat goes on... (See Chapter 6 for more details.)*

Proactive reviews are the only professionally sound method a business can use in actively managing its technology environment. This process has been proven to consistently reduce technology costs and protect companies from, or substantially reduce exposure to, the vast majority of compliance enforcement events. Proactive audits will reveal a multitude of weaknesses and inefficiencies in any technology environment. Whether you are searching for hardware or software statistics, licensing and documentation resources, or conducting patch and anti virus management initiatives, an effective proactive technology asset discovery and management process will help provide accurate and timely information.

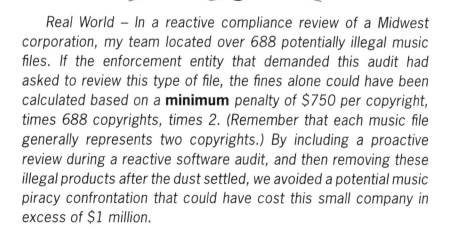

Real World – In a reactive compliance review of a Midwest corporation, my team located over 688 potentially illegal music files. If the enforcement entity that demanded this audit had asked to review this type of file, the fines alone could have been calculated based on a **minimum** *penalty of $750 per copyright, times 688 copyrights, times 2. (Remember that each music file generally represents two copyrights.) By including a proactive review during a reactive software audit, and then removing these illegal products after the dust settled, we avoided a potential music piracy confrontation that could have cost this small company in excess of $1 million.*

Settlement: TX – eBusiness Services Co. - $100,000

Where does all of this stop?

Based on extensive experience with enforcement activities—both personally and through hundreds of technology asset managers around the globe—I can honestly predict that this confrontational process of maintaining compliance with copyright laws is not going to stop. In fact, our exposure as piracy targets will grow at a steady rate. As systems and copyrighted products become more complex, it will become more and more difficult for ethical companies to monitor compliance and maintain their legal balance. Mistakes will happen with greater frequency and the costs will pile up.

> *In 2003 and 2004 we began seeing a significant increase in aggressive enforcement of music copyright on the parts of Recording Industry Associations of America and other entertainment entities. Their controversial approach to MP3 file sharing has been labeled both confrontational and draconian, even by some of this industry's most loyal supporters. Intelligent companies realized that they now had to aggressively monitor **every** computing device for copyrighted music products along with software. Less than effective companies kept their non compliant heads in the sand.*

In terms of confrontational copyright enforcement, the motion picture industry hasn't been far behind the music industry. Thanks to incredibly fast Internet connections, corporations are discovering that employees now download movies from warez sites, using corporate systems and on company time. As noted, the movie industry has been very active in drafting and supporting legislation that makes it easy to track illegal files from their source to their precise destination. The end result

---

Settlement: TX – Hospital Gift Shop - $100,000

(Remember the SDMCA laws?) is that in many states music and video industry investigators are capable of peering right through your previously *secure* firewalls to identify the specific desktop where the download was transferred.

Real World – A professional software asset manager contacted me in mid-2005 to report the following event: An employee, working inside the corporate firewall, illegally downloaded music through a peer to peer file sharing service. One of the major copyright enforcement entities tracked the downloads, through the firewall and company security systems, directly to the individual desktop. (With this in mind, I'm curious: how is it that this level of investigative focus is possible in copyright piracy but nobody seems capable of tracking down and confronting individuals who send spam?)

> *In a quote from a 2004 press release, the MPAA Director of World-Wide Anti Piracy Operations stated, "...if you illegally trade movies online, we can find you and we will hold you accountable."*

Here is another interesting thought. A significant number, (well over 50%) of your employees have PDAs and/or cell phones—many of them provided to the employee by the company. These products can, and do, contain copyrighted operating systems, software, graphics, music, fonts, games, and even video files. Each of these categories of product, if not currently controlled by license, can become controlled without your knowledge—exposing your company to copyright violations. Also, it frequently doesn't matter whether the hardware belongs to the company or to the employee. If personnel use the corporate Internet to download incorrectly licensed materials to a desktop or server for later transfer to their own hardware, the company could easily be part of the evidence trail and may be held accountable—*will definitely* be held accountable if the PDA or cell phone is company owned. Any of your personnel downloaded any copyrighted ring tones lately?

> *While I have not yet encountered an instance of a company being audited for copyrighted products on PDAs or cell phones, these products represent a significant potential revenue stream for the software and music industries. How long do you think it will take for them to start cashing in? If you do not currently monitor these items, I strongly recommend that you begin doing so.*

What have we learned?

First and foremost, no matter what company you represent; no matter how ethically you use computers, you will eventually be audited by a copyright holder. They will have very specific questions that will be focused on the terms and conditions of the product licenses and agreements—legal documents to which you or your personnel have bound the company.

In general, auditing entities will want you to prove the following:

- What copyrighted products do you actually have on your systems?
- What copyrighted products are you legally entitled to possess?
- Can you identify and produce all the necessary documentation?

Settlement: IL – Engineering Firm - $249,000

- Is the documentation accurate and acceptable?

- Are any copyrighted products, documents, or media counterfeit?

- Can you prove that you are compliant with all contractual requirements?

- A forced audit, though relatively rare (at least in the States), usually occurs after a company refuses to heed warnings of non compliance or refuses to conduct its own forced voluntary audit.

- A forced voluntary audit occurs when a company has been accused of non compliance by a copyright holder or an enforcement entity. While voluntary in nature, this audit scenario carries with it the threat of a forced audit if the target company does not comply with the request.

- An ongoing series of proactive voluntary systems reviews (audits) is the most effective defense against externally controlled audits. These systems reviews are not instigated by any enforcement entity. They are completely internal ongoing reviews of corporate compliance status that allow the company to adjust copyright product inventories without penalty. These proactive audits have significant cost saving potential and should become regular processes conducted by any corporation that utilizes computing devices as part of its ongoing business best practices.

- Most important: if you are not being audited by a copyright holder or its representative, you have every right in the world to identify and remove copyrighted products that are not correctly licensed or that may be counterfeit. However, once you receive that formal audit notification, you must follow the instructions. Once the letter arrives, do not illegally remove copyrighted products or modify systems in any manner not permitted by the audit entity.

Settlement: CA – Engineering Firm - $147,000

Questions to consider

1. Based on the information in this chapter, would you be prepared to deliver the correct information in an audit?

2. If not, what items do you need to begin collecting — now — before someone knocks on your door?

3. Document this list and begin locating your audit materials.

4. How close is your company to implementing an enterprise-wide proactive review process?

5. What steps can you take to initiating this process or enhancing existing processes?

Moving right along...

Now let's take a look at the ways companies tend to slide their own necks into the copyright violations noose.

Chapter 5

COSTLY COMMUNICATIONS MISTAKES

Chapter Goals: First, recognize that loose lips do, indeed, sink ships!

Why worry about communications?

Who are the players?

What you say can, and will, be used against you!

Are *they* talking to *me*?!?

As we've discussed, the global copyright enforcement teams work without any apparent formal regulation or oversight of their tactics or activities. They can determine their own requirements for escalating non compliance events from simple cease and desist requests to full blown forced audits. The enforcement entities can often essentially make their own rules and decisions as to whether or not to pursue your alleged non compliance as a criminal or civil violation of copyright laws.

The enforcement entities have a wide range of laws under which they can threaten action against your company or you as an individual. They also have huge litigation budgets that they are more than willing to match against your (*meager?*) legal funds in case of a formal litigation confrontation. When these folks speak, only a foolish or uninformed individual would even consider failing to listen.

Sadly, there are *so* many businesses that absolutely fail to listen to the messages. When this occurs, the enforcement reaction can range from patient education efforts to threats of immediate litigation. While no solid public evidence appears to exist supporting a progressively more emphatic approach to copyright violators, we certainly hope that common sense would prevail in confronting violations. Unfortunately, the nearly industry-wide *cone of silence* that appears to surround enforcement operations has achieved near mythical proportions (*Much more so than Maxwell Smart.*). A fraction of the individuals interacting with the enforcement industry have very carefully hinted that they follow a basic approach such as this:

- Initiate communication with non compliant companies informally and ask that they check their use of copyrighted products,

- Follow up with a letter making the same request in a more formal manner—this is quite possibly the cease and desist phase,

- Formally request that the target company conduct a compliance audit and report the findings,

- Offer to conduct an onsite *voluntary* audit using the enforcement entity's own auditors,

- Obtain a search warrant and conduct a forced audit raid

We would hope that there are additional steps throughout this process but, since the enforcement industry is not regulated, they technically do not have to follow any formal process; also, as they have repeatedly implied in our actual discussions, they certainly do not have to reveal or discuss their operational details with anyone.

Unfortunately, the consumer is being thrust into a literal maelstrom of frequently conflicting approaches to compliance enforcement. Corporate consumers regularly receive multiple compliance enforcement letters requesting audits. Some of these letters are genuine, some are merely psychological nudges seemingly designed by the software or copyrighted product industries in an effort to dupe unaware corporate personnel into conducting and submitting self-audits — even when the companies have not been reported for non compliance.

The focus of many of these pseudo-letters appears to be a sort of bizarre form of educational awareness, or consciousness raising — an effort to wake up clueless consumers. But, wait: which letter is serious and which is a semi-blatant attempt to sell more software by forcing companies to reactively over-purchase instead of establish a process to effectively manage copyrighted products? How is the average business owner expected to react to this barrage of intimidating personal touches? The dozens of letters I have reviewed appear to be so much alike that it is nearly impossible to differentiate the fishing expeditions from the honest and ethical warning letters.

Real World – It is little wonder that I have actually received phone calls from small business owners across the United States who tearfully read me a bogus audit warning letter—bogus, to me, but earth-shattering for them.

To compound the confusion, many pseudo-audit letters are sent to multiple individuals within a given organization—including people who have no authority over, or knowledge of, compliance issues. When three or four letters are discovered floating around a multinational corporation it is extremely difficult to determine the individual credibility of content. Perhaps it is time for this consumer awareness education process to take on a little more form, function, and credibility?

Settlement: MN – Manufacturing Co. - $45,500

So? *Are* they talking to you?

Sure thing! After all, the letters are addressed to you as well as to several other corporate personnel, right? Absolutely. And what prompted many of these letters? Could it be evidence of non compliance? Is the company actually violating copyright laws? Did someone make that fateful toll free call? Is Jimmy down in the mailroom after the top secret $50,000 reward for frying his non compliant boss and potentially destroying the company financial prospects? Not necessarily.

In reality, the enforcement group or software publisher could easily have simply purchased a mailing list of corporate personnel for a given zip code or range of zip codes. That *audit right now* warning letter you just received could quite possibly represent a simple fishing expedition. You know, don't you? Sales are down and we need to generate revenue for the end of quarter books? Then again, that same audit letter may be a serious opening salvo in a soon to escalate copyright litigation war. If you ignore the former letter, you will probably face no particular consequences. If you ignore the latter — *death to the non-believer!*

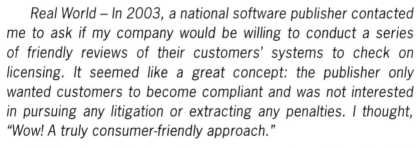

Real World – In 2003, a national software publisher contacted me to ask if my company would be willing to conduct a series of friendly reviews of their customers' systems to check on licensing. It seemed like a great concept: the publisher only wanted customers to become compliant and was not interested in pursuing any litigation or extracting any penalties. I thought, "Wow! A truly consumer-friendly approach."

Well, at least I believed that concept until, well into the third discussion session, a member of the publisher committee let slip that they were having a bad fiscal year and that each customer license violation I located could easily represent a $1,000,000

Settlement: CO – Engineering Firm - $150,000

license reconciliation fee. (So much for the nice guy approach. No. I didn't accept the project.)

Are they talking to you? Yes, most certainly. However, it is up to you to determine which side of the enforcement mouth the words are emerging from. This is where many companies make their initial communication mistakes.

Mistake: "It never happened."

In the scenarios above, the tendency of most corporate employees is to pretend the letter never arrived. This can be discussed as a three-pronged potential threat. First, many individuals who receive the audit letter are simply in no position to initiate any corrective action. In fact, in many of these cases, the addressees would be seriously risking their jobs if they presented the letter to management or made any attempt to conduct a quiet localized audit review. Although this is frequently a result of the enforcement entity incorrectly identifying corporate personnel, their miscommunication with corporate management could easily be considered a valid attempt to notify the company of a non compliance situation.

Real World: Although UCITA does not directly apply to this scenario, this legislation **does** *clearly state that* **blind notification** *can be legally binding. Could this be interpreted by the enforcement industry to mean that, based on the potential legal precedents resulting from UCITA, the copyright holders could eventually place a notice of non compliance on any industry web site—without directly notifying the offending company—then, after a designated response period passes, immediately charge*

Settlement: NV – Pathology Laboratory - $150,000

the company with criminal infringement? Based on the concepts
behind legitimizing blind notification, this could technically become
a working scenario. (Think UCITA can't impact your company?)

Aren't you glad you don't live in a UCITA state?
Then again, have you checked all of your agree-
ments to ensure that none of them cite Virginia or
Maryland as state of governing law? You may not
be living in a UCITA state but you could still be liv-
ing with UCITA.

Mistake: "You have no authority over me."

As noted earlier, there are so many audit letters circulating
in the business world that the average business owner has no
idea which to consider valid. The result is that many corporate
personnel simply throw the audit letters away, often without
fully comprehending the actual content. Common reactions include:

- "After all, the licensed product doesn't belong to these
  people so who are they to intrude on my right to quiet
  enjoyment of the products I purchased."
- "I've never heard of these people. They must not have
  much authority."
- "Let them try to audit me. I won't let them in."
- "I asked several other people who received the same
  letter and threw it away."
- "I'm too busy to address this issue right now. They can
  wait."

Unfortunately, these concepts are dead wrong. In almost
every major software license is a right to audit clause. This

clause, generally something along the lines of, "The copyright holder...has the right to audit for compliance," gives the copyright holder the right to audit your company for compliant possession and use of its products. Most of these clauses also contain a little side bet nestled between those ellipses above that we tend not to notice. This side statement usually takes the form of, "or its representatives" and when placed after, "The copyright holder," means that virtually anyone or any entity may audit you—provided they have power of attorney from the copyright holder. In practice, the copyright holders can significantly extend their reach and intimidation factor by extending this right to audit to additional entities.

Real World – I conducted a fairly comprehensive but informal series of software license compliance discussions with a local lawyer over a one year period. We had lost track of one another for several months when he called to discuss a client who was being audited by a compliance enforcement group. His reaction to the notice, even after all our discussions, was, "They can't do this to my client." (Actually, yes they can—and they did.)

Mistake: "I'm afraid to ask for help."

Again and again, it all comes down to a definite lack of solid understanding of, or trust in, the enforcement industry, the laws, and the limitations of the license agreement terms and conditions. Business owners and their personnel constantly rely on assumptions and speculation instead of checking out the facts. Unfortunately, the enforcement industry subtly encourages this lack of knowledge by fostering an aura of fear and mystique surrounding its activities.

Settlement: TX – Real Estate Investment. Co. - $312,000

I constantly speak with business professionals who inform me that they are literally afraid to contact the enforcement companies or the copyright holders about their problems because they fear doing so will put them on the radar screens as a target. Essentially, business people believe (*justifiably?*) that any discussion with these groups will only lead to enhancing the enforcement agenda. Executives and asset managers are under a constant barrage of intimidating public relations messages that tend to foster much more fear than encourage honest and mutually beneficial dialogue.

Real World – During 2003 and early 2004, I made well over 100 calls to enforcement industry toll free confidential anti-piracy hot lines. In each call I asked for assistance in initiating a **proactive** *anti piracy program in my company. In each and every contact, I encountered personnel who were thoroughly trained in encouraging me to report piracy but had no clue or interest in helping me* **prevent** *piracy or non compliance in my company in the first place. My attempts to connect with supervisors were either ignored; my messages not returned; or the supervisors were only interested in my piracy report potential. In one instance involving a major software publisher, the supervisor told me: "(Company name omitted to protect my future)...does not accept unsolicited consumer suggestions." And, yes, I asked for, and received, permission to quote her.*

Further, my calls for assistance to private compliance enforcement companies were actually rewarded with statements along the lines of: "We do not represent or work with software consumers. We work on behalf of our industry members and their interests."

Finally, the major software publisher mentioned above actually gave me a follow up call to measure my satisfaction with the

results of my original call. The individual recited from a script that •
had nothing to do with my requests. When I interrupted him to
reply that I was not satisfied with the results of my call he merely
continued his script reading as if he were on mental rails. After
several more questions he simply hung up on my futile requests
for additional supervisory follow up.

It appears that the **anti piracy** hot lines are, in reality, **report
piracy** hot lines. As an update, recently many enforcement groups
have jumped on the software asset management and software life
cycle management band wagon. After years of ignoring consumer
requests for help, suddenly they want the corporate consumer—
the same ones that they have been penalizing for millions of
dollars—to place complete trust in their proactive services. Think
about this concept. (Review the white paper: Who you gonna call?
[For compliance assistance] on the biztechnet.org web site.)

The web sites of governmental enforcement and assistance
agencies were not much more help. Their educational materials were essentially—*you guessed it*—authored by the corporate anti piracy enforcement industry players. The anti piracy
materials that were posted were also hopelessly out of date and
incomplete. Few of the real world issues that confront the corporate technology consumer are even addressed on these state
and national business support sites.

Real World – Most non compliance enforcement actions
require the target company to put in place policies addressing
piracy and illegal use of copyrighted products. However, I have
yet to locate any significant level of discussion on the part of
the anti piracy education industry that clearly emphasizes the

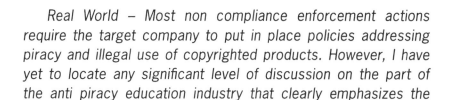

Settlement: IL – IT Consulting Co. - $31,784.75

*absolute critical nature of actively **enforcing** those policies. The failure of executive management to seriously enforce policies is one of the most frequent complaints I've heard from the asset managers who represent the few companies that actually have these policies in place. Why doesn't the enforcement industry give this critical element of compliance assurance the serious attention it deserves? Could it be that when copyright compliance policies are actually enforced, the results tend to reduce violations which tends to reduce potential fines, penalties, and settlements?*

(If we're really in this enforcement business to encourage change, shouldn't we be documenting all the changes necessary to avoid violations? If, on the other hand, we're only in it for the money, then it probably makes perfect sense to inadvertently downplay a few key items. Please tell me this isn't what's happening.)

It seems that for years many of the enforcement industry players have wanted to complain about piracy and non compliance with copyright but few have been particularly concerned with preventing non compliance from occurring in the first place. Again, as mentioned, I believe that this is because piracy prevention is simply not as profitable or easily accomplished as post-violation enforcement. Even the multitude of consulting and copyright compliance assistance services that have popped out of the woodwork in recent years seems to frequently be composed of marginal experts who have strong secondary agendas that they are following—and that they expect you to follow if you want their help—such as:

- Those who predicate their services on the consumer purchasing their compliance-related product line (I'll help you if you buy my products.),
- Those who ultimately represent the enforcement industry players (Again, a practice akin to setting your cat to keep an eye on your canary),

---

Settlement: IL – Marketing Service Co. - $225,000

- Those who understand and address only a minor fraction of the software or technology life cycle management process (We can help you get compliant but we can only do it for the products we represent.),

- For-profit groups that are more concerned with their bottom line than their effectiveness (These folks will provide advice and help, but it'll cost you pretty hefty dollars),

- Slightly crazed fringe groups that want you to believe that you need not be concerned with copyright—the sky is not falling—so forget your worries (These folks tend to provide some really scary advice. They also fit in well with the ones who advise you not to pay your federal taxes.).

Who can you trust for non biased and accurate information? You could invest hundreds of hours combing the Internet in search of product-neutral elements of effective systems asset management and compliance assurance techniques. Next, you could double that time in your efforts to cull out the entities and perspectives that are based on private, corporate, or industry agendas that supercede your needs. After this significant investment in time and focus you will actually have compiled a fairly comprehensive overview of possible options—most of which are prohibitively expensive, time consuming, and generally without correctly balanced costs and benefits.

My best advice is that you should begin building a support network of other software and technology asset managers—one that has not been contaminated with members of the copyrighted products industries. Communicate regularly with one another and share your experiences. Listen carefully to, or carefully read, discuss, then filter out the less than accurate options and pursue the ones you agree as a group are realistic. Test and evaluate, then share the results. Pick up on someone else's tests and expand their results, then share again. Commu-

Settlement: NJ – Software Development Co. - $125,000

nicate with one another. When the global corporate technology consumers openly communicate with and support one another, the copyright holders will have a much more difficult time dividing and conquering.

Or, you can always ask for compliance advice of the people who are suing their own customers into submission. Keep in mind, though, that the average compliance enforcement entity is only expert with desktop computers and PC or Mac-based server environments. Frequently, too, they're only interested in their own products, or those of their members. In addition, is it really in their best business interests to help you cut the costs of your operating systems, software, support, or maintenance? Who do the enforcement players really work for? The consumer or the copyrighted products industries? (*Hint: where do they get most of the money or power?*) Please be careful to watch who you talk to.

Mistake: "We've been targeted by the Feds."

The audit letter arrives. It looks very official and — almost — governmental. Is this entity a little known IRS governmental auditing agency clone? The letter is from Washington, D.C. so it *must* be official. Time to panic? Only if you're guilty.

Remember our discussion in Chapter 2? Contrary to common misconceptions, the compliance enforcement, or anti piracy, companies are not affiliated in any formal manner with the American government or, we hope, any other government. In general, they are non profit, privately held, member-based corporations that represent industry product copyright holders. As mentioned, they derive their authority from power of attorney granted by their copyright holder members.

Unless the communications you receive are clearly from an agency of the government, you are about to interact with another business. The key issue in this case is that many consumers react differently to government agencies than they do

---

Settlement: MD – eBusiness Co. - $65,000

other businesses. Do not panic and attempt to placate your way out of the audit. Know your rights. Know your systems status and acquire effective legal help to prove your innocence.

If you have conducted a proactive audit and you are *absolutely certain* that your company is in compliance with the products they represent, tell them. Counter the non compliance or piracy accusations with solid supportive facts and statistics. If you are solidly compliant, you have every right to refuse to play their game. Just make very sure that you are, indeed, fully backed with true figures. It isn't necessary for you to counter their hard ball attitude with one of your own. Merely refuse to be intimidated, state the facts, and invite them to visit your conference room and review your data—at their expense, of course.

Communicating confidence—confidence that evolves from being certain that you have proactively managed your systems—is one of the most critical steps in making your company a hard target for the enforcement industry. If you do this correctly, they'll move on to another company that is less effectively prepared. After all, easy targets represent easy money, right?

Mistake: "I wasn't aware."

In our next scenario, many executives who receive compliance enforcement audit letters simply throw them away. After all, they have seen so many false audit letters that the initial impression is that the one on the desk at any given moment is probably just another fake. During a 2003 compliance awareness event, businesses in a single municipality received a letter from a membership-based enforcement company asking that they conduct an immediate audit and report their findings. The letter made a further statement along the lines that the enforcement entity would not hold them liable for non compliance if they cooperated fully. Addressees were given thirty days to comply. Realistically, the letter held no authority to initiate any audit proceedings, but consumers were not made aware of this. Even more interestingly, *consumers do not need anyone's permission to become compliant*, on their own, in their own time, and without penalty—they may do so at any time and without registering their identity with the software enforcement industry.

The first letter was followed up within a week by a letter from a major software publisher *implying* that the publisher expected its customers to conduct audits to assure compliance. Less than a week later, the audit enforcement company delivered a second letter warning of the necessity to conduct the audit and report findings. Which letter was credible? Which was an attempt to educate or which was an effort to sell more product? Precisely what element of this process represented the consumer *education* process? What if these letters arrived around the same time as one of the recording industry's mass mailings? Or one from the movie industry? There is nearly enough confusion around these uncontrolled, unregulated procedures to convince any respectable corporate executive to run screaming from the corner office—never to be seen again! Well, maybe not.

Here are some of the credibility problems we see with these tactics:

- Giving a company less than a month to conduct a compliance audit is an essentially empty concept. This is an action that most companies simply have not historically had the time, talent, or tools to complete since the day they installed their first computer. Software compliance management is an ongoing process that should be implemented in phases and should never be rushed.

- High speed reactive audits simply cost so much that the average executive concludes the audit with a very nasty taste for compliance assurance—dooming the company to repeat prior compliance mistakes. The wrong tools are purchased and results, at best, are inconclusive.

Settlement: CA – Sales & Marketing Co. - $40,000

- In companies of any size, we have found that an effective long term compliance assurance *process* generally takes at least several months to implement. This is certainly not a credible business process that should be completed in less than thirty days.

- Reactive audits are conducted outside the corporate budget. An instant question after receipt of an audit letter is, "Where are we going to find the money to implement this process?" This is a valid reaction that frequently leads to harsh relations between executive management and the audit letter originator.

- Then the credibility factor slips into the equation: "Who are these people to audit me?" Followed by, "They have no authority over my use of these products." Unfortunately, as noted, many legal representatives will agree with their client on this question and the trouble begins.

- How about, "I have three audit letters, here. Which should I consider real?" Yes, we have seen as many as four audit letters on an executive desktop in a single thirty day period. The end result? Every letter is considered bogus and ignored.

- Then there is, "I've seen these letters. Seems like everyone down at the Chamber received one. Looks like a mass mailing to me."

- Realistically, these letters are from a single enforcement entity that represents a narrow range of copyright holders—even if you comply with this letter, yet another enforcement entity, or any number of individual copyright holders, could still audit you for compliance at any time for products not represented by the first. Left unsaid by these educational programs: "you are not safe until you are completely compliant with every

Settlement: CA – Graphics Co. - $35,000

single copyrighted product, until you can prove it, and until you can remain that way."

- And, yes, once again, the list goes on and on...

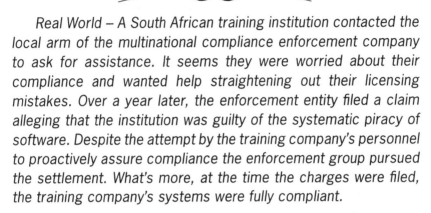

Real World – A South African training institution contacted the local arm of the multinational compliance enforcement company to ask for assistance. It seems they were worried about their compliance and wanted help straightening out their licensing mistakes. Over a year later, the enforcement entity filed a claim alleging that the institution was guilty of the systematic piracy of software. Despite the attempt by the training company's personnel to proactively assure compliance the enforcement group pursued the settlement. What's more, at the time the charges were filed, the training company's systems were fully compliant.

(In late-2003, I communicated with a New York company that was confronted by an enforcement entity shortly before the tragic events of 9/11. It seems that the enforcement entity was just getting around to following up on the non compliance allegations. How many years was that, again?)

It certainly appears that the enforcement industry is not succeeding in their efforts to educate, or litigate, compliance. Perhaps it is time to change the approach?

Mistake: "Don't tell me. I don't want to know."

Seriously. I hear this statement with distressing regularity. It seems that many corporate executives are under the impression (a sadly mistaken one) that, if they don't know about the violations, they can't be held accountable. Please permit me to

---

Settlement: CA – Home Builder - $225,000

set this straight: "Technically, if you suspect non compliance or piracy, or you have been told that you are out of compliance and you ignore that information, you could very easily be confronted with criminal infringement." Why? Because you were to some degree aware and you continued to allow the violations. With this inaction you could very easily have shifted your exposure from the *accidental* (civil offense) category into the *willful* (criminal offense) category and doubled your potential fines.

Real World: I have repeatedly heard from practicing software asset managers that their corporate executives have forbidden them to discuss any non compliance issues. The attitude here appears to be that management will eventually attempt to transfer responsibility for non compliance events over to the employee who is charged with monitoring licensing. Wrong concept. Management remains responsible for compliance and, as a quick aside, any software asset manager who is the least bit knowledgeable will maintain accurate records of all notifications— whether management approves or not. In addition, keep in mind that ethical employees also report non compliance. Ignoring the advice of your software compliance manager could very easily conclude in finding your company reported for non compliance in return for that (up to) $50,000 confidential "turn in your company" anti piracy reward.

Listen to the software managers. Correct the problems. Enforce the policies. Monitor the systems. Become a hard target. Save huge money. Protect the corporate image. Incidentally, I do not know of any *trained* software compliance manager who has reported their own company for non compliance. Most of

Settlement: CA – Home Builder - $225,000

the professionals I have trained or who have reported being placed in these situations have managed to proactively help bring the company out of the target zone.

Who are the players? - Internal

As noted previously, in many potential audit events multiple corporate personnel will receive the same letter. Frequently, as a direct result of this divisive contact the company's response is fragmented and less than effective. Unfortunately, this inadvertent (we hope) multiple notification process can lead to more than one corporate employee communicating with the enforcement group. Result? Each person handles the audit discussions in a slightly different manner. Since the enforcement entity contact generally remains constant, the methodologies of "divide and conquer" can easily govern the exchange—in favor of the audit entity.

It is critical that you set in place a formal strategy and process for reacting to and responding to any copyright audit letter. The larger and more dispersed your corporation, the more crucial this process will become. I strongly recommend that you set in place an audit reaction team and communicate its existence to every staff member. Any audit communication that is received by any employee should be instantly brought to the attention of a member of this audit team. The team then activates and becomes responsible for all audit actions and communications. (See *Forming a Strategic Review Team* in Chapter 7.)

At a minimum, your company should identify a legal professional who will manage any and all communications with an audit entity. This individual should be supported with up-to-date strategic information detailing license and usage status for the copyrighted products targeted for audit. If your legal counsel does not have quality compliance assurance data, or if they respond inappropriately to the enforcement entity, you will find yourself well down the road to losing the audit.

Settlement: CA – Engineering Firm - $43,500

Next, the corporate software asset manager (SAM) (You *do* have one, don't you?) should be the key person to identify and coordinate the information required by the legal representative. In many audit events, the target company provides significantly more information regarding its exposure and possession of copyrighted products than necessary. This additional information can easily serve to expand the scope of the audit—there-by expanding the cost and impact of the audit. An effective SAM should have a good understanding of compliance audits and will be capable of filtering information so that it applies only to the specific issues.

I am not suggesting that you withhold information during an audit. Far from it. It is critical that you cooperate fully and provide whatever information the audit entity requires. However, it is just as critical that the SAM and legal counsel *know when to say no* to information demands. To effectively filter the information required during an audit, you must be well aware of the requirements and limitations of the license agreement in regards to that information. Your license agreement should clearly state what documentation and data are required during an audit.

Most licenses do not clearly define compliance requirements.

The lack of requirements in a license essentially means that the auditing entity can demand whatever documentation it chooses. An effective SAM will ensure that these requirements are clearly spelled out in every copyrighted product license or agreement. In this specific case, proactive up-front negotiations will help protect your company from significant future compliance audit costs—giving your legal representative some really solid negotiations ground from which to work.

The final corporate employee whose communications we need to discuss is none other than your CEO. While in some companies another executive staff member may participate directly in the audit, the CEO is generally the lead compliance audit player. Now, I know this is going to be painful but: during an audit event, the CEO needs to be either extremely aware of the copyright compliance audit process or the CEO needs to be very, very silent.

Noisy CEOs who are understandably upset over an audit event tend to say things that directly interfere with the audit damage control process. For CEOs, there is a nearly overwhelming urge to communicate reactively (or, shall we hint at violently?) with the audit entity. While understandable, this reactive response will usually result in much more damage to the corporate credibility than it could divert.

There is a definite place for the CEO or other executive officer on the internal audit team—their authority level is absolutely critical. But always keep in mind that the company must react to an audit threat with a calmly calculated series of effective pre-planned strategic steps to develop and present its compliance confirmation case. Any mistake during this process, whether it be incomplete data or ill-considered comments, will cause significant damage to the potential audit conclusion.

Work as a team. Prepare the correct data. Follow a clear audit plan and communication process. You will significantly cut your costs. External compliance auditors exist in many shapes, sizes, and temperaments. Unfortunately, a significant number of them come with a genuine confrontational attitude. Prepare yourself and your fellow employees to respond strategically—not react inappropriately.

Who are the players? - External

An external audit team will hold—and deal—all of the cards that guide the audit event. If you negotiated compliance assurance into your license agreements, you will have an opportunity to influence which cards may be played and you should have a clear understanding of what will be required to

---

Settlement: CA – Image Technology Co. - $30,000

state and prove your case. If you didn't, you will have little control over the game guidelines. So, who are the players?

Copyright holders have the primary right to audit the consumers of their products. For instance, audit team representatives from a given software publisher will contact your company with a request to review your acquisition documents, licenses, and install base. The contact may be informal and friendly or it may be confrontational and distinctly cool. Remember, they have the right to conduct compliance audits—this is clearly spelled out in the license agreement your company accepted.

In the case of a copyright holder requesting, or demanding, the compliance audit, they can only audit for their own copyrighted products. Technically, the company could also audit you for any other products that may be illegally utilizing its copyrights (as in derivative works) though this type of action is comparatively rare.

Keep in mind that, while you may be working directly with a software publisher sales representative, that rep will be reporting everything that occurs to their company's corporate expert in the legal niceties of copyright law. If the initial approach is friendly, this is usually a good opportunity to straighten up your environment—sometimes without penalty. I strongly recommend this approach. After all, the soft touch can preserve the supplier/consumer relationship and become a win/win experience for all.

Unfortunately, and in some cases rightly, the friendly approach is simply not effective. Altogether too many companies will ignore friendly reminders and requests for voluntary compliance reviews. When this happens, the audit entity reaction tends to take the form of a significant consciousness-enhancing event. This might be the time a copyright holder chooses to send in the serious audit teams. The auditors may take the form of copyright holder audit teams or they may represent one of the member-based enforcement companies. In general, when

Settlement: CA – Software Development Co. - $45,000

you face one of these teams, the entire audit process will very strictly follow the letter of the law. In these cases, you will be communicating with an expert in the details of copyright compliance—generally a lawyer or a paralegal, but occasionally this might be a CPA who works directly with the enforcement entity legal team. Welcome to the world of compliance hardball. Play carefully. You might want to wear your helmet and Kevlar vest.

Finally, you may encounter agencies of the government under which you live. In the U.S., these agencies tend to only enter the picture during criminal investigations, but, since copyright violation is a federal offense, they could knock on your door at any time. In fact, in some cases, if your crimes involved use of the Internet, you could have committed crimes that cross state and national borders—things could become very, very, scary. And, yes, enforcement entities have been known to visit, and search, the homes of individuals who, for instance, are violating copyright through illegal downloading—this includes your dorm room if you are a member of the college downloading or P2P set. Again, the letter of the law is the guideline for all communication and interaction. Play very, very carefully.

What you say can be used against you!

You remember the television cops show, don't you? "Anything you say can be used against you in a court of law." Sound familiar? Let's keep this simple: you must strictly control the people permitted to communicate with an enforcement entity as well as what they are permitted to say.

Remember the noisy CEO we discussed? The concept applies to any corporate employee. With the exception of a fully trained and experienced legal professional, none of us has the knowledge or skills necessary to verbally spar with an enforcement expert. Do not even try. Listen to, and document, the requests and reply that you will follow up with the caller. Then

---

Settlement: FL – Engineering Firm - $130,000

hang up. From this point onward, only a single designated expert should be the corporate point of contact — preferably your legal counsel. If you don't have one — get one before you speak with the enforcement entity again.

What you say can — make that, *will* — be used against you. Loose lips do, indeed, sink ships — picture your corporate name instantly changing to *Bismark*. Respond according to a carefully structured proactive audit plan.

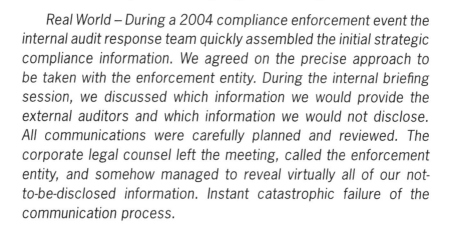

Real World – During a 2004 compliance enforcement event the internal audit response team quickly assembled the initial strategic compliance information. We agreed on the precise approach to be taken with the enforcement entity. During the internal briefing session, we discussed which information we would provide the external auditors and which information we would not disclose. All communications were carefully planned and reviewed. The corporate legal counsel left the meeting, called the enforcement entity, and somehow managed to reveal virtually all of our not-to-be-disclosed information. Instant catastrophic failure of the communication process.

Plan, monitor and control all communications. Review every communication before and after it is delivered. Ensure that more than a single person is present during all conversations. While only one will speak, the other, or others, can ensure that should a mistake be made, damage control will be immediate. This includes *accidentally* disconnecting the call if your communicator falls off the wagon like the one in the example we just covered.

What have we learned?

- We need to be seriously concerned about communications with copyright enforcement entities. Inappropriate communication with an enforcement entity can, and does, significantly complicate the audit and will increase costs.
- We need to clearly identify the internal and external players so that we can plan and control communications.
- What we say can, and will, be used against us!

Questions you might care to ask yourself.

1. Do we have a pre-planned compliance audit communications process?
2. Has our legal representative bought in to this process?
3. Is the process clear to senior management?
4. Has the plan been clearly communicated to all other managers?
5. Who have we designated as players?
6. If we were contacted, today, what would we say?
7. What is our state of readiness?
8. What can we do to improve our hard target capabilities?

Plan your responses carefully. Control all communications and communicators.

What's next?

Are you ready to conduct the basic audit? Let's look over the process.

Chapter 6

HOW DO I CONDUCT THE COMPLIANCE AUDIT?

Chapter Goals: First, we have to determine...

What copyrighted products do you have?

Where are they?

What products are you legally permitted to have?

How did you pay for these products?

What did your payment cover?

Where did you get the products?

When did you acquire and load the products?

Are the products genuine?

What documentation can you produce to prove it?

Why should you conduct an automated audit?

What physical documentation do you need to identify and collect?

What tools do you need?

Conducting a compliance audit

We discussed the surface characteristics of several audit scenarios in Chapter 4. Now let's expand that short version: "The auditors want you to be able to prove that you are using the products you are legally entitled to use, in the numbers and manner in which you are entitled to use them, that your documentation is accurate and clearly covers every purchase and license count, and that the products you are using are not counterfeit." I've found over the years that this is usually a much easier topic to explain if I run through a detailed compliance audit.

What do you have?

The key to compliance and copyright assurance audits is an accurate determination of which products are physically loaded on every computing device. The externally motivated audit will also usually include any systems and hard drives you may have in storage. For our purposes, let's hallucinate that you have diligently wiped all excess systems and drives. During any type of audit, your system by system check of hard drive content generally requires you to use an automated audit tool.

For most of the enforcement industry's history, auditing entities would only accept automated audits, most likely because their theoretical accuracy was preferred over hand audits. This makes sense, up to a point: a company under audit could easily modify results during a hand audit—an exercise that becomes much more complicated (yet still possible) during an automated audit.

However, in late 2003, I began receiving reports from companies targeted for audits indicating that some enforcement entities were becoming willing to accept the less accurate hand audits. Was this an attempt by the enforcement industry to be more user friendly? I'd sure be interesting in confirming that possibility. Although by no means overwhelming or conclusive as evidence, there were some discussions among software asset managers—many of whom had been targeted—that the sudden change of heart might have had a lot more to do with a combination of some of the following factors.

Was the enforcement industry encountering a lower percentage of non compliance events in developed countries? Did interest shift from building relatively expensive solid cases against accused pirates to, in some instances, building less so-

Settlement: CA – Manufacturing Co. - $12,900

phisticated cases and relying on the knee-jerk mentality of, "Pay the fine and make these people go away"? Did the change of heart coincide with any newly publicized offers of rewards for reporting piracy? Logically, much of this could make a certain amount of sense when based on the software industry's own statistical evidence of falling piracy rates in certain developed countries. Could those lower rates mean that there might possibly be fewer easy targets to harvest? Fewer potential targets could, in turn, possibly imply that lightening up a little on the physical audit *burden of proof* would actually permit more marginally non compliant companies to be confronted based on lesser degrees of violation.

Real World - Of interest in terms of the potential credibility of this concept—at least in the United States—is a very small amount of evidence that suggests that fines against American businesses appear to be enormously out of proportion to those levied in countries where the piracy rate is double or even triple that of the States. Could it be that American companies, with the lowest piracy rate in the world, simply have the spare money to pay the fines that could very easily represent the most significant contributions to the global funding coffers of the copyright enforcement industry?

Yes, we're well aware that American businesses are the ones best capable of paying. As well, we're aware of the software industry surveys that imply evidence that, since American businesses must pay more for software and since American businesses use more software, then American businesses must be the most expensive pirates on earth. (*For a vendor neutral discussion of the relevance and impact of piracy studies you*

Settlement: CA – Ceramics Manufacturer - $68,890

might want to look at the "Playing the Statistics Game" article series on the biztechnet.org web site.)

However, since the enforcement industry is unregulated, there are no apparent independent studies that remotely document which countries carry the load of supporting global anti piracy efforts. But, interestingly enough, you might want to consider the case of a single software compliance enforcement company that:

- Collected nearly $3.4 million in accumulated fines in the United Kingdom over a *five year* period.
- Collected over $3.1 million in fines from American businesses during a *single week* in June 2004.

So? You are probably asking yourself, "What does this all have to do with enforcement entities permitting a higher percentage of hand audits?" If the industry could pay less to pursue target companies but still reap the same dollars in fines and penalties, why not loosen up? Remember, in many cases, almost all the copyright cops have to do is send out a threatening registered letter and some petrified business person writes a check. What would be the sense in complicating things with a lengthy implementation of an automated tool in every case? Besides, since most hand audits are extremely inaccurate, the chances are just as good that those inaccuracies could favor the enforcement entity as easily as they could favor the target company.

On the other hand, maybe the global copyright enforcement industries have seen the error of their confrontational ways and they want us all to know what great folks they are.... *Dream on....*

The automated audit

The automated audit tool can represent a significant investment for medium to large corporations. Although many auditing entities offer an audit tool at no charge, the majority of the free tools will only review a limited number of systems (usually from fifty to one hundred). Beyond that number of systems, the target company has to purchase additional short term — usually referred to as "project" — licenses. This makes the free tools relatively convenient for small companies but represents a potential trap for larger companies.

Even those who receive the free tool will find themselves in need of continued service after the initial audit. Remember: we discussed the probability that a majority of targeted companies are required to conduct periodic follow-up audits for three to five years following the initial audit. Those audits must be accurate. As a result, the company would, logically, wind up purchasing an enterprise-wide automated configuration discovery tool. As well, most settlements will clearly require the target company to implement an ongoing compliance assurance program. Again, regular audits are a part of the process, which supports the ongoing need for an automated tool.

Real World – A relatively complete hand audit will generally take a skilled technician approximately two hours per computer. During this two hour period, the tech must review all files or directories (folders) on the system to determine which copyrighted products are loaded. At the most simplistic level, the tech will search for all command, system, and executable files linked to specific applications. Technically, a review of desktop icons should be conducted to determine the number of applications being executed from the local computer but operating off a server. A proper documentation process would then demand a printout of the directories and file structures of the folders in question. This printout would report, at a bare minimum, any .com, .sys, and .exe files applicable to the copyrighted products involved in the audit.

Settlement: CA – Biotechnology Co. - $65,000

If you have a small environment, say two to ten systems, this hand audit process could be considered cost efficient. But, irregardless of whether you win or lose the audit, once you have paid your dues you will want to conduct periodic reviews to confirm ongoing status. When you consider the cost of the technicians' time, as well as their downtime while they are distracted by the audit; and you multiply this lost productivity by the number of systems, then multiply again by the number of audits conducted over a given time period, the cost of an automated audit tool, even at forty to sixty dollars per seat, becomes downright cheap.

Either way you might view the issue, your company will still eventually purchase an automated discovery tool. The problem is that during the pressures of an actual enforcement audit, you may have little choice as to which audit tool you'll have to use. On the other hand, if you acquire the tool without being forced by an audit event, you will be able to carefully select the tool that best matches your environment, your criteria, your tech skills set, and your budget. Is this something you should consider?

Automated tools include the **configuration discovery tool** *which documents the individual hardware configurations as well as the copyrighted products that are actually installed on each system; the* **metering tool** *enables you to monitor and control who can use products and how many licenses can be used; the* **asset management repository** *in its most simple form is a database which you use to track licenses and documentation (You're probably already using a series of spreadsheets, right?); and an* **uninstall tool** *which does—guess what?*

Settlement: CA – Interactive Agency - $175,000

Once the configuration discovery tool is installed on your servers (and/or distributed to the desktops) you should merely have to re-start the computers to initiate the automated audit. Each tool is different so your implementation will vary in this respect. Also, be aware that some tools will not audit servers without shutting them down first—a potentially significant problem. Take time to consider the capabilities of the tool before you commit to buying it. Small to medium sized companies should be able to implement an entry level discovery tool in a week. Frequently, this can be as little as a day or two. If you find yourself trapped in a seemingly never-ending implementation, you have probably acquired the wrong tool. (Refer to white paper: *Criteria for Selecting and Using the Asset Management Discovery Tool* on the biztechnet.org web site.)

Filtering the audit

A good audit tool should be capable of reviewing every computer on a small to medium sized network over an initial period of one or two days. You will want to be able to generate reports from the tool that permit you to filter, scrub, or modify, the report content to display only specific copyrighted products. Next, you'll want to ensure that the reports are sorted by the copyright holder company, followed by the products produced by that company. Each report should only contain the filtered information for the specific company (or companies) and products that you request. This is important because you will be sending these reports to the auditing entity. Yet another key factor in an enforcement audit is that you should provide *only the information requested by the enforcement entity*. If your reports cannot be filtered and you submit a raw audit you could be at risk of additional copyright infringement problems.

Real World – The auditing entity will pressure you to submit a raw audit. This is a report showing every product loaded on every computer. Submitting a raw audit is a significant mistake that could cost you substantially more in fines and penalties. You have a right to push back and demand that the audit entity provide a list of the specific products you are accused of using illegally. Be reasonable and cooperative, but firm, in your expectation that the enforcement entity provide you with this specific list. Once you receive the list, limit all discussions and reports to only the products noted there-in. Reducing your exposure in this manner will be the first test of effectiveness for your legal counsel's abilities to interact with the enforcement group.

Note that I did not say you were filtering or scrubbing the data to hide your mistakes. Far from it. In this process, you are merely ensuring that you limit your exposure *and your reports* to cover only the products requested in the audit notice.

Now, where is all of that documentation?

Are you bored yet? I didn't think so. While the techies are implementing the audit tool, you have an equally serious job. Unless your company is among the tiny minority that has already done so, you get to circulate throughout the corporate infrastructure in an effort to collect and centralize all of the acquisition, licensing, and other forms of documentation applicable to your audit.

Real World – Microsoft™ Corporation is one of the few software publishers that clearly defines the documentation it requires to prove compliance. Take a look at their web site: www. microsoft.com/ and conduct a search for your specific license.

Interestingly enough, though, you will note that documentation requirements (not necessarily involving this publisher) tend to be posted to an easily modified web site that is (here's a surprise) subject to *change without notice*. (*Did someone mention the blind notification clause in UCITA?*) When planning a compliance assurance program, if you fail to plan for the worst case scenario, would you care to guess which requirements you will be expected to follow during your enforcement audit? You know as well as I do that the chances are good that you'll be required to produce precisely the materials you did not maintain. Remember Murphy? (Consider reviewing the *Software License Terms and Conditions* training program on the biztechnet.org web site. You will learn how to correct this problem.)

If you exist within the average corporate environment, you will find yourself being bounced from department to department, division to division, or desk to desk in an intense game of "Who has the paper." You will definitely become the bearer of bad tidings when you ask already overworked people to drop everything they're doing and aid you in locating papers and documentation. Realistically, these folks simply won't have the time, or the interest, in locating your papers.

The issue of "too busy" will tend to evolve into a possessive form of interpersonal or inter-departmental turf warfare. After all, the mentality that "These documents belong to me" can, and usually does, frequently represent a massive problem for internal compliance audit teams. When one department *owns* the proofs of purchase; another department *owns* the licenses; a third department *owns* the master media; and a fourth department *owns* the actual configured product, you

---

Settlement: KY – Dining & Entertainment Co. - $41,366

have a neatly convoluted recipe for disaster. Nonetheless, interpersonal or interdepartmental turf wars have no place in the
compliance audit process. Every item of documentation you
can locate will contribute to reducing the company exposure
to substantial fines and penalties.

> *Ensure that you have visible and well-communicated*
> *executive support before you embark on your docu-*
> *mentation search. You are about to play legal hardball*
> *against a highly skilled and experienced adversary.*
> *Your corporate CEO must be made aware of the seri-*
> *ousness of your search. In turn, that CEO must make*
> *absolutely certain that all management personnel un-*
> *derstand your search will take precedence over any*
> *other activities—including, for many key people, lunch*
> *breaks and days off. The first time some manager*
> *informs you that their personnel don't have time to*
> *locate the required documents the CEO must step in*
> *and correct the miscommunication. If this process is*
> *not followed, you will not be capable of amassing the*
> *supportive data the company needs to defend itself.*
> *You'll pay more.*

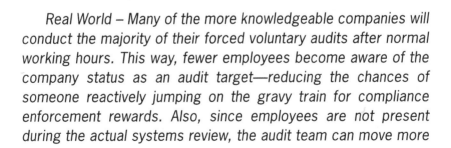

Real World – Many of the more knowledgeable companies will
conduct the majority of their forced voluntary audits after normal
working hours. This way, fewer employees become aware of the
company status as an audit target—reducing the chances of
someone reactively jumping on the gravy train for compliance
enforcement rewards. Also, since employees are not present
during the actual systems review, the audit team can move more

---

Settlement: IN – Telecommunications Co. - $71,810

quickly through the environment and the documentation process will be more secure.

Purchase Records

First, and foremost, find all of your proofs of purchase. You must have, and produce, a clear purchase trail for every single copyrighted product your company has loaded on its computer systems. This trail is composed of paid invoices, cancelled checks, receipts, credit card vouchers, and other items as requested. Proof of purchase documents are your physical proof that you actually paid for the products being reviewed — you didn't steal them and the price was realistic — that the products weren't pirated, and that you acquired the products from a recognized reseller — not an online auction or Vinnie down in the parking deck.

The purchase records are some of the most frequently misunderstood items requested during an audit. When the audit entity reviews the receipts, it does so with nearly microscopic attention to detail. Any mistake or missing information on any receipt item may easily be considered grounds for not accepting the documentation. The more of these records that the audit entity can challenge and disallow, the more you will pay in fines and penalties. (*Sort of sounds like our best buddies from the IRS, doesn't it?*)

To be considered valid, receipt records must, at minimum, clearly state the following:

- Precisely what product was purchased? This should include the exact product name, version or release, as well as serial numbers if applicable.
- Exactly how many licenses of the product were acquired, the types of license, and the cost per license?

This is the actual count of the number of installations for which you will be held accountable.

- Where was the product purchased? The receipt or document must contain the full address and contact information of the company that supplied you.

- On what date was the product purchased? If you are missing the date, among other issues, you might not be able to prove that you didn't simply go out and buy up licenses after the audit letter arrived.

- Then there's the big one: you have to prove that the product was, indeed, paid for by producing that cancelled check or invoice marked *paid* by a proper vendor. Do not even consider presenting a receipt from an Internet auction site—you'll only become entangled in endless dialog regarding this generally unacceptable resource. (*Isn't it interesting how none of your license documentation clarifies—up front—that this type of receipt might be considered invalid? Wait, there are hardly any licenses that even remotely hint at the need to retain the proof of purchase.*)

Real World – You purchase twenty fully configured computers from a brand name hardware provider. The provider sent you an advertising slick detailing the copyrighted products it would load on each system you purchased. Your receipt clearly stated **twenty computer systems** *along with the specific hardware configuration data. However, the receipt did not detail the copyrighted products that were delivered pre-loaded on those systems. The vendor informed you that your ad slick was your record of these products. Wrong. Technically, you do not possess any proof that you legally acquired those copyrighted products unless they are specifically and clearly listed on the paid invoice. The hardware vendor has no clue that they are setting you up to lose a compliance audit.*

Settlement: PA – Metal Building Co. - $100,000

> *Nearly all of the retail establishments, and a large number of the general wholesalers, of technology products have essentially no clue what the compliance enforcement documentation must look like. The chances are excellent that more than half of your acquisition and possession documents are incorrectly completed by the reseller. I'm sorry but, too bad. It is your responsibility to ensure the proofs are complete and accurate.*

Other critical records:

- Items such as credit card vouchers and cancelled checks should contain information linking the purchase to the completed receipt or paid invoice.
  - » Linking to a purchase order is a good initial step, but purchase orders generally cannot be utilized to prove you paid for products. You need the *paid* invoice.
- Paid invoices should also contain full information regarding the specific product that was purchased and should be clearly marked by the reseller as paid. The data they contain can, and should, be linked to all other documentation.
- Do not permit any supplier to *reassure* you that any given item of documentation is acceptable. Review all licenses and contracts with the copyright holder and *assure yourself* that you have the proper documentation as required by the copyright holder. Remember, your name — not the provider's name — will appear on the litigation documents.
- Believe it or not, you may have to actually negotiate — or argue, if you prefer — with the provider to ensure that you receive proper documentation. This is incredibly

wrong, but you may have to do it to gain the documents you need to protect yourself from non compliance litigation.

- Remember, if you do not negotiate compliance requirements into the license documents, the copyright holder can demand any proof of legal possession or authenticity that they chose to demand. If you cannot produce the requested documentation — pay up.

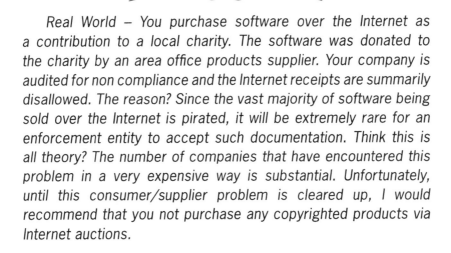

Real World – You purchase software over the Internet as a contribution to a local charity. The software was donated to the charity by an area office products supplier. Your company is audited for non compliance and the Internet receipts are summarily disallowed. The reason? Since the vast majority of software being sold over the Internet is pirated, it will be extremely rare for an enforcement entity to accept such documentation. Think this is all theory? The number of companies that have encountered this problem in a very expensive way is substantial. Unfortunately, until this consumer/supplier problem is cleared up, I would recommend that you not purchase any copyrighted products via Internet auctions.

There are many perfectly valid software providers available through the Internet. The only semi-effective due diligence process you have in choosing one is to check with the copyright holder that this is an authorized supplier and that the supplier is *currently* in good standing. Get the reassurances in writing if possible. Keep in mind, though, that no matter what that supplier does, or doesn't do, with your documentation, *you* are still the one who is liable for illegal software on your systems. Incidentally, if the advertisements for the products

Settlement: PA – Service Organization - $90,000

are loaded with misspellings and grammar errors, you might want to reconsider the reseller.

Is it Counterfeit?

Second, you must be able to prove that the products you possess are not counterfeit. Do you keep up to date records of which copyrighted products in your environment require certificates of authenticity (COAs) or some other seal, proof, or stamp of authenticity? Where are these documents stored? How quickly can you assemble all of the COAs for all the products for a given range of software publishers? Comfortable with all this? Good. You just received an audit letter: produce the COAs for all of the products for the five companies mentioned in the letter. You have three weeks, starting—now...

Welcome to the real world. One of the significant reasons compliance auditing frequency has increased over the years has been the massive growth in the numbers and range of pirated products. The copyright holders are well aware of the global need to acquire software and related products at the lowest possible cost. The odds are incredibly high that, irregardless of how ethical and careful you are, your company probably has some counterfeit products on its systems. Think I'm kidding?

Real World – Microsoft™ Corporation has found itself in the frustrating position of having to sue some resellers of its own products for illegal distribution of Certificates of Authenticity (COAs). If any of your hardware dealers are putting these products on the street illegally, what are the chances that you may have purchased one? Or two? Or a hundred?

See: http://www.microsoft.com/presspass/press/2005/ jun05/06-15FourVACAPR.mspx

Settlement: NJ – Graphics Firm - $45,000

Curious? – *Want to see if one of your suppliers is playing an ethical game? Check Microsoft's litigation site at:*

http://www.microsoft.com/presspass/legalnews.mspx

Here is a tricky question: Based on the previous information, what are the chances that every one of your COAs is valid? How would you find out without setting yourself up for a non compliance audit? Would you be able to identify the counterfeits yourself?

Real World – A small Midwest company asked me to review some of their software to check its authenticity. They were afraid to approach the software publisher because they wanted to solve the problem, not become embroiled in a piracy confrontation. I collected their documentation and—guess what?—it even looked counterfeit to my tri-focal eyes. To protect the company from an audit I confidentially submitted the documentation to the publisher for an authenticity check. The publisher confirmed that each copy was counterfeit and immediately wanted to know which of my clients possessed the product. Sorry, (remember my promise?) it was confidential—can't tell you. We removed all the illegal software; negotiated an excellent price from a local trusted reseller for all new product, re-installed the new product, and brought the company into compliance with virtually no penalties or confrontations. We were lucky.

There was an interestingly quiet case brought to court in Canada involving a business owner who unwittingly acquired counterfeit software. She was confronted and sued by the software publisher for piracy. However, during the court case, the software publisher expert on the witness stand could not distinguish the authentic product from the counterfeit one. If the publisher's own expert can't tell the difference, what are the chances of the folks down on the loading dock, or your resident techies identifying the same differences? Slim? None? Case dismissed — and it was.

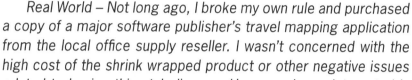

Real World – Not long ago, I broke my own rule and purchased a copy of a major software publisher's travel mapping application from the local office supply reseller. I wasn't concerned with the high cost of the shrink wrapped product or other negative issues related to buying this style license. However, I **was** *interested in obtaining the $10 rebate prominently advertised on the front of the package. When I opened the box, became locked into the license, and reviewed the requirements for the rebate, I discovered that the software giant expected me to submit the box top (with its bar code and other information) if I ever wanted to see the rebate.*

Interestingly enough, the label on the box top also contained the product certificate of authenticity. If I had been foolish enough to submit the box top for my rebate, I would have immediately given up my primary defensive document should I ever be involved in a counterfeit-product-related piracy audit. Not a bad concept: save the customer $10 to expose them to a potential $150,000 copyright violation fine. Doesn't it seem like this software publisher's marketing department needs to communicate its rebate expectations a bit more effectively to its own compliance enforcement team? Or is it the other way around?

Settlement: NY – International Law Firm - $45,000

Got licenses?

Did you obtain, and retain, valid and accurate licenses with your products? Do you have any clue where the long-gone consultants put the documents for those products they installed three years ago? Unfortunately for you, if you didn't maintain the licenses correctly, vanished documents like these are just that many more items you will have to ask those busy people in other departments to produce during your corporate-wide game of seek and find. This time the game could easily progress all the way down to the individual user over in accounting who purchased and configured that shrink wrap product from the local office supply store (or from good old Vinnie).

Real World – I worked with a corporation that discovered that its software reseller was habitually registering the licenses, not under the purchasing company name, but under **the reseller's** *company name. Again, technically, the corporation that purchased the products had virtually no paper trail to prove that it legally acquired the licenses. The copyrighted products it was using were licensed to the reseller. This reflected an instant massive legal problem if the corporate consumer was audited. We cleared the licenses up without penalty because of a proactive internal review—supplemented by several stressful discussions with the supplier. Do you have any licenses that do not clearly identify your company as the licensee? Are you sure?*

When you finally locate the licenses, make absolutely certain that they reflect your actual process for using the products. Are your licenses upgrade licenses? If so, you will also need to locate all the documentation for every product along the upgrade path—otherwise, your upgrades will quickly be

Settlement: SC – Financial Service Co. - $95,000

rendered invalid. Are the licenses linked to specific computers, departments, people, and/or locations? If so, you will have to ensure that this information is available when requested. Do the licenses clearly identify the product they cover? If not, you could be in for some interesting discussions followed by not-so-interesting fines.

Real World – Many software publishers issue license documents that state, "The (software publisher named) product covered by this license..." Instead of including the name of the actual product, the documents are designed as generic licenses. Incredibly, a publisher might actually get away with generic licenses because consumers don't consider the future ramifications of possessing an empty license. If your licenses do not clearly identify the product, version, release, or other identifying characteristics, how are you going to prove you have a license for that specific product? Answer: you aren't going to be able to prove it. You'll pay the fine because the copyright holder saved a few pennies by giving you pre-printed generic licenses. Back then, before they had your money, they were your buddies—they wouldn't even think of suing you. Today, they are the poor pitiable representatives of starving developers who you have sorely wronged with your evil piratical ways. Interesting potential process, isn't it? Make sure the paperwork is correct **before** *you hand over your money.*

"You should know better, but please—Don't ever do 'trust me' deals with copyright holders."

Where do we stand?

Here is what we've accomplished so far: first, you have initiated the automated audit tool and it is quietly running in the background—detailing every product loaded on every computer.

While your audit tool may appear to be locating every computer the company owns, it could easily miss a few. Remember that this tool generally only sees the systems that access the network, either via onsite login or alternate, remote, access. It does not see or audit computers on service benches or those stored in closets. It does not necessarily audit systems that are transported outside of, and returned to, the facilities. You will be expected to audit any of these *misplaced* systems either manually, via floppy/CD, or by using other hand or automated audit methods.

Real World – A Midwest company I know downsized, reducing staff by nearly one fourth (Let's say from 1,000 employees to 750 just to keep this simple for my fellow mathematically challenged friends.). Shortly there-after, the company was audited by a major software publisher. Even though the 250 computers in storage were no longer in use, the auditors required the target company to include them in its count. The company paid a substantial fine for unused software that should have been uninstalled before those 250 systems were put in storage. Lesson learned? Those computers are technically fully operational, along with all installed software. If the system is out of service, it must be stripped of copyrighted products and those licenses placed in (virtual) storage until they are required.

Second, you are simultaneously locating and recovering all related documents—beginning with receipts, COAs, and licenses—that prove you legally possess the copyrighted prod-

---

Settlement: FL – Manufacturing Co. - $120,000

ucts in the proper configurations and numbers, and that the products are not counterfeit. By this point in your audit process you should know which software publishers or copyright holders are auditing your company so you will be somewhat limiting the recovery operation to documentation relating to those specific products.

Real World – One of the many hidden costs of being forced by threatened litigation to conduct a hurried audit has just slipped through your fingers. Because you have no choice during the required audit, you have to limit your search to only a narrow range of copyrighted products and documentation. When this audit is over, you will have to go back and do it all over again to pick up on any the other copyrighted products your company uses. Doing this more than once will cost you huge invisible dollars merely in labor and downtime of corporate personnel. Do it right the first time.

While you are searching for specific documentation, if any other copyright-related documentation crosses your path, scoop it up and place it in a box or cabinet for later review. This will save you time and frustration when you centralize your software asset management and IT asset management processes in the very near future. "What? Centralize asset management? Why would I do that?" You will do it because, contrary to what all of the theoretical research institutes advise, it is the *only* way you can effectively manage technology assets. (Go online and check out the biztechnet.org knowledge briefing covering *Technology Asset Management Centralization.*)

Third, you have brought all of the reports and documentation back to a secure conference room in which you are gradually tabulating the identities of all products you are entitled to have (by virtue of your documentation) and all the products you actually have in place (by virtue of your automated audit tool or other systems audit process).

⌒

Real World – Secure this room at all times. Do not permit anyone—including custodial personnel—into this room, other than the internal audit team. Do not post critical information on the white boards in this room if they can be viewed from the doorway. If you must use the boards, cover them so they cannot be viewed from outside the room. Remember, in many cases, someone from inside the company reported the incorrect or illegal use of copyrighted product. If that person can also keep the enforcement entity informed of your subsequent actions, your adversary has an edge in the settlement negotiations. Paranoid? You bet your assets we are.

⌒

Consider the Oklahoma company that was under audit and couldn't figure out why auditors had such up-to-the-moment information on their environment. It seems that a former employee kept calling technical personnel and describing ongoing changes in the network—changes the other employees would not confirm. This employee always seemed to be aware of what the internal audit team was working on.

On the last day of our review, my assistant determined that the former employee was capable of logging on to the systems via a wireless access point (and a user back door) and reviewing network data. He simply waited for the employees to go home at the end of business then parked at the company next door and accessed the network via his wi-fi-equipped notebook computer. Is your wi-fi secure?

Settlement: NC – Manufacturing Co. - $35,000

But, wait. There's more...

The following two items are of much less importance in an audit event. However, they have played their parts and companies have been penalized for not retaining them. Trust me on this one. I am not totally out of my mind. Someone else might be but it certainly isn't me — *I think*.

While you were searching for documentation, did you also locate and retrieve all the master media? Yep, there are distinct probabilities that you will be asked to produce the original CDs (or whatever other media) that came with the product. This will certainly be the case if any items such as your licenses or COAs prove to be counterfeit. *Please don't shoot the messenger.*

Real World – I was helping a company survive an enforcement audit when I happened to glimpse a master CD that **just didn't look quite right.** *After close investigation I was pretty sure it was counterfeit and asked to see the entire stock of that particular product. Sure enough, every copy was, if not a completely sloppy counterfeit job, a pretty fair example of counterfeit work. They looked decent by themselves, but when we placed them next to a master CD and other documentation that we knew was authentic, the resemblance started to slip. By an incredible stroke of luck, the auditing entity did not represent the copyright holder of the counterfeit product. Had this product been part of the audit, the fines and penalties the company eventually faced might have been, at the very least, quadrupled. Instead, after the audit, we ensured that the product was brought into licensing alignment and the company dodged at least one of the dozens of non compliance legal bullets.*

Settlement: LA – Service Organization - $28,750

There is just one more thing you might have to locate and provide. In a few audits, the copyright holder requires the consumer to produce the original product manuals as part of the compliance documentation. I know. I know. You didn't keep all four thousand manuals. You only kept six in case they were needed and you tossed the rest. Don't become fixated on this single issue. The manuals rarely come into play in an audit. Just keep in mind that the copyright holder can demand pretty much any documents it wishes and be prepared. Unless, that is, you actually negotiated this requirement out of your license agreements. (Refer to biztechnet.org for *Software License Negotiations* and *Software License Terms and Conditions*.)

Let's take a look at several audit process scenarios

These scenarios should lend additional reality to the positions in which your company might find itself. Combined with the previous discussions, they should give you an excellent overview of the realities of preparing your company for an audit or protecting your company with a proactive review.

Reactive Scenario: The reactive process of managing copyright-related documentation assumes (rightly, for most companies) that you have no formal process in place to control the flow of documentation across the product life cycle. As a result, when you receive the audit notice you are forced into reactive (panic?) mode. Incredibly, this scenario is both the most costly and the most common in small- to medium-sized businesses. This failure to manage assets is generally driven primarily by the near-invisibility aura that seems to surround copyrighted product acquisition, distribution, use, control, and disposal. Also, since copyrighted products are generally electronic, therefore not physically *there*, companies simply do not realize the risks they are taking by not controlling their documentation.

Settlement: NC – Architectural Firm - $25,000

> Control is not a bad word. In terms of copyrighted products it is your legal responsibility to firmly control the product for its entire life cycle. Control does not have to be evil, but it does have to be meaningful. If you have obviously failed to control a copyrighted product you will not be capable of defending your violations. Your lack of due diligence will be among the first issues cited in court. Get, and maintain, control of copyrighted products.

Real World – Someone in your company decides that they absolutely must have a specific software application—and they need to have it **right now**. They either rush out to the local office supply store and purchase it themselves with their personal credit card or they demand that one of your techies make the emergency purchase. The new product enters your environment through this **acquisitions back door** and promptly disappears from the known universe. You might know that it is present because Joe down in accounting is using it or because the credit card reimbursement shows up in accounting. However, the master media, license, certificate of authenticity, and other related documentation have gone the way of last year's asteroid sighting. You receive an audit notice that applies to this particular product and the fun begins. To avoid paying a possible six figure fine for this single product, you have to completely backtrack the purchase and hope that you can locate all the documentation. Where did you go wrong?

First, remember, we're looking at a reactive scenario in this instance. You aren't trying to correct software asset management problems—yet. You are merely trying to save your collective assets from the enforcement entity. The most important problem you are going to run into with this example is that the employee purchased the software with a personal credit card. Technically, this means that the software is licensed in that employee's name and does not legally belong to the company. In order to be fully legal, the employee would have had to formally request that the product copyright holder transfer the license into the company name, in writing. Until that request was granted, in writing, you are using illegal software. Strike one.

Second, the product entered your environment as a reactive purchase so it was not processed through any formal accounting methodology. This means that there is most likely no paper trail of the actual purchase: no effectively completed documents showing where the purchase was made, precisely what was purchased, the company that made the purchase, the license type, and the precise cost. These documents must be absolutely complete and accurate or, even if they are partially valid, the copyright holder may deny their use. Strike two.

Third, the employee who purchased the software loaded the product themselves. Since the user has no training in license compliance management, the certificate of authenticity meant nothing to them—they threw it in the trash. The master media was originally tossed in a desk drawer but eventually disappeared because other employees wanted to see how the product worked and borrowed the media. The credit card receipt defined the purchase simply as *software* and documented the price. The employee filled out the registration card in their own name because, after all, it was *their* software. Strikes three, four, five, and six. You have a significant problem—not only did you lose the inning, you lost the game. Pay the fine. And be prepared to read about your company in the global piracy enforcement press release.

Settlement: FL – Media Organization - $53,500

Unfortunately, the majority of your software and copyrighted product purchases are missing at least one or two of each of the necessary documentation items. When you conduct the audit, you discover fifteen products that do not have complete documentation. Your problem just grew by a factor of fifteen. Pay the fine, times fifteen.

Now the good — *good?!?* — news: you were forced to audit and reorganize your licenses and documentation. Theoretically, these materials are all correct, *at this time*. Now keep them that way! Otherwise your efforts will have been wasted. Centralize and control this documentation into the foreseeable future and your exposure to future pain will be reduced by at least the number of products covered in your first audit. Keep in mind, the first audit is called the first audit because there will most likely be a second, third, fourth, or — you get the idea? — audit. You haven't safely run the bases back to the protection of home plate. You are only temporarily safe at first base. Batter up!

Welcome to the Reactive-Proactive Scenario

Now that you have suffered through a failed audit, and paid your two pounds of gold, you will be required to begin constructing, or reconstructing, your acquisitions and software life cycle management processes. Yes, this requirement is usually part of non compliance settlements. Not only does this mean you must develop effective documentation procedures for ongoing acquisitions, but you should be *very* concerned with straightening out the documentation for all the products that were not covered in the audit. Remember: you can never predict how many copyright holders will eventually audit your company.

This is without a doubt the most common and least understood, compliance audit scenario. Most companies that are audited assume that lightening doesn't strike twice. Unfortu-

Settlement: IL – Auto Leasing Co. - $75,000

nately, there are many instances of non compliance audit lightening striking three to six (more?) times over periods that may last from three to five years. Consider the following method of reducing, or avoiding, future shocks:

Bring your audit to closure. Take all of the accumulated — and now rendered correctly documented — materials and file them in a central location. At this point you are only breaking even with that narrow range of compliant products. Your next focus should be to review your environment to identify all other copyrighted products that are present — in whatever numbers they represent. Following this step, you need to accurately prioritize bringing those products into compliance according to the potential audit risk each one represents.

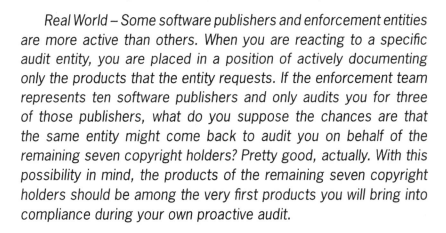

Real World – Some software publishers and enforcement entities are more active than others. When you are reacting to a specific audit entity, you are placed in a position of actively documenting only the products that the entity requests. If the enforcement team represents ten software publishers and only audits you for three of those publishers, what do you suppose the chances are that the same entity might come back to audit you on behalf of the remaining seven copyright holders? Pretty good, actually. With this possibility in mind, the products of the remaining seven copyright holders should be among the very first products you will bring into compliance during your own proactive audit.

The reverse holds true if you are audited by an individual software publisher. After the audit, you have straightened out the documentation for that publisher's products, but the publisher belongs to a certain enforcement member organization with nine other publishers. Think they don't pay attention to

---

Settlement: IL – Financial Organization - $54,500

one another's audit activities? Think again. If this enforcement group is active, you would be very wise to proactively review and correct any licensing issues for the remaining nine copyright holders. This may, or may not, prevent an audit from any individual copyright holder in the group or by the over-all group—minus the original copyright holder that has already audited you. However, after you have been hit by one copyright holder, if you have cleaned up all of the licenses applicable to the other nine, your exposure to the risks of their potential for audits will be significantly reduced.

By now, you should have developed a clear view of your environment and the copyrighted products that are present. You have probably also been overwhelmed by the sheer volume of documentation that has apparently vanished. Overwhelmed is usually a gentle word. Most companies are, quite frankly, blown away by the amounts of missing documentation. Fear not. Your next step is to separate out the top four or five (Seven? Ten?) copyright holder companies that are the most active in compliance enforcement confrontations. Begin a phased process of proactively self-auditing your company for this first small group of copyright holders and their products. Use the template of your painful audit experience to identify the documentation you must locate and the filing process you must create to ensure that these products will pass an external audit muster. (A template for organizing audit data is discussed in Chapter 7 and there is a sample on the biztechnet.org site.)

Next, move on to another prioritized group of four or five (or more) companies and their products. Continue the process until you have brought your entire environment up to speed. While you are doing this—yes, I know, you are totally bored and have nothing better to do with your time, right?—you must ensure that the correctly documented products remain that way. Keep in mind that an effective technology environment is constantly flexing, with moves, adds, and changes shuffling licensed products from system to system or from system to shelf

Settlement: GA – Law Firm - $108,679

and back to system. Yes, you have to track the licenses through these evolutions, too. Still bored? Great, let's discuss the process for doing this right without being forced by a group of armed governmental agents accompanied by steely-eyed software publisher audit teams supported by legions of litigation-happy lawyers.

Proactive Scenario: Build the ship so it can't be sunk. It might get battered, but it won't go down. (And don't go all over pessimistic on me by thinking about any of those old Titanic, Bismark, and Lusitania stories.)

Here is the conundrum: if you can avoid fines that reach up to and beyond six figures, is this a valid business justification for implementing a proactive copyright compliance initiative? If you can keep your company name out of local, national, and international headlines as a software or music pirate, does that avoidance represent a sufficient cost/benefit for executive management to get behind your proposal? If you could invest as little as 1% of your annual IT budget in preventing the company from losing as much as 50% of that budget in potential fines, penalties, and audit costs, would someone notice that you are doing your job? It is difficult to justify a proactive asset management process when the company doesn't recognize the need. We'll discuss the justification options you can use to build this program in the closing chapters. For now, let's consider a phased approach to implementing the compliance assurance portion of the over-all asset management process.

Take a careful look around—ask questions of others in your network of fellow software asset managers. Which copyright holders are the most active in confrontational compliance audits? Which membership-based enforcement companies are the most active in areas where your company has facilities? These questions relate to the question I asked in previously: which products in your environment represent copyright holders that are active in confrontational audit events? These specific products should become your first priorities in conducting the proactive audit. After all, these products and the companies that own them represent the most immediate threats to your enterprise.

What quality of ground are we standing on right this minute?

Did you gather everything together? Great! Now, at the very basic minimum of operational effectiveness, here is what you'll need to do:

- Create filing boxes for each software publisher represented in your audit.

- Inside those boxes place individual file folders (the paper ones, not the virtual ones) for each product the software publisher, or auditing entity, mentions in their audit letter—including the ones you *know* you do not have.

- Inside each of those product folders, place the receipts; authenticity proofs, certifications, or documents; licenses; master media; manuals; and any other documentation relating to that specific product. (Okay, I'll have mercy. Just place one or two master media items and one manual in the file—store the rest but make certain your count is correct and you can locate all the documents in case you are asked to produce them.)

- Also, inside each product folder, place a copy of your automated audit results carefully filtered for that product only. These reports should clearly show which computers have the product loaded and the total number of licenses actually in use.

  » These reports will fluctuate with changes in your environment and should be updated regularly.

- If you have multiple versions or releases of a given product loaded on enterprise computers, you will need to create a unique folder for each version or release. This includes any upgrade licenses you have present, along with cross references to locate the upgrade fodder (prior products) used to justify the upgrade.

- Finally, create a spreadsheet showing each product, how many copies are loaded, where they are loaded, how many receipts you have, the numbers of authenticity documents you have, and all other significant documentation for each product. Summarize the number of products you are legally entitled to possess and the number of products you actually have loaded. Print that spreadsheet, filtered by copyright holder, and place a copy in the front of each publisher or copyright holder folder.

The nice thing about the process noted above is that all of this paperwork will become the master data you will use as input for the automated asset management repository (database) you will eventually implement. (See *Selecting and Using a Technology Asset Management Repository Tool* on the biztechnet.org web site.)

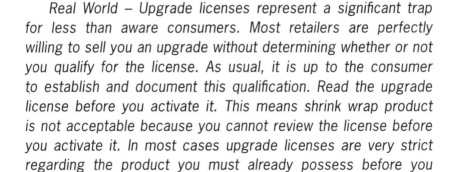

Real World – Upgrade licenses represent a significant trap for less than aware consumers. Most retailers are perfectly willing to sell you an upgrade without determining whether or not you qualify for the license. As usual, it is up to the consumer to establish and document this qualification. Read the upgrade license before you activate it. This means shrink wrap product is not acceptable because you cannot review the license before you activate it. In most cases upgrade licenses are very strict regarding the product you must already possess before you qualify for the upgrade license. Here is the shocker: If you cannot

document legal ownership of the previous product you will most likely not be able to prove that you legally possess the upgrade license. Even if you retain all the actual final upgrade product documentation perfectly, if you do not have proper documentation for the previous product, you could still be out of compliance and exposed to violation of Federal Copyright.

Picture this: you purchased 100 seats of WordPerfect™ in 1990. In 1995, you used the WordPerfect products as competitive upgrades to the Gnorf word processor product (Name changed to protect me from being sued). In 1998, you upgraded that initial Gnorf product to 100 seats of a new Gnorf version using a version upgrade. In 1999, you are audited for compliance and discover you cannot prove legal possession of the original WordPerfect product from 1990. Every upgraded Gnorf license since that time could easily be invalid due to the missing original documentation. Lucky you: you get to pay the non compliance fines **plus** *the cost of replacing the software you already purchased. Yes, I was there when this happened.*

I'll call your six and raise you 3,994!

At this point your audit is coming together pretty nicely. All the numbers are in and you are feeling confident. The documentation is as pristine as you can make it. Now it's time to play the negotiation game. In this not-so-pleasantly interactive activity, the enforcement entity will try to invalidate your documentation, your audit, your results, your lawyer's college degree, your marriage, and maybe even your first born's date of birth. Or so it seems... Your legal representative will use

Settlement: CA – Engineering Firm - $63,765

the strategic information you provided to counter the auditor's moves. You *did* provide your legal team with carefully filtered and accurate strategic information, didn't you? Talk about a real life game of...well...Life®?

The bottom line is that the quality of that documentation you have produced will determine how well your legal representatives can defend you. If you are missing the receipts for 3,994 copies of product "X", you will most likely find yourself in serious trouble—with little negotiation leverage. If you find yourself with only six manuals instead of the four thousand you received with (for instance) the operating systems you acquired two years ago, you will still be very capable of defending your rights of possession. Be aware of this key point: in compliance audits, nearly every point is negotiable. For instance: in many cases, the amount of money you give away is inversely proportional to the public damages you incur. Pay more and the potential press release goes away. I often wonder if these settlements are about intellectual property protection or if they are more accurately a matter of how the money changes hands. Guess that could be the bottom line of the entire relationship, couldn't it?

Knowing your compliance strengths prior to the negotiations process will give you a really accurate estimation of your exposure and possible audit costs. Not knowing your strengths makes the entire exercise a craps shoot. Careful, though: the compliance enforcement industry can, and does, change compliance requirements at any time. (You can find the cures for many of these issues in the *Software Agreement Terms and Conditions* self-paced training program on the biztechnet.org web site.)

What have we learned?

- It is best to use an automated discovery tool to conduct a compliance audit. This tool both discovers and identifies the precise products on your computers and documents the number of computers present.

- You must produce, in general order of importance, correctly completed receipts, licenses, and authenticity documents for every product you have loaded on your computers.

- You could also easily be responsible for producing master media and original manuals for audited products.

- The numbers of valid documents of possession must match, or exceed, the numbers of loaded products being audited.

- Be prepared to defend and negotiate any individual item in the audit.

- Know that, for you, there are three basic audit processes: the reactive audit, the reactive/proactive audit, and the proactive audit. The proactive audit and management processes are, my apologies for the term, the only sane approach to compliance.

Keep in mind: the compliance enforcement entity only has to audit your company for compliance once and for limited copyrighted products. **You** *have to check the company for compliance every day for every copyrighted product.*

Questions you should be asking yourself.

1. What copyrighted products do I have?
2. Where are they?
3. What products am I legally permitted to have?
4. How did I pay for these products?
5. What did my payment cover?
6. Where did I get the products?

Settlement: OH – Truck Manufacturing Co. - $54,000

7. When did I acquire and load the products?

8. Are the products genuine?

9. What documentation can I produce to prove it?

10. Why should I conduct an automated audit?

11. What physical documentation might I need to identify and collect?

12. What automated tools do I need?

What's next? Let's get proactive with a compliance wall of due diligence!

And let's do it with a process you can afford...

Chapter 7

WHAT IS MY BEST DEFENSE
AGAINST PIRACY?

Chapter Goals: First, we need to be secure...

Is a good offense the best defense?

What is the wall of due diligence?

Why should I create a strategic audit team?

Changing the future - Playing Offense

You should now be fairly well aware of the enormous range
of enforcement industry players. You should also be aware of
the basic laws governing the misuse of copyrighted products.
We've even discussed some of the enforcement industry audit tactics and processes. Now let's consider methods you can
actually use to remove that copyright piracy target from your
forehead. Basically, considering the issues and the risks, it's
high time that you quit being reactive and defensive and begin
the process of going on the offensive in the ways you acquire,
use, manage, and dispose of copyrighted products.

There is an important distinction to be made here. Going
on the offensive in your copyrighted products management
process does not mean that you have to become belligerent or
in any manner unpleasant with the copyright holders. Far from
it. Instead, you are going to become aggressive about proactively managing and controlling the existence and utilization
of copyrighted products on corporate computing devices.

By now, either people are no longer reading this book or they have come to the conclusion that it is time to seriously consider changing their perspectives in regards to copyright compliance assurance. The fact that you are still reading these words indicates that, at least on the surface, you intend to become more aware of the issues and solutions.

Proactive Due Diligence

Option three is where the concept of effective technology asset management makes its appearance and evolves into real savings for the company. A word of caution here: a truly effective technology asset management program does not spring full-blown from the earth beneath our collective feet. In spite of the claims to the contrary being broadcasted by many software solutions providers there is no silver bullet technology asset management application. There is no tool that does anything and everything for you. Don't expect to configure a single software application then sit back and watch as everything becomes automated, easy, and accurate. Instead, this type of process begins simply and grows as you grow.

Unfortunately, a majority of budding software compliance assurance or asset management projects are essentially ignored until the company finds itself up against the audit wall. When confronted by a compliance enforcement audit, companies tend to try and force the implementation of every asset management element, tool, and process into one massive reactive step. The result is almost always project failure. Slow down. Get it right. Let the processes evolve and invest your time working out the kinks one step at a time.

I can recognize that you may have been trying to work technologies into your front line corporate infrastructure since the late seventies. There hasn't been much time for formally organizing and managing software and hardware assets. Technology asset management seems to have been historically relegated to a back burner and permitted to simmer with little or no formal guidance or attention to detail. In fact, the detailed processes for effectively managing copyrighted products were virtually non-existent—often, even to many of the copyright holders themselves—until post Y2K when software sales revenues began to lag. Around that time, the frequency of compliance enforcement audits began to increase all across the globe, leaving technology consumers essentially clueless as to the steps necessary to counteract the wide range of litigation threats. Let's discuss how you can begin to reverse the trend—without breaking the bank.

Basically, by now we should all be on the same page: we want to change our technology life cycle asset management processes but we're just not certain about where we should start. Here is what we are going to do: we are going to begin building a *wall of due diligence* to protect ourselves from the copyright cops and the software police. Then, once that wall is strong, we will use it as a foundation for creating an effective long term technology asset management program for the company. Step one is to form a team of people who have a clue. After all, if you are going to build an effective wall, you'll certainly need skilled brick layers, right?

The Strategic Review Team

As we have discussed, you can either manage your technology assets in a knee-jerk reactive manner, or you can begin a phased approach to managing the essentially narrow range of assets that represent the greatest risk to the enterprise—copyrighted products. Once you have control of the copyrighted assets, you can move on to more extensive technology asset management processes.

A primary control mechanism that you must set in place is the proactive copyright compliance due diligence process. Like any process, this one requires a knowledgeable team to guide

---

Settlement: GA – Graphics Firm - $35,000

its effectiveness. There are key considerations that every company must bring to bear in building this process. Each item of strategic data from each category we discuss will become an individual brick in your wall of due diligence. First of all, you need to determine precisely where the company stands—right this minute—in terms of its use of copyrighted products.

- What products are present?
- Where did they come from?
- What documentation do you have that applies to each product?
- What documentation might the copyright holder expect you to produce?
- What are the contractual controls that govern product existence?
- Who uses the products?
- How is usage monitored and controlled?

The questions continue, but the environmental analysis, process analysis, and risk analysis are the most productive places to start. Unfortunately for many companies, these processes require knowledgeable people to drive their success. Lacking the expertise, companies constantly approach these asset management programs in an ad hoc manner.

The way this usually works out is that some helpless employee finds a stack of paperwork on their desk—usually right after they return from vacation. While they were gone, management decided that changes were necessary. This particular employee was drafted into the position simply because they weren't around to defend themselves. The employee is further hampered because they are provided with no authority or training in performing the necessary tasks. Recipe for failure? Yep. Responsibility without authority? Absolutely. Think this doesn't happen? In interviews with hundreds of technology asset managers, this ad hoc appointment process has been the most frequent method of making people responsible for managing technology assets. Let's change the pattern.

Instead of appointing a single scapegoat—*did I say that right?*—we need to create a knowledgeable team of technology asset life cycle management resource experts. This team should be composed of people who *do* things, not people who observe things being done. Effective technology asset management—anti piracy management—is *not* a spectator sport. It is either being accomplished and your company is reaping the benefits, or it is not being accomplished and your company is already paying the penalties. There are no other options. Pick your team carefully.

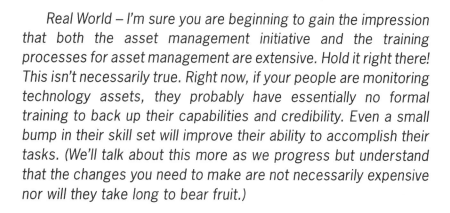

Real World – I'm sure you are beginning to gain the impression that both the asset management initiative and the training processes for asset management are extensive. Hold it right there! This isn't necessarily true. Right now, if your people are monitoring technology assets, they probably have essentially no formal training to back up their capabilities and credibility. Even a small bump in their skill set will improve their ability to accomplish their tasks. (We'll talk about this more as we progress but understand that the changes you need to make are not necessarily expensive nor will they take long to bear fruit.)

In a small company of up to one hundred computers, with only fifteen or twenty copyrighted products to support, and with a relatively simple environment, a single person can generally manage these responsibilities. As the company and technology environment become more sophisticated, the number of qualified asset managers should increase. When you build

Settlement: GA – Consulting Firm - $155,000

the team it is critical that members be selected based on skills and knowledge criteria determined in advance and not simply based on whether or not the prospective team member has a core body temperature above seventy degrees.

Consider the following criteria as a starting place. Team member skills should represent a mix or general understanding of:

- Copyright compliance management,
- Software licensing terms and conditions,
- General negotiating techniques,
- Hands-on hardware and software operations,
- Effective organizational management and human relations skills,
- Clerical organization skills,
- Strong ethics

Further, the team must have the direct, visible, and ongoing support of executive management. Understand that without this support your team will be rowing with at least half of its oars out of the water. Need I mention that their course would be decidedly circular? If executive management is still unconcerned enough with anti piracy and technology cost reductions that they will not support the initiative, you might as well save the money of creating the team and hold it as an inadequate down payment on the fines and penalties you will be paying *when* you are audited. Or you could simply burn the money. That pretty much constitutes the same quality of investment. To put it more bluntly: if executive management doesn't consider this process important enough to show their support, why would any employee be expected to stick their neck out for the audit aftermath executioners to chop off?

Settlement: GA – Manufacturing Co. - $125,000

Real World – Remember those guys in Washington D.C. — Sarbanes and Oxley from Chapter 3? One of the key goals behind the Sarbanes-Oxley Act is to ensure accountability in corporate spending and financial processes. If your company is covered by SOX (not your feet—your finances), you should consider the percentage of costs being sunk into the technology that makes the company competitive. Are these revenues being invested wisely, or foolishly? More to the point, when you have to pay all those Federal Copyright violation fines and penalties, will you have to report that significant unbudgeted expenditure under SOX? Care to guess the reactions by your Board of Directors or your shareholders when you try to explain that the non compliance settlements and adverse publicity outcomes were results of poor technology asset management? Ouch!

Consider this important distinction—a non compliance confrontation with a copyright holder or enforcement entity does *not* represent a resume enhancing opportunity. On the other hand, what if you are responsible for implementing a proactive software asset management program, one that substantially reduces the risks of copyright violation audits and reduces technology costs while dramatically increasing the real world return on your software and other technology investments? Would this constitute a positive resume entry? What if the same processes, tools, and procedures you put in place for software management, were also used to monitor hardware, support, maintenance, and other asset management issues on systems ranging from PDAs, desktops and servers, to routers and mainframes?

Settlement: PA – Telecommunications Provider - $45,000

As your company grows, so should your software asset due diligence and technology asset management team. Consider a mix of personnel with such knowledge as:

- A trained software asset manager,
- An effective member of the executive staff,
- A member of the corporate purchasing or accounting staff,
- A member of the corporate legal affairs staff,
- A skilled process analyst, risk analyst, or certified project manager,
- An experienced technician,
- A member of the personnel department.

I know what you are thinking: why should we commit all of these valuable resources to managing software and other technologies? You should do this because software and hardware represent not only substantial risks but they also represent highly significant uncontrolled monetary investments on the part of the company. I would be quite willing to bet that someone in your company is already tracking every desk, office chair, and portable partition module the company owns — including the pictures (art?) on the corporate walls. Why would you allow software and hardware to run wild when they both represent much more significant litigation risks in addition to being major long term financial investments?

Real World – In the East coast compliance review example, the corporate president considered our concerns over the value and risk potential of desktop and server software to be of no consequence. He was absolutely certain that the value and services provided by his mainframe environment were far more

---

Settlement: TX – Video Production Co. - $55,000

crucial to the company. Then we demonstrated that his desktop and server environment investments and compliance risk values were actually over triple the mainframe investment and risk values. Instant astonishment. Remember: it isn't that we're collectively ignorant. Instead, we simply do not know what we do not know. Time to find out?

The executive mentioned above is certainly not alone. Once again, due to rapid technology growth and the often subtle evolution away from mainframe environments, we basically haven't seen the forest for the trees. The value and risks represented by copyrighted materials on corporate systems have simply been a huge surprise to executive managers who weren't looking in the right direction at the right time. Frankly, for a massive number of companies, this entire process has been one big, *Surprise!* Don't get caught staring the wrong direction.

Okay. Do you have your review team conceptualized? Let's move on to building the actual wall of due diligence.

Building the wall

Initially, your wall of due diligence is, quite simply, a series of compliance assurance steps that will come together to protect your company from the vast majority of non compliance confrontations. Keep in mind that until you regain full control of your contractual negotiation process the copyright holders will continue to control your ability to prove compliance. Until the industry is regulated and mutually beneficial standardized compliance assurance processes are created, you will be at the mercy of any copyright holder demand.

Building the wall will not completely protect you from being audited. Instead, *the wall of due diligence will make you an extremely hard target to hit.* In my experience, the enforcement industries are looking for easy targets—companies that will pay big fines because they have no significant defensive potential. Companies with an effective wall of due diligence definitely do not represent easy audit targets. Here is how the wall of due diligence works.

Remember, we've discussed how difficult it is for you to know where you should begin? Attempting to implement every aspect of a compliance assurance initiative at once is a recipe for failure. However, collecting each of the following items and building on each like protective bricks in a documentation wall can, and will, significantly reduce your exposure and carry you forward into a long term compliance assurance process followed by a life cycle asset management process for all technology assets. Consider the following strategy.

Organizing documentation

When you first begin your document management system, create a simple spreadsheet. This spreadsheet will help you ensure that you can track the various documentation and report bricks that will compose your wall. Consider this simple plan:

- Use column one for copyright holder names,
- Column two will contain product names produced by that copyright holder,
- Column three can contain versions or release numbers for each product,
- Column four can contain the number of actual installs of each product,
- Columns five, six, seven, and eight (etc) can contain the types of proofs of purchase—checked if they are present—unchecked if they are absent,
- Columns nine, or more, (we'll just use this but remember the proofs of purchase may extend beyond columns

five through eight) will contain authenticity documents or other genuine seals or marks,

- Column ten, or more, will contain the license types and whether the given product can be traced directly back to a specific license,
- Column eleven can contain details relating to upgrade licenses
- Column twelve can contain the master media,
- Column thirteen can contain the status and count of manuals,
- Other columns may come into play as necessary.

Organizational style will vary but I think you can get the idea. As you create your physical filing system, print out the cells for each product and place the printouts in the proper file folder. Next, print out the copyright holder name, range of products, and their status, and then place the printout in the master folder for the given copyright holder. (A sample of this spreadsheet is posted on the biztechnet.org web site.)

Real World – If you are extremely proactive (and one of those super-efficient people who drive the rest of us crazy), you might want to construct this spreadsheet to mirror the record or input structure of the high end asset management repository (database) of your choice. Doing so will reduce the frustration when you eventually upgrade to the professionally developed system—the entry fields will be more closely matched.

To keep it massively simple, let's assume you only have four copyright holders representing the products on your systems (*Dream on—our lives should be so organized—though I could name several software publishers who would just love this dream to come true.*). Each file drawer of a four drawer cabinet will be dedicated to a single copyright holder and its products. Drawer number one will be labeled company number one and will have individual folders for each product, further subdivided by version or release. The other drawers will each hold the product documentation for the other three copyright holders and their products.

Within each product folder you will place the applicable product license and any other legal agreements, the proofs of purchase relating to the product, the COAs or other authenticity seals or symbols, at least one copy of the master media, at least one copy of the manual, and any other item that you predict may become necessary. If you staple these together, and/or place them in an envelope, they're less likely to grow legs and toddle off. Also, and this is important, you will use your discovery tool to maintain current counts of actual installations of each product and include these reports in the proper file. If you are efficient you will also include in these counts the precise system MAC addresses where each product is installed.

At the front of each file, you will place the latest printout for the proper product that summarizes the counts and documentation present.

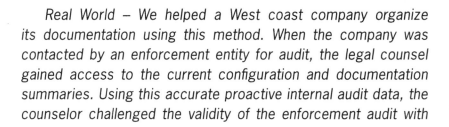

Real World – We helped a West coast company organize its documentation using this method. When the company was contacted by an enforcement entity for audit, the legal counsel gained access to the current configuration and documentation summaries. Using this accurate proactive internal audit data, the counselor challenged the validity of the enforcement audit with

Settlement: TX – Engineering Co. - $30,000

documented proof that the company was **not** *out of compliance. It required a few forceful phone conversations, but the bottom line was that the enforcement entity dropped the accusations and moved on to another (easier) audit target. This particular* **wall of due diligence** *had held back the invading hordes.*

Documentation elements

Which products are present? (Bricks in your wall)

- Research, identify, and implement an effective auto-mated systems discovery tool that will work within your organizational culture. Do it before you are audited. If necessary, and this is especially true with smaller com-panies, select a temporary product or a project license that you intend to use just to get started. Then plan a competitive upgrade to a more robust product later in the process. The important thing is to ensure that you get a quick and fairly accurate image of your en-vironment right away—one you can refer to in the next steps. Getting that ultra-powerful discovery product can wait until you have reached initial compliance with the products that represent the most immediate audit risks. Companies constantly either freeze because they cannot decide which discovery tool to use, because they cannot afford a given automated tool, or because they acquired the wrong tool and cannot get it to work. Don't freeze. Keep it simple and move forward with a phased approach.

  » Cost of this phase is nominal. Make use of the free evaluation products available on the market to con-duct a pilot review of a representative range of cor-porate systems. Then use the pilot data to justify acquiring an enterprise tool. (Chapter 10 discusses the pilot review as well as some relatively painless methods of paying for the entire process.)

Settlement: CA – Architectural Firm - $100,000

» Acquiring and fully implementing this discovery tool is a major brick—the foundation—for your wall of due diligence.

• Identify every product that you have on every one of your computer systems (servers as well as desktops). At this point it doesn't matter if the products are copyrighted or not. You simply need to know precisely which products are out there—the publishers, product names, versions, releases, and etc. Knowledge, and this should eventually become ongoing knowledge, of what is actually present on your systems will keep you up to date on your effectiveness in managing the copyrighted products representing the most risk.

» If financial constraints make it necessary, you can always begin with a surface review of systems using a hand audit. Again, conduct the review of a representative sample of corporate systems, and then expand the results.

» Knowing which products are present on your systems, and the copyright holders who might audit you, are additional major bricks in your wall of due diligence.

Which products represent the greatest risk? (More bricks)

• Conduct a review of compliance enforcement activities and determine which copyright holders are confrontational and which are willing to work cooperatively, without penalty, with their customers. This simple review will provide a good prioritized checklist of which copyrighted products, copyright holders, and enforcement groups represent the highest risks to your company.

» Cost of this phase can be essentially zero. A simple web search of anti piracy web sites will give you access to non compliance press releases. Each release will generally note which companies were involved in the take-down. Or, try contacting other software asset managers and simply asking them which companies are the most cooperative. Take a look at the biztechnet.org web site for a quick training video covering the process of creating a *settlement trends folder* for use in monitoring and communicating compliance litigation activities. This folder is priceless in helping others become aware of the realities of the illegal use of copyrighted materials.

» This analysis permits you to identify which copyright holder "bricks" should be placed in the wall first and which can be temporarily delayed.

• Begin an aggressive campaign to bring the products representing the highest risk into compliance before addressing the products that represent a lower risk. I am not suggesting that you ignore non compliance issues. Quite the opposite. If you locate a product that you know is out of compliance, that product should immediately be included with your top compliance assurance priorities.

» Remember—you have to start somewhere. Start with the most significant risks and move down the line of products until you have covered them all.

» Cost avoidance: if you identify an illegally loaded copyrighted product at this point, you have every right in the world to remove it from your systems. If you consider that an average cost for each copyright violation could have been $30,000, you will immediately show evidence of savings to the company. Keep close track of the savings you identify. Every penny you save at this point will be justification for expanding and formalizing the long term process. (The biztechnet.org web site has a Compliance

---

Settlement: TX – Optical Lens Co. - $85,000

Avoidance Calculator you can use to estimate the potential non compliance costs you locate and correct.)

» Your wall should be taking shape now. Identifying and documenting savings and cost avoidance numbers represents another solid step forward in building the wall. Tracking this information also permits you to more effectively justify your initiative.

• How do you set these priorities? As noted, first address any products that are obviously out of compliance. Once you have cleared these copyright violations, move to the products represented by the confrontational companies you identified in the first step. Then move to any major products present on your systems that are not represented by the companies noted in step one. Finally, address the compliance assurance of the rest of your copyrighted products.

» Remember: *if you have not been notified that you are being audited, it is not only your right but your responsibility to remove illegally used copyrighted products from corporate systems.*

» Caution: I strongly recommend that you acquire an effective uninstall tool. Do not rely on the generic uninstall tool on your corporate systems to complete a full removal of all traces of illegal copyrighted products. If you miss even a single critical file, you could, technically, still be in violation. (Check biz-technet.org for the white paper covering Criteria for an Uninstall Tool.)

» Each product removed or brought into compliance is a brick. Each document located or eliminated is a brick. Is your wall becoming higher and thicker? It should be.

Settlement: MN – Hospitality Organization - $80,000

Where is the documentation? (More bricks)

- Identify, collect, and centralize every proof of purchase item the company possesses. Document and file these items, first according to software publisher or copyright holder, then according to the products held by each publisher or copyright holder. Again, work the high risk products first — but locate and hold everything for eventual inclusion in your filing system. Each time you cull through the company records you should reduce the levels of misplaced (rogue?) documentation and increase the volume of documents that you are bringing under control.

  » Cost savings: knowing precisely where all the documentation is located will save significant process costs should you be audited. Also, you will be able to use this organized documentation to develop ongoing cost reduction savings once your compliance concerns are eliminated.

- Identify, collect, and centralize every license agreement, then file it according to copyright holder and product.

  » Cost savings: you will most likely be astounded by the sheer number of license styles and conditions you are expected to follow. Many products will be covered by multiple license documents, styles, terms, and conditions — some might actually conflict with one another. Gaining control over these documents will enable you to begin a process of standardizing your acquisition, licensing, and utilization criteria — another series of cost savings opportunities.

- Identify, collect, and centralize every certificate of authenticity and place them with their applicable products.

  » Some products do not come with authenticity documents (COAs). However, with the increase of piracy activities more copyright holders are producing their own COAs every day. Be certain that you know which products require these documents. Be certain the documents are always under control. Keep up to speed on this.

» Caution: Some products contain COAs as a portion of the packaging (Remember the example in the previous chapter?). Check every box before you destroy it to ensure that there is no critical documentation stamp, seal, or mark *inadvertently* concealed on a minor flap, edge, or in a remote corner. Toss the box without checking and you could lose this documentation.

- Identify, collect, and centralize every master media item you can locate. Place at least one copy of each in the file with the appropriate product. Depending on the license agreement, the master media may have to be retained in bulk. If so, hold a single copy or two in the file and place the duplicates in a secure location.

  » Corporations are constantly losing master media. For some interesting reasons, master CDs tend to wander off on their own. If you enhance control of these assets, you will probably be able to show significant savings by reducing the amount of replacement costs relating to the mysterious disappearance of master media.

- Identify, collect, and centralize every original manual you can locate. Place a single copy in the file for each product. Include in these files a spreadsheet or paper that notes the location of each additional manual, either its bulk storage location or the location of the individual who uses the manual. Ensure that personnel know that they are responsible for retaining the manuals in their possession.

> » I agree that this one is a pain. However, and again, until you have gained a detailed knowledge of the copyrighted products in your possession you will not be capable of changing this requirement. Preparing for any requirement that the copyright holder may decide to throw your way is a direct cost avoidance process.

Are you achieving balance? (More bricks)

- Once you determine the number, version, release, and license style of each product loaded on your systems, you will want to reconcile — or balance — this number with each item of license, authenticity, and proof of purchase documentation you can locate. If you have 120 copies of product "X" present on your systems, you need to ensure that you can justify legal possession of those 120 copies with accurate purchase and payment records.

- Also, you need to be certain that each of your 120 licenses is genuine and that you do not possess any counterfeit copies of each product. That means you have authentic COAs for 120 precise items.

- Missing or incomplete documentation should be acquired from vendors or resellers. Be careful you don't stick your head into a non compliance reporting noose. If necessary, use a neutral third party, such as *The Institute* at biztechnet.org for this process.

- Documentation that you suspect is counterfeit should be checked for authenticity by a neutral third party (You can use *The Institute* at biztechnet.org for this, too). Again, you need to take care that you do not inadvertently report yourself to the copyright holder.

- In short — you need to ensure that your actual copyrighted product possessions match your licenses (both

Settlement: CA – Police Federal Credit Union - $60,000

count and style), and that these numbers match your
proofs of purchase as well as your certificates of authenticity. If necessary, depending on how pressed you
are for time and your compliance status, you will include the master media and manuals in this count.

*Real World – Let's predict that you locate six incorrectly
licensed products on your systems during a proactive compliance
review. You decide that these are necessary products and
immediately purchase complete licenses and full documentation
for each of the products. Did you also consider removing and
reinstalling the older, incorrectly licensed, products? If not, and if
you are audited, you could still be non compliant. Why? Because
the dates of installation of the six products on your systems do
not match the dates of your brand new receipts. In fact, once
again, technically—those early dates could actually prove that
you were illegally using those six products up until the time you
made the reconciliation purchases. Uninstall and destroy the old;
install the new; make sure the install dates are correct. How much
did we just save you in cost avoidance? Track it.*

*Well over half of all technologically sophisticated busi-
nesses actually purchase **too much** software. The
belief here is that, by buying too many licenses, the
company shouldn't have to be concerned about non
compliance audits. That belief is wrong; the cost is
unnecessary; and the entire concept is a (pardon the
expression) sloppy way to cover an ineffective technology asset management process. Doing it right in
the first place is significantly cheaper.*

Settlement: CA – Unified School District - $300,000

Where do you stand?

How solid is your wall of due diligence?

Create milestones that clearly show where you stand in your process at any given time. Each of the milestones should represent a clear step in bringing your environment under control. Examples of milestones would be:

- "Our company is in full compliance with all products represented by software publishers that are members of the (specific) compliance enforcement entity."
- "Our company is in full compliance with all products copyrighted by the following software publishers..."
- "Our company is in full control of all MP3 files present on all systems."
- "Our company has removed all gaming applications from all systems."

In addition to the progressive milestones, you should create an over-all process plan that details the precise steps you are taking to bring your company under control and the order in which you are taking those steps. Examples would include:

- "Our company has implemented *and enforces* formal policies for the acquisition and use of copyrighted products."
- "Our company has implemented an automated systems and configuration discovery tool."
- "Our company conducts periodic compliance reviews according to the following rolling formal schedule and plan."
- "Our company has a formal process to control all copyrighted product documentation."

Each and every one of the previous bullet points represents a strong individual brick in the wall of due diligence. There

Settlement: CA – Real Estate Organization - $170,000

are considerably more of these potential points but, if you do nothing more than address the ones listed here, you will drastically reduce your exposure to revenue loss due to non compliance confrontations. You will have started your compliance assurance program. Don't stop there.

Just another brick...

Do you have a formal disaster recovery plan? Does the plan include your software and copyrighted products? Does every one of your software license agreements clearly cover the processes for recovery should your company become victim of a disaster?

Real World – Your company has recently become proactive and developed a fairly effective basic copyrighted product compliance management program. All the documentation has been collected and most of it is filed accurately. Much of the documentation has not been fully brought under control but it has at least been secured in bulk along with the other materials. Your company facility is decimated by a tornado and you must move to your disaster recovery plan. Unfortunately, all of your proofs of purchase, licenses, authenticity documents, and master media went down with the facility.

*When you begin resurrecting the facility and reconfiguring all the new computers, you discover that one of the software publishers or compliance enforcement companies has determined that, since you now cannot prove you legally possessed valid software before the disaster, you must re-purchase all copyrighted titles. Or, a more likely scenario is that the forced voluntary audit will not occur until a few years **after** the disaster. You still won't be able to prove you legally possess the products.*

Settlement: CA – Telecommunications Co. - $70,000

Could this happen? Very easily. Consider the victims of Katrina and other disasters. Unless you have clarified the necessary documentation in writing—in your license agreements—when you are audited for compliance, the copyright holder may demand any documentation it wishes. *(Again, I'll keep repeating this until you fully understand the concept.)* In this case, you will be completely at their mercy because every item of your documentation is now cruising around in the jet stream somewhere over central Kansas. You cannot prove which operating systems or software you owned. You cannot prove what license or support agreements were in place. You cannot prove the numbers or locations of any copyrighted products within your company. Technically, and we know absolutely that the enforcement industry is very fond of quoting the letter of the agreement or the law, you no longer own any of the copyrighted products that built your business. Prepare to beg for mercy and prepare to pay.

> *Make copies of all critical compliance and acquisition documentation. Place either the copies or the originals in your secure disaster recovery site. Place the alternate documents in your functional and operational central repository. If either location is inadvertently teleported to Mars you will still be capable of proving legal possession and your recovery will proceed with considerably fewer difficulties.*

Just another brick...

Do you perform periodic live effectiveness testing of your disaster recovery processes and systems? Have you included written and detailed permissions for live testing in every applicable copyrighted products license and contractual document?

Settlement: NJ – Housing Authority - $175,000

Real World – I have encountered dozens of companies that included permission to maintain copies of systems for disaster recovery purposes in their software and hardware contracts. Unfortunately, many of these companies did not also include a permission and schedule for actually testing those systems to ensure that they would be effective in an actual disaster situation. When these companies brought their recovery systems up to speed for the live test, they immediately violated their licenses and were open targets for paying non compliance penalties. Ensure that your license agreements not only include permission to create a disaster recovery system but also permission to perform live testing of that system.

Can you avoid these scenarios? Absolutely, yet very few companies that I've encountered have even remotely considered these problems. The initial portion of the solution is simple as noted in the side bar—but it bears repeating. Merely make copies of all the documentation that you have collected during your compliance assurance and asset management operations project. Then, ensure that those copies, or the originals, are relocated to your off-site disaster recovery repository. This way, should the records at the corporate facility meet with an untimely end; you can recover all licensing and other documentation without delay.

Just another brick...

When disaster strikes your company, how do you know precisely which computers contained specific copyrighted products as well as which versions or releases of those products were actually being used by individual employees?

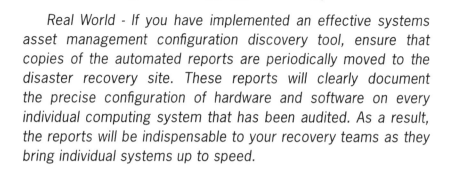

Real World - If you have implemented an effective systems asset management configuration discovery tool, ensure that copies of the automated reports are periodically moved to the disaster recovery site. These reports will clearly document the precise configuration of hardware and software on every individual computing system that has been audited. As a result, the reports will be indispensable to your recovery teams as they bring individual systems up to speed.

If you have followed this advice, you have just saved yourself a huge hit on your revenue stream. Quantify and document the savings and cost avoidance. Don't forget the savings you will probably realize from not having to battle with your insurance carrier over the costs of replacing and reconfiguring systems.

What have we learned?

- We've learned the basics of creating an audit review team as well as an ongoing asset management team.
- We've learned which items of documentation we should maintain and a basic process for organizing the documents.
- We've learned the process for developing a wall of due diligence and the necessity of maintaining the program.
- We have learned about some of the blind spots in disaster recovery planning.

Settlement: NY – Fabric Manufacturer - $100,000

Questions to consider

1. How thick, tall, and effective is your wall of due diligence?

2. If every proof of purchase for every product you have loaded on your systems was a brick in a single defensive wall, would there be any gaps? List them.

3. Who should you include in your team?

   a. Phase this in gradually.

   b. If you do not have a "who", consider what skill sets you should begin looking for.

4. Which documentation gaps could you fill without accumulating costs?

5. What other savings opportunities have you discovered?

6. Have you started your list of savings produced by your initiative?

   a. I would be amazed if you haven't already begun to accumulate savings at this point in your reading. Document it to show how effective your processes have become.

Shall we continue?

Chapter 8

Paperwork And Peoplework

Chapter Goals: First, we need to understand...

What paperwork should I consider critical?

How should I manage documentation?

Where do I start?

What if...?

What paperwork should I consider critical?

In any given software management initiative you will have to implement and maintain accurate records. Remember, since compliance is rarely defined in license agreements, the copyright holders are capable of demanding virtually any element of documentation (or any combination of elements) that they choose to identify as valid. Unfortunately, this places you in a position of retaining every item of documentation for every copyrighted product. It also means that you may have to retain this documentation for a very long time. Let's discuss an effective method of documentation collection and management.

First assumption: you don't have the dollars to convert every item of documentation to digital format, so you have to play the paper game. This isn't as much of a problem as you may think. Remember that at this point you should be considering both reactive and proactive documentation management. Also keep in mind that the process is the same for companies that have ten copyrighted products on their systems as it is for companies that have ten thousand copyrighted products on their systems. The applied procedures are merely a matter of differing scale and your chosen approach to phasing in the initiative.

Virtually any company that begins a software management initiative from scratch will use the same method we discussed in Chapter 6. You'll begin with stacks of boxes filled with a literal mess of documentation that you may have collected from desktops and divisions all across the company. You'll take the boxes to a conference room and sort through the papers to separate each of the following according to the products they cover:

- Valid proofs of purchase,
- Licenses,
- Certificates of Authenticity,
- Registrations,
- Master media,
- Copyright holder manuals,
- And any other documentation you can locate.

Logically, if you have never done this before, you have to begin by finding everything, or at least as much as you can. Take your time and ensure that you have a comfortable procedure for keeping things organized as you progress through the process.

Real World – I am consistently frustrated by the number of companies that regularly dispose of paperwork without understanding the risks that each item represents. Altogether too many corporate accounting departments, evidently acting upon their industry best practice recommendations, have policies of disposing of records when those records exceed three to five

years of age. If your copyrighted products proofs of purchase are controlled by the accounting department and their policies follow this trend you could easily find yourself incapable of documenting legal ownership for software during a compliance audit. This single simple miscommunication between departments could very quickly result in the company having to pay massive penalties along with having to repurchase the offending products. Think this doesn't happen? Think again. One of the first questions I ask a company that is under an audit notice concerns the frequency the accounting department uses to define disposal periods for records.

Do not become frustrated if you can't locate every individual piece of paper at this point. Merely document on your spreadsheet (Discussed in Chapter 6 but detailed at biztechnet. org *Document Management Processes*) the items you have located and which ones you still need to find. Once you have collected and organized this initial mess, you'll go back and cull through the file systems to locate the stragglers. Depending on the complexity of your environment, and the number of people you can apply to the job, this document collection could easily take months to accomplish. As you work, constantly remind yourself of the phased approach to a beginning compliance management program (Chapter 6 and below). You will want to focus initially on the companies and products that represent the most significant threat of confrontational audit.

How should I manage documentation?

There are many approaches to document management. You can spend huge money on a monstrous enterprise document management system that can consume an incredible amount of implementation and operational time. Or, you could start simple and grow as your needs grow. Personally, I strongly recommend that any company, regardless of how large and complex, begin with the basics and expand—after you get the processes down as close to perfect as possible. Please, please, please, don't rush out and buy that big money application; and please don't attempt to force your existing ineffective document management process into the new and improved operational evolution you want to create.

Dirty Data

If you are like most of us, if you track documentation or systems at all, you currently track these assets with a combination of paper files, spreadsheets, home grown databases, and—maybe—some successful or unsuccessful commercial application. A significant amount of the data collected was not scrubbed for accuracy or for consistent entry format. Much of the data is no longer valid and none of the formats or records are compatible. The average company will find itself in such a hurry to implement their new asset management software and process that personnel will literally cram all of this defective data into the new system, trashing the new system before it gets off the ground. Sound familiar? Again, this is a scenario I have encountered too many times. Don't get caught. Pre-plan this entire process before you begin.

Format or for-mutt?

Remember our discussion on the critical nature of developing your own criteria? How about the concept of cutting implementation costs through advanced planning? Your company can, and will, save significant revenue if one of the new policies you implement governs setting and following acquisition criteria. (Policies are covered in Chapter 9) Set full and accurate criteria and ensure that the project addresses those criteria.

Settlement: AZ – Educational Consulting Co. - $45,000

Here is another place where we tend to crash our projects: we try to accomplish too much, too fast, and we plan for the wrong time frame. We've touched a little on the *too much* concept but it bears expansion. When companies initiate a new document management system they tend to try to force every problem they have ever encountered into the new solution option. This tends to doom the project. A process more likely to conclude in success is to group the problems you would like to address, and then prioritize the groups. Phase the project into existence so that it addresses each problem in its prioritized order. Implement and fully test the solution for each prioritized group before moving on to the next group. If you locate, solve, and test any defects in your new solution as they occur, you'll be less surprised by costly upstream fixes later on.

Another example of too much, too fast would include the company that chooses to implement the entire asset management operational spectrum in one huge chunk. This company starts looking for and sorting documentation at the same time it is implementing its automated discovery tool and at the same time it is implementing its asset management repository (database). In addition, the same company will be completely revamping its policies and procedures along with its acquisitions through disposal processes. *Order to go: one recipe for complete disaster.*

In terms of planning, the majority of companies that plan technology-based solutions tend to plan for a future they cannot foresee. As a direct result, the criteria they address either fall incredibly short of their eventual needs or they become outdated before the project is completed. If your company determines a good balance between planning ahead and implementing in short well-tested phases, you will have more opportunity to ensure project applicability and success across a wider range of time and requirements.

If you are currently undergoing an externally controlled audit process, you have little choice in the scope and sequence of your planning. You have little opportunity to carefully plan a long range document management process. This situation is normal and acceptable—for now. The secret is in how well you handle the long range plan based on the requirements of the moment.

Consider: You can force your company to use the automated discovery tool recommended or supplied by the auditing entity. This product may or may not meet your ongoing needs but it is there and you might as well continue using it, right? Wrong. If you are forced by time constraints to use a product you haven't thoroughly tested, license that product via a time limited project license. If the product turns out to be one you like, you can always upgrade it to a full license at a discount. However, if the product does not meet your needs you can cut your losses and move to a product that does.

In my experience, at least half of the companies that attempt to implement an asset management initiative encounter near or total failure. The general scenario shows that a company will spend years trying to force an automated asset management product to do what the product cannot do simply because the company personnel refuse to admit they selected the wrong product in the first place. Most frequently, this trend will apply to implementing the configuration discovery tool, but it also frequently applies to any asset management tool. If you cannot implement the tool quickly and begin harvesting accurate and useful data, you have the wrong tool.

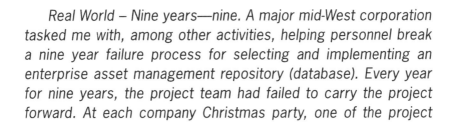

Real World – Nine years—nine. A major mid-West corporation tasked me with, among other activities, helping personnel break a nine year failure process for selecting and implementing an enterprise asset management repository (database). Every year for nine years, the project team had failed to carry the project forward. At each company Christmas party, one of the project

Settlement: NY – Audio Video Co. - $125,000

team was tasked with sitting on Santa's lap and explaining the latest failure. Humorous? Well, yes and no. I guess it depends on whether or not you were a shareholder. A more descriptive word for nine years of project failure would be "costly."

It only took us eighteen months to select, fully implement, and begin using the new enterprise asset management repository. Project over.

Studies have shown that over half of major IT projects will fail. If you purchased the right product, one of your major criteria should have been an accurate expectation of how quickly that product will become fully operational. If your technology asset management program is reactive, you will shut down the project after losing considerable revenue. If you are proactive, you will select a product with care and cut your losses very early in the implementation phase if you discover problems.

Where should I start?

"There are legions of copyrighted products on my systems. Where do I begin?" Consider the software and copyright enforcement member-based companies. In the country, or countries, where your company operates, which of these entities is the most active? Once you determine this level of activity, document which software publishers or copyright holders belong to these organizations. How active are the individual copyright holders in non compliance confrontations? For this list of active copyright holders, which of their products does your company actually use? Which product could be present without your knowledge? The picture that will develop in your mind is a pretty accurate rendition of the outline you need to follow in building your documentation management system.

Settlement: MO – Services Co. - $91,694

Address the documentation for the big name and active compliance enforcement entities first. Make certain you are covered with them, and then move down your list of priorities a group at a time. What should you cover after you are sure you are compliant with this first prioritized list? Look at your environment again. Which other products are present in the highest concentrations? What copyright holders do they represent? Review and reconcile this group next. Finally, move on to the less frequent products and less active copyright holders.

> *One of the most important concepts you can keep in mind to protect your company is: The copyright cops only have to monitor your company for copyright violations once and for one range of products. You have to monitor your company every single day for every single copyrighted product.*

Consider these questions:

- Why should I embrace change management?
- What is peoplework?
- How can these concepts help me make a difference?
- What roles should policies and procedures play in my company?

Change Management

For most of you, this will be a tough section to read through. Please stick with it. The concept of human change management is absolutely critical to your success as a technology asset manager. In order to work effectively with those around you, you have to understand the way they will perceive your proposals and projects. With a solid understanding of change management, of the audience for your projects, and your unique corporate culture, your success rate will improve significantly with every asset management process or initiative you attempt.

Peoplework

One of the absolutely decisive obstacles to technological change and growth is also the least often considered by planning teams. Who are the people involved in, and touched by, this project? How can we gain their buy-in and overt support for what we are attempting to accomplish? We consistently fail to plan for the real human beings who are going to interact with the new process or product.

Many of us have grown up being inundated by constant changes. We're used to modifying our behavior to match the most recent change and then moving forward with our lives. However, there is still a solid majority of human beings out there in the real world who simply cannot comfortably flow with the speed and complexity of technological change. Projects very frequently fail because the people impacted by those projects are being forced into a solution they cannot readily comprehend. After all, the project has been developed from the perspective of the local tech wizard—not the actual users. When people aren't ready, willing, or able to change, change will not occur—no matter how hard you push those people.

Real World – As the newly appointed software license compliance manager you want to implement a new corporate policy that applies to the acquisition, configuration, and use of copyrighted products on company computing devices. Up until today, the corporate Internet represented a sort of Wild West cornucopia of freely available software, graphics, music, videos, games, and other really cool toys. Now here you stand, wanting to

Settlement: NJ – Advertising Agency - $70,000

end the era of infinite partying on company time. Worse yet, your policy also includes those stock ticker applications that poverty-stricken executives absolutely must keep streaming across the bottom half of their monitors. Think your new policy is going to be accepted?

More to the point: based on the reaction to this request, do you think your long range job prospects are high? The answer to both questions is a sincere, but apologetic, "probably not." You are attempting to change your corporate culture — the comfort zones of your fellow employees — with the intellectual equivalent of slamming a fist on the desk. In our current societies this is simply not going to happen.

Think about this. People have become used to doing whatever they want to do with their — Do you see that word? *Their!* — computers. This will be your first major hurdle in changing the company tech environment: most employees honestly believe that the computer on their desk belongs to them. Since the computer belongs to them, all the data and software on that computer is also theirs. This means that when you step forward and try to change the way the technology is managed — controlled — you are taking away their personal toys. Let's put this all in a perspective that nearly everyone can comprehend.

When we were all tiny people, with empty heads and full diapers, what happened to us on the playground when we took someone else's toy? How did we react when someone took our toy? Think life has changed now that we're all grown up and our toys of the day are corporate *personal computers*? Hardly.

*Real World – They are no longer **personal computers**. Don't use the phrase. Slowly but surely we have to evolve away from*

personal computer to **corporate computing device**. *As long as the reference to the asset implies personal ownership, you— the lowly asset manager—will not manage any significant level of control over how the device is used. Try gently changing the mindset in order to change the process.*

It all comes down to this.

If you intend to change the way your company acquires, distributes, and uses or abuses copyrighted products, you must absolutely come to terms with the process behind human change management. If you honestly intend to stop piracy in your company, it is essential that you implement the new process—from day one—with a keen eye toward human and organizational personalities and perspectives. Your sense of audience—the people who you want to support you—will determine, in large part, your potential for success. What are the risks of failure? If you cannot gain the cooperation of the entire company in supporting your anti piracy initiative, you should plan on a very expensive interaction with the copyright enforcement industry. In fact, you can probably expect more than one confrontation.

A brief history: How did we arrive at this topic?

Consider: For nearly the entire history of the human race, the average person has been told what to do and told when to do it. There has always been an authority figure that controls and guides ongoing activities as well as changes. This leader may have been the head hunter of the pack (*That's head hunter—not headhunter.*); they might have been the most knowledgeable local farmer; or they could have been the military groups with their leadership hierarchies. In the early industrial age, former farmers and guildsmen suddenly found their actions being

guided and controlled by factory owners and operators. There
has always been a leadership differential between the knowledgeable and the not quite so knowledgeable. Bosses—the
alpha males or females—have always directed the efforts of
those they work with. Get the picture?

But the world has changed, hasn't it? As advanced education opportunities have become more accessible to more people, the boundaries between alpha leadership and intellectual
leadership have blurred. In the industrial age, the alphas and
knowledgeable individuals were a significant minority. After
the mid 20th century, we suddenly found ourselves with a sur-
plus of bright, motivated workers—people who could think for
themselves. Political leaders somehow hadn't managed to kill
off the majority of the best and the brightest in global warfare
and, there they were, questioning everything. The so-called
common man and woman discovered that they could exert
control over their personal and professional worlds through
intelligent interaction. Around the halfway mark of the industrial age, the alpha minority discovered that its assumed power
base was somehow dwindling. When they issued orders from
on high, people were actually beginning to question the validity of those orders. Then, we were all slammed head-on into
the technological age.

Ouch! Suddenly changes were progressing much faster
than the average person could comprehend or manage them.
The alphas struggled to maintain control—they still do—but
they rapidly found themselves overwhelmed by the incredible
complexity and specialized needs that technology brought (and
still brings) to the corporate cultural table. Entire societies began to shift from the right by might control paradigm to the
right by unique knowledge paradigm. Merely being the boss
simply no longer gave executives the cultural right to personally set and direct human action. The alphas of the new day
had to earn their leadership positions through their capabilities—not their birthright or birth sex.

Settlement: NJ – Kitchenware Sales Co. - $60,000

There was turmoil in the so-called lower ranks as well. Real world people found themselves challenged by such incredible—at the time—inventions as the calculator and the memory enhanced electric typewriter. The everyday worker had barely mastered these highly complex inventions when they were introduced to computers—first the behemoths, then the midrange systems. For a while, the knowledge of the mysterious workings of these technologies was closely held by such wizards as the mainframe gurus and advanced software programmers. Then, in what a seemed like a single rotation of the globe, the personal computing device whimpered onto the scene. The birth was not particularly spectacular, at first.

Once upon a time, the tiny Sinclair computer popped into being. This little gem of a toy could actually utilize your own personal television for video and a handy tape recorder for data storage. Computer programming was instantly thrust into the hungry hands of a curious and relatively well educated populous. Real human beings discovered that they could learn to program a computer on their own. As the computers and software became more complex, huge numbers of everyday normal people began to take formal training in programming. Control of the magical inner workings of the corporate master data vault began slipping from the hands of the alphas and into the hands of the technically adept rank and file. The computer geek was born.

The remaining rank and file wasn't yet prepared to follow the technology curve, though. A majority of these folks were perfectly comfortable taking their marching orders from their neighborhood alpha. They had no interest in making, or desire to make, decisions on their own. So rank and file split into those who could innovate and were willing to do so using their knowledge of, and comfort with, technologies and those who were comfortable in the follow orders life-style they had always enjoyed. The alphas quickly realized that their entire power base was shifting toward the techies so they graciously took the newly arrived techies *under their wing* and offered their enlightened guidance and experience. The techies were young, impressionable, and more than willing to leave the heavy business thinking to someone else so they became a sort of collective Robin to the executive Batman—not quite bright enough to run the company but bright enough to create, maintain, and operate the systems that could be used to run the company.

And here we are today. The alphas remain in precarious control—precarious because it is becoming more and more difficult to lead by force of will. The individuals who are techno-savvy will remain in demand because so many of their skill sets reside at the edge of mystical. The other rank and file group—real people who just want to do their jobs and be left alone—is growing larger by virtue of technology growth and infestation into less developed countries. And here-in lies the problem—a significant majority of the rank and file human beings are, quite simply, not receptive to any changes that take them out of their comfort zones. However, these same people are intelligent enough to, at least internally, question the executive *word from on high.*

Your job, should you choose to keep it...

There you have it. A simplified concept of incredibly condensed history of the working world, part one—in seven short paragraphs. Why have I submitted you to my ravings? Because the basic human personality types will directly impact your ability to change the way your company manages technologies. If you cannot gain a core understanding of what makes these personalities embrace change, your projects will fail. Who are these people?

- Executive Management – alphas who still control the corporation,

- Techies – create, operate, and manage the hardware and software environments,

- Tech Savvy – rank and file who are comfortable with technology changes,

- Tech Wary – rank and file who view tech changes with suspicion,

- Anti-Tech – individuals at all levels who fear and oppose technology changes,

- Unconscious – usually the ones management puts on your project team.

In actuality, whether you choose to do it or not, your corporate responsibility is to modify the processes by which your company identifies, acquires, distributes, tracks, uses, and abuses technologies. Your job success potential is dependent on gaining a basic working knowledge of human change management so that you can ensure the front line human support necessary to save the company from itself.

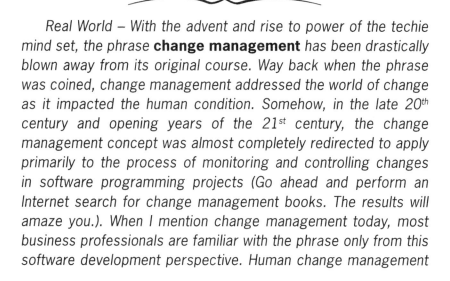

Real World – With the advent and rise to power of the techie mind set, the phrase **change management** *has been drastically blown away from its original course. Way back when the phrase was coined, change management addressed the world of change as it impacted the human condition. Somehow, in the late 20th century and opening years of the 21st century, the change management concept was almost completely redirected to apply primarily to the process of monitoring and controlling changes in software programming projects (Go ahead and perform an Internet search for change management books. The results will amaze you.). When I mention change management today, most business professionals are familiar with the phrase only from this software development perspective. Human change management*

had somehow nearly disappeared from the scene until it began to
warily reappear in isolated pockets of resistance. But, the ability
to read an audience and help them embrace changes is absolutely
key to the success of virtually every corporate project. The need
for corporate change agents has never been more acute.

Becoming an Agent for Change

If your company is like the majority of corporations in developed countries, it was literally blasted into the technological age. Changes occurred so quickly and in such a complex manner that a majority of corporate personnel found themselves barely hanging on for the ride. The company rocketed forward toward tech infinity, accepting *the next big thing* as if it were the corporate equivalent of the elixir of (business) life. Technology projects failed right and left, in part because the alphas — read: executive management — were taking their cues from business-challenged techies who were into the latest and greatest software and hardware toys. We won't even discuss the dot com fiasco.

For nearly three decades, corporate rank and file personnel have been practically buried in promises regarding the vast improvements that technologies will bring to their work and leisure life. If you were around at the time you should remember such interesting promises as:

- Your job will be secure after this change.
- Everyone will be working four days a week.
- Life will be easier.
- You're gonna love this new system.

Are these promises of corporate cultural and personal growth and improvement; or are they often repeated precursors of pending personal peril? (*Don't you just* hate *alliteration?*)

Settlement: VA – Employment Services Co. - $160,000

How does all this affect organizational change?

Let's take a quick run through the assurances in the previous section. First, and foremost, your job was definitely not secure. Corporate management quickly discovered the myriad ways technology could increase the efficiency of the individual. Instead of accomplishing more with the same number of people, they used technology to perform the same amount of work with fewer people. Companies began a series of downsizings that reached all the way to middle management. Now that fewer people were producing the same amount of work, the idea of a four day work week rapidly disappeared and became mandatory overtime. Nobody noticed that the prescribed work load was measured based on past work flow requirements, not the requirements to improve and expand the company.

Did I miss the part where our lives became easier? Instead, they seem to have become much more complex — both in the workplace and in terms of our private lives. The phrase, "You can use your computers to work from home, now," was supposed to mean more time with the family. Instead, it came to mean, "Work your normal extended shift, then go home and finish filing those reports on line." Or, the ever more popular, "You're on call 24/7 this month. Wear your pager at all times." Should we even mention the huge numbers of people who can't seem to extract their cell phones from their collective ear canals?

And the big one? "You're gonna love this new system," became a technology project introductory phrase that inspired instant terror in the hearts and minds of employees who were trying to sustain a family. It meant the pattern was about to start all over again. The new system probably meant that jobs were about to be lost. Other employees, people you cared about, were probably about to be downsized. Worse yet, *you* could be about to lose your own job.

The empty promises of technology projects have piled up over the years to such a degree that even the least aware employees are well aware of the incredibly low chances of any given tech project even surviving its implementation. It is little wonder that our current crop of employees have little faith in technology projects and many are, in fact, perfectly willing to sabotage your latest proposal in order to, hopefully, hang on to their jobs for just a little longer.

Real World – Let's see. I keep hearing the compliance enforcement industry radio spots encouraging me to call the toll free confidential hot line to report the company for non compliance. I also heard that there were rewards of as much as $50,000 for successfully concluded cases. How could I get back at a company that has treated me in a manner that I consider disrespectful? Maybe I need to ponder this. Nope. What was that number again?

Violating copyright is wrong!

Absolutely. I'll give my complete support to this concept. But, again, we have to begin focusing very closely on the perspective of each individual user; taking the time to fully understand more of the reasons why people ignore copyright in our times. Note that I didn't say we had to agree with those reasons, but it is critical that we understand them. In your own corporate environment, consider the wide range of copyright perspectives that are present. To be successful in initiating a new process for managing copyrighted products, you must come to understand the meanings behind *all* of these points of view. If you don't thoroughly know your audience, how will you communicate with them? Consider these:

- Every global society has a different perspective of personal possession and the validity of copyright. In many socialist countries, resources belonging to one are often considered as the shared property of many. At what point does one society have a right to impose its values on another? Are the wealthy multinational corporations sincerely concerned with the rights of the people who create products or are they interested only in their own profit margins? When these huge companies complain about the consumer practices of an impoverished rice farmer in China, do they actually think that rice farmer cares?

- The latest generation of copyright thieves—read P2P file sharers—is also the first generation to have passed through the copyright education and awareness programs developed by the enforcement industry. Could this be interpreted as a testimony to the effectiveness of those programs?

- For decades we have been hearing of the abilities of the entertainment delivery industry to greedily consume the profits from sales while forwarding a miniscule fraction of the revenue to the creative artists (if they forwarded anything at all). Did anyone honestly think that the consumers were unaware of this trend? Does anyone honestly consider where the consumers' loyalties might actually lie?

- Way back when, we bought record albums containing one or two songs we liked and ten or twelve songs we didn't want. Then we moved up to tapes and, now, to CDs—same story—we buy for that single song and are charged for all the rest. (Sorry, but you 8-track people are *still* way out there on the cosmic edge of *whatever*.) Again, for decades the consumer has been asking for a copyrighted product delivery process that delivers, and charges for, precisely what we want without including, and charging for, materials we do not want. If the industries that supply these products do not respond to

Settlement: NC – Commercial Builder - $45,000

their consumers' desires, what is so surprising about consumers who locate and use a delivery process that meets their needs?

- Have the copyrighted products industries considered that, what they view as charging what the market will bear could actually be over charging? Could it be that the reason people steal copyrighted products is that the consumers' perception of relative value is vastly different than that of the supplier? Oh, and by the way, is this practice of cramming those products with unwanted functionality to boost the perceived value an effective method of concealing price gouging? Doesn't the relatively new phrase "feature bloat" pretty well cover a high percentage of these issues?

- But, our surveys say... Could it be that, time and again, consumers have witnessed research and studies sponsored by a given industry that report precisely what that industry wanted those studies to report? Could it be that consumers perceive that the majority of industry sponsored studies are biased, therefore invalid?

Do you honestly believe that your fellow employees aren't thinking thoughts like these? Look again. Your challenge, our challenge, is to humanely bend and reshape these perspectives so that a given employee's personal beliefs about piracy cannot damage the corporation.

And, here you are.

Now here you come, strolling up to other employees' desks and asking that they provide you with information regarding their possession and use of technical devices. You, read: "nearly one of *them*" — an *almost techno geek* yourself — are asking rank and file employees to once again look at a new process for using technology. This time, however, the process includes the potential for you and any other person with access to the

---

Settlement: NC – Accounting Firm - $23,229

reports, to electronically look over the computer user's shoulder at the inner workings of *their* computer. Now, each employee is being given a very personal stake in the anti piracy project: if they have added any software or unapproved files to their computer they could be at risk of their jobs. Great. This should be a fun and highly productive project.

Why do policies and procedures fail?

What are you attempting to accomplish? Why do you want to accomplish this task? How should the task be accomplished? These questions will form the developmental backbone of any corporate policy or procedure process. To put it briefly: policies cover the *what and why* of corporate expectations. Procedures cover the *how* of the way things are accomplished.

Remember what we discussed a few pages back? If you do not provide today's employees and contractors with a credible reason—one that *they* will buy into—for your policy, your policy will not be followed. Again, it all comes down to audience. If you want communications to be productive, you absolutely need to ensure that your *send* is followed up by a *comprehended receive*. Order me to do something and you will probably not get very far in terms of cooperation. Explain to me why it is vital and necessary to our mutual interests and the chances are infinitely better that I'll follow your lead.

If you want to be effective, recognize that the employees of today always require a valid *why* for any policy you create. If you want that all-important buy-in, you will have to thoroughly explain the reasons a given policy must exist and those reasons must be valid. Remember the questions I asked a page or two back? Remember that your fellow employees will be considering many of the same issues. If you can effectively communicate the necessity of addressing those questions, you will be successful in implementing your policy. If employees perceive a taint of dishonesty or a touch of insincerity in your policy, it will most likely fail.

Settlement: FL – Internet Co. - $23,768

> *A policy should cover **what** task you want to accom-*
> *plish **and why** the task needs to be accomplished. A*
> *procedure should cover **how** the task should be ac-*
> *complished.*

Got Policies?

In terms of compliance with Federal Copyright Law, one of the most frequent mistakes that companies make is to have no clear policies governing copyrighted products. In multiple surveys, conducted with hundreds of global software and IT asset managers, I have asked the question: "Does your company have a policy addressing illegal software or copyright violations?" With near perfect precision, in virtually every case, fewer than 25% of those in attendance raised their hands. Since there was essentially no risk to answering this question honestly, it appears that a substantial majority of small to middle sized companies have not created anti piracy policies. Failure to create and publicize an internal anti piracy policy is an accurate indicator that the company does not take copyright violations as seriously as it should.

In terms of copyright and anti piracy enforcement, it will be extremely difficult for you to prove your due diligence if you have not bothered to create a company policy covering the necessity of following copyright regulations.

Enforced any Policies Lately?

The second major mistake I have encountered indicates that over half of the companies that actually have policies in place do not enforce them. As a lawyer friend of mine said recently: "That un-enforced anti piracy policy will become the copyright holder's Exhibit A in their court case against your company." Realistically, a policy that you do not enforce is essentially equivalent to having no policy at all. The core concept we need to consider, here, is that un-enforced policies tend to become invisible because executive management does not actively—visibly—support enforcement.

Again, audience is critical. When you made your first proposal for this policy, did you fully explain the critical nature of the follow up in a manner that executive management could relate to? Did they buy in to supporting the policy itself, the processes and consequences of enforcement, and the consequences of non enforcement? If there is no enforcement follow up, then they were not made fully aware. Time to explain everything to them again.

Finally, a minor though very serious mistake we make is that companies develop policies that are distinctly industrial age in their approach. As noted previously, people in our current corporations are much more intellectually sophisticated than they were as little as five years ago. Most of them are very aware of their respective value to the corporation and their potential for employment elsewhere. Quite often, they have very saleable skills and experiences. Combine all of these traits in a single individual and you will encounter someone who does not respond well to psychological intimidation. To put it bluntly, you cannot simply demand that they comply.

If you attempt to build your policies and procedures on that industrial age philosophy of demanding that personnel blindly follow instructions, you are most likely going to encounter a few unpleasant surprises—the least painful of which will be simple refusal to comply. Remember: audience is critical. To create a successful policy, you have to involve the expected audience. You need their approval and buy-in at an intellectual level before they will follow up on your expectations. (For comprehensive details regarding *Creating Effective Policies*, go on line at biztechnet.org.)

Have I struck any cords? Any discords? My goal with this chapter was to start you thinking about the myriad ways that

people perceive the copyrighted product industries as well as
the ways they will perceive your efforts to manage company
technology assets. The quality of your abilities to initiate and
encourage change will determine to a great extent your success in implementing an effective anti piracy program in your
company. Whether you are a software asset manager or a CEO,
you must cultivate an in-depth knowledge of audience and an
ability to anticipate the inner motivations of your fellow employees.

Once more into the breach, my friends!

Q. Isn't this where we started out?

A. Yes

Q. What is the bottom line of all this confusing rhetoric?

A. Before you propose your compliance assurance project
   (or any project), you must understand the needs, perspectives, and agendas of your audience.

Q. Are you suggesting that policies can help reduce the
   costs of a compliance audit?

A. Absolutely—provided they are well written; the employees are made thoroughly aware of them; and that
   you enforce the policies.

Q. Where do I start?

A. If you actually read this entire chapter, you have already started. With any luck, you are beginning to perceive that there is a process that is much more effective
   than merely demanding change. Check the book list on
   the biztechnet.org web site for further reading.

Settlement: TX – Robotic Computer Co. - $107,500

Q. How does this change management concept fit into my overall asset management program?

A. I'm glad you asked!

Questions you should ask.

1. Is my paperwork process effective?
2. What documentation do I have available?
3. What documentation will I need to locate?
4. Am I forcing defective data and practices into a new process?
5. Where am I going to actually start?
   - What will my phased approach look like?
6. Do I understand my corporate culture?
   - What about the individual perspectives?
7. Do I need to learn more about being a change agent?
   - Where will I get the knowledge?
8. Are there other change agents in the company?
   - Can I connect with them for support?
   - Can I connect with other asset managers for support?
9. Am I communicating, or merely making noise?
   - How will I change the trend?
10. After reconsidering my policies, what should I change?

Ready to move on?

Chapter 9

WHAT ARE MY REACTIVE &
PROACTIVE COST SAVINGS OPPORTUNITIES?

Chapter Goals: First, money talks...

Given my existing environment, how can I save money?

How am I going to pay for all this?

What are my reactive opportunities and savings?

What are my proactive opportunities and savings?

Today is the first day

Every process has to have a starting point. Hopefully, as we have moved through this material, you have kept that list of questions and potential issues that your company needs to address. If so, you will have a relatively complete initial set of possible software asset management criteria. If not, you might want to go back through the chapters and revisit the questions on each concluding page.

Rarely do companies effectively include copyright compliance assurance, software asset management, or technology asset management in their budgets. Wait. Let me guess. You were drafted into this job. You have no budget and no direct executive support. You're lucky to have your own cubical and a battered four drawer file cabinet that doesn't lock, right? Is this mission doomed to failure? Not necessarily. Let's start at the beginning and run through the process of gaining support, locating funding, and reducing apathy.

> *The core goals in technology asset management are not necessarily focused on the non compliance issues you will discover. Your most important goal is to gain operational control over your technology assets and the related processes. Once you control the paper, the products, the services, and (hopefully) the nego-tiations, you will gradually find yourself identifying more and more options for avoiding problems, reduc-ing costs and delivering more service and more prod-uct per invested dollar. Again, as noted early in the book—***control*** is not a bad word. It is your job.*

You need to know what is out there

If you want to increase your abilities to be effective, the initial expense for any software asset management (or overall technology asset management) program is the presence of a good configuration discovery tool. If you are going to invest any money or effort in your new asset management process, this is where you should put the most intelligent dollars.

Essentially, in terms of collecting and organizing documen-tation, any basic asset management program can easily begin operating on brain power, alone. This phase is mostly clerical in nature until the environment reaches a sophisticated level of complexity. However, if you are just beginning the document organizational process, people power will accomplish the nec-essary tasks just fine.

Unfortunately, the heavy lifting part of an asset manage-ment program is identifying and monitoring systems along with the products that make those systems operate and serve the business. The only efficient way to perform these tasks is through an automated configuration discovery tool. (Take a look at the biztechnet.org white paper covering *Selecting and Using an Asset Management Discovery Tool* for details

Settlement: GA – Insurance Co. - $100,000

of these critical products.) The good news is that many of the more credible discovery tool providers will permit you to conduct a *live test drive* of their product.

The free functional test drive might appear to reflect a certain process we refer to as the Columbian Marketing concept *(See Real World page 273)* but, in this case, it is a *good thing* for the consumer. After all, would you purchase a car without driving it? The key to avoiding a drug-induced withdrawal scenario is to not permit yourself to become professionally dependent on the evaluation product.

Start with the Free Pilot

You have been given the problem of either proactively creating a compliance management process or proactively creating a software or IT asset management program. Either way, if you want to do this right, you will have to phase the entire process into place one step at a time.

One of the first issues you'll recognize is that you quite likely have no idea which copyrighted products are loaded on your systems. This is simply status quo and to be expected—for now. You may not currently have an automated configuration discovery tool but you're aware that you'll need the statistics that the tool can produce if you expect to get the ball rolling quickly. You may have identified a few asset management acquisition criteria as noted earlier, but more probably this project is a knee-jerk reaction to outside pressures—such as an audit. Where do you start?

If you are not under an audit notification, without an automated tool or any formal process, go ahead and use one of the free configuration discovery (audit) tools to conduct a *proof of concept pilot audit*. Acquire as many free licenses as you feel necessary and prepare to review a representative sample segment of your corporate computer systems. This initial sample should include around 3% to 10% of the enterprise computing systems (more if you wish) selected in such a manner that you include computers being used by a range of departments or divisions.

> *As with any copyrighted product or technical prod-*
> *uct read the license agreement very carefully prior to*
> *making the license valid. Significant hidden costs are*
> *frequently concealed inside the plethora of terms and*
> *conditions.*

With many of the more effective automated discovery tools, you have the option of conducting the configuration review via a floppy disk (older systems) or a thumb drive. Doing so will eliminate the need to modify your network as well as bypass the need to complicate the process by having to schedule a technician to load, configure, and manage the tool on a server. You are looking for a quick survey in this phase, not a definitive set of numbers. However, you *are* looking for numbers — numbers you can use to estimate the overall level of compliance across the enterprise.

The initial pilot review will also give you an opportunity to become familiar with the potential of the discovery tool you select. You will quickly get a feel for the positive and negative aspects of possessing and using this tool during the pilot review. How easily does the tool implement — in terms of your abilities to get it set up? How long does it take to begin producing useful results? What level of talent is required to load and manage the tool? What level of talent is required to actually make use of the tool? How accurate is the tool and how difficult is it to customize?

Big hint, here: if your company does not have the technical talent to work with this tool, you'll find yourself throwing away scarce revenue on consultants who may *or may not* have the required capabilities. Make certain your own people can manage the tool across its operational range—and do not take, "Yeah. I think I can handle this one," as an accurate indicator of capability. Remember, the average techie views learning a challenging new program from scratch as their most exciting fantasy. You, on the other hand, will be paying the bills for a hunt and peck learning curve.

Part of the beauty of this phased implementation process is that you can select several free tools and conduct multiple pilots simultaneously. This gives you the chance to compare the tools as well as check their accuracy against one another. It also gives you more coverage for your initial audit because your multiple samples can span across the license limitations of each free product.

Alright, let's guess that you have acquired two free audit tools licensed for one hundred users each. You can conduct two pilot audits of, say, ninety representative systems with each tool. Remember: you'll want to check these tools against one another so you will conduct dual audits by using the tools simultaneously on ten (or so) systems.

Here's how it works

In general you will be able to create an automated hand audit for each of the free tools. This audit is automated because the tool conducts the actual review of each machine via a floppy disk or thumb drive. (Other methods are certainly possible, but we'll restrict our discussion options to these two.) The automated audit is combined with a hand audit process because you will physically move around the facility with the floppy or thumb drive, visiting each computer.

When you arrive at each computer, you will activate the discovery tool on the portable media (floppy or thumb) and the tool will conduct an audit on the system. When the individual audit is concluded (usually a couple minutes), the tool stores the results on the portable media and you will move on to the next system. An effective automated tool will not touch any data on the computer with the exception of identifying and counting the individual files relating to program activation and operation—user files are generally quite safe from potential intrusion. However, if the tool you are using should impact any user files that you did not specifically set the tool to discover, you may want to very carefully investigate that tool for possible undesirable systems impact. Conversely, if you cannot adjust the discovery tool to locate specific files, such as MP3s, differing graphics formats, or font systems then, once again, it may be the wrong tool for you.

*Real World – If you are using an automated discovery tool that cannot be set to discover music, graphic, gaming, font, or video formats, you will be essentially defenseless should an enforcement entity from those industries choose to audit you for compliance. If the product does not identify these formats by default, ensure that you will be capable of **easily** resetting the default to include them.*

Once you have visited each of your selected pilot computers and conducted the review, you will return to your administration computer to check the data. Most automated tools have an administrator's console from which you can combine the audits and filter the results into reports. If you cannot quickly understand and use this console, you may have the wrong tool. If the audit tool does not provide a wide range of pre-designed reports, you may have the wrong tool. If you cannot easily modify the reports, you may have the wrong tool.

Settlement: IL – Manufacturing Co. - $81,437

*Real World – One of the major required characteristics of a configuration discovery tool involves its day-to-day operation. If you are going to be managing the tool, (and you should be) it has to be easy for **you** to use. Otherwise, if the tool is too complicated for you, or if it requires the regular attentions of a highly trained technician, or you have to have a specialist available to modify and generate reports, your ability to actually use the product is marginal. A good tool is one that nearly anyone can use with very little training. Inattention to this area of concern is one of the reasons tools—and projects—fall into disuse and, possibly, failure.*

Next, when you combine all the system audits into a single review database, you can begin filtering the data. Generate a simple report that details the total number of products configured and group them according to copyright holder. This will give you the information you will use in the next section.

The better discovery tools will contain an internal database that already contains the names of software publishers and other copyright holders. The database will also contain details of each product produced by the copyright holder such as file names, file sizes, the date and time that the file was finalized by the developers, and the copyright holder's embedded copyright data. The quality and currency of this database is critical to the effectiveness of the product. (You'll find more detail on this in the Selecting and Using an Automated Discovery Tool white paper on biztechnet.org.)

Settlement: AL – Software Development Co. - $32,000

Real World – An effective configuration discovery tool will actually document every file on every computer it reviews based on its defined search settings interacting with its internal database. Here is the place where you should be able to modify the application to highlight music or other formats. However, once you set the tool to monitor your specified range of files, the tool should continue monitoring that range until you change the settings. Using the example mentioned previously, if you were not auditing for music files, and you needed a quick review, you could reset the audit tool to run a specialized review including those files you are interested in checking. Then you could filter that review based on a lower volume of raw data. Or, you could simply add the .MP3, or other, extensions to the general list of products already being reported. When the tool runs the next scheduled general audit, it will simply add the new files to the data it collects.

Remember: the configuration discovery tool is there to make your job more efficient. *It* should work for *you*. You are not there to invest your valuable time and energy in gaining a PhD in intensive configuration discovery tool operations. If you cannot implement the tool quickly and begin harvesting accurate data right away, you may have the wrong tool.

Also remember that many of the recommendations included in this book apply most directly to small and medium sized companies. Usually, these companies do not generate the revenue necessary to have massive and highly trained technology support teams. In my experience, the majority of asset management operations are built upon a small number of vastly overworked and (often) under-trained personnel. Overly complex tools that require extensive knowledge and techno skills are not the best choice for efficient operations in this environment.

Settlement: KY – Commercial Real Estate Co. - $36,554

Real World – An attendee of one of my advanced technology asset management training programs commented that her company possessed a top of the line systems configuration discovery tool. The tool had consumed more than twenty months to implement yet it still wasn't fully functional. Further, the tool was being attended to by an entire team of highly trained technicians. When I asked her how it was working for her, she replied that she had no idea. The technicians would not share the data or reports— even though she had repeatedly requested the information.

Was this very expensive and very complicated tool a good investment for the company? Or was it a good investment to ensure the future aura of mystery and employment prospects of an elite technical team? Maybe it was more appropriately used to ensure that company executives or techs would have bragging rights because *they purchased the best*? Remember the commentary about Guido? Did good old Guido decide the company must have this product above all others? If I made the observation that I encounter situations such as this way too often, would it suggest a trend?

*Real World – In many companies, way too many, there is a near drug addiction-like need to acquire certain products and services. This need manifests itself in actions closely mimicking substance abuse withdrawal when the **new product fix** doesn't come about on a regular basis. I haven't encountered any reports of techie suicides yet, but I've listened to dozens of stories of despondent technicians literally drooling over the prospect of a*

Settlement: WI – Manufacturing Co. - $33,500

soon to be released new product from software publisher "X."
This, then, represents the Columbian Marketing concept.

Are copyrighted **soft** technologies the new designer
drug of choice? Consider how easily many of us become totally addicted to certain technical toys. Also,
consider how easily a company can become locked in
to a given product or product line. It becomes more
expensive to displace (eliminate) these products than
it would be to simply put up with the addiction. Are
you hooked on technologies? This sort of sounds like
a certain product line out of Columbia, doesn't it? And,
no, I'm not talking about coffee. **(My sincere apologies to Juan Valdez.)**

Can't you just visualize a meeting of Techno-Junkies
Anonymous? "Hi, my name is Vinnie and I'm addicted to my
desktop productivity suite."

Interpreting the representative sample

In our example we've come to the step where you locate
your justification for gaining management support and funding to acquire a tool for conducting enterprise reactive audits.
One of the most frequent problems I encounter in the fields
of software and technology asset management is a failure to
understand the need to quantify — set in numbers, or measure —
existing processes and results of process changes.

Consider, in your company, which items of strategic information always seem to gain the active attention of executive
management? Are they facts and figures? Absolutely. Yet asset
managers consistently fail to utilize solid facts and figures in

proposals. Is there any wonder that a majority of those proposals tends to fail? (Check out the biztechnet.org training program in *Quantifying and Measuring Asset Management Processes to Improve Your Success*.)

Here is where we're heading with all this. Let's guess that your company has four hundred computers. You conduct two overlapping reviews totaling two hundred of those systems with your free tools—that's 50% of the corporate computers. Scrub and filter the resulting data to identify and report every copyrighted product. For this exercise, just print out the reports showing the copyright holders and the total number of each of their products located on the pilot study systems. How many products did you discover that are not a part of the usual corporate computer configuration for your users? If you don't know what products the company should have configured, this is a prime example of the trend of non management of technology assets. For now, I'll guess there were plenty, but let's say you found potentially illegal products loaded on fifty of the two hundred sampled systems.

Now you should have generated some solid foundation figures to use in justifying your new initiative. If fifty of two hundred systems contain illegal software, you can accurately predict the overall percentage of systems in the entire environment that may also contain unauthorized copyrighted products. Now we can accurately state that, statistically, one fourth of the enterprise computers will contain copyrighted products that may expose the company to compliance enforcement audits.

Our sample was 200 systems out of four hundred. Violations occurred in one fourth (50) of the 200 systems. Multiply the 200 system sample times 2 to reflect the entire environment of 400. Then multiple the 50 violations times 2 and you'll find that you might predict as many as 100 of the total 400 systems will contain incorrectly licensed copyrighted products. Are these decent starting stats? Are they more solid than those you have used in the past?

Settlement: WI – Sales & Distribution Co. - $25,000

Caution – We are not launching a probe to Mars with these statistics. Don't rush out and sign up for a graduate level statistical analysis course at Harvard. Simply establish a numeric valuation system that makes basic sense and use it throughout the examination process. As long as your measurements are consistent and accurate, you will obtain the numbers necessary to support your case.

Want to go further? If you expect to get the attention of executive management, you should. Let's guess that on those 50 non compliant systems you located a total of 150 questionable products. This number could easily represent an average of three illegal products per system. (150 products divided by 50 systems—remember, we're being pretty rough, here.) You can now apply that figure of three products per machine in the pilot to the one hundred potential computer violations you located in the previous paragraph.

Your results? Statistically, based on a 50% sampling of corporate systems, we have determined the 25% of your computers potentially contain approximately three or more incorrectly licensed products. That number would reflect 300 (or more—or fewer) potential copyright violations, times a potential fine of $30,000 to $150,000 per copyright. (Remember, that's per copyright, not per instance of the same copyright being violated.) Technically, according to Federal Copyright Law your company *could* be looking a maximum fine of nearly $9 million. Would that figure wake up a few executive managers from asset management nap time?

Are you afraid you might cause some fatal heart damage with this announcement? Fine, we can work with that. Let's assume that, of the one hundred potential violations, only twenty-five actual copyrights were involved. Well, that's a relief. The company could only be exposed to $750,000 in fines and penalties (at the $30,000 per copyright penalty mark). Go ahead and use this number. Don't be afraid of giving management an estimated range. However, after they have breathed that collective sigh of false relief, you might also mention that technology asset managers who have been audited estimate that actual audit costs tend to range near, and exceed, 3 to 6 times the published fines. That $750,000 just jumped to $2,250,000 (4.5 times 750,000). Think you could use these figures to show how much your initiative could save the company? Did we forget to calculate the impact of all that negative publicity on the corporate image? How about the costs of company down time during an enforcement audit? Isn't it a great feeling to be able to justify what you are trying to accomplish? Look at it this way — we finally get to be the folks in the white hats.

What have you spent so far in this example? I would estimate maybe twenty hours of your time and virtually no company revenue (These tasks *are* part of your job, aren't they?). The free tools were...well...free, so the cost of the tools was nicely acceptable. You didn't search for any documentation yet because you weren't focusing on that side of the equation. Not to worry — when you do factor in the documentation search, the potential for fines will only increase due to all the paperwork you won't be able to locate. You didn't interrupt any of the busy technicians because you were able to conduct the review yourself using portable media. You didn't interrupt the desktop workers because your review of each machine consumed maybe two and a half minutes.

Now, what if I told you that you could easily acquire an asset management discovery tool for around $40 per seat (or less)? That would work out as $40 times your 400 computers or an investment of $16,000 to put a pretty solid end to potential copyright violation issues — issues that, statistically, you have demonstrated might cost the company in excess of $750,000. As well, the discovery tool is a long term solution so it will provide services other than mere compliance assurance. But, wait, there's more: the tool that I have in mind for your 400 seat company can be implemented in a single day by a single moderately skilled technician; it will be producing strategic

Settlement: WA – Technology Consulting Co. - $300,000

data within twenty-four hours; and you will be capable of managing the tool operations yourself. Is this a good deal?

Will people shoot holes in your neatly prepared proposal? Absolutely. However, even your most optimistic appraisal will still represent a significant potentially negative financial impact to the enterprise. Not many companies with approximately four hundred employees can afford to drop three quarters of a million unbudgeted dollars on a single copyright litigation settlement. (The number of computers is usually a close indication of the number of employees.) Also remember, if your company is covered by the Sarbanes-Oxley Act, executive management might find itself explaining this litigation expenditure and adverse publicity to the Board of Directors as well as the shareholders — a tough process when it could have been avoided so easily.

Consider this bottom line to what you have just read: the majority of companies represented by this scenario can begin recovering lost revenue or avoiding unnecessary costs with what I have told you here. In fact, many of you will be able to use this material, alone, to locate enough savings to initiate a pretty solid technology asset management program for either very little — or zero — investment on the part of the company. *(Still doubting me? Check the biztechnet.org web site for ongoing savings observations.)*

Okay, now you know what is out there. So what?

You now have a very basic glimpse of your environment that cost essentially nothing. Keep in mind that there are plenty of holes in our example — simply because it is an example — and because I'm not standing here physically discussing this with you. For instance, you probably did not review the servers in your audit — and servers nearly always have plenty of violations hidden in their massive storage and delivery capacities. Every company is different (as if you needed me to tell you that), so every company will encounter different issues in selecting and implementing a discovery tool or license assurance program. If we were together right now in a full training session, we could address your individual issues but, since we aren't, we can't—and the book has to remain pretty generic.

The bottom line is that you should now have shown a definite potential for impressive cost avoidance opportunities. If you made use of the details in Chapter 2 regarding the high potential for confrontational litigation represented by the software police and copyright cops, you can certainly speak knowledgeably about the probabilities that your company may be audited. If you paid surface attention in Chapter 3 you will be capable of explaining how even basic copyright-related laws enhance and support the efforts of enforcement audit teams at the expense of the consumer—in this case, your company. You now know, and can probably communicate, how serious the risks have become as well as how they will inevitably grow. Are you following my process, here? Hope so. *(If not, drop me an email with your questions.)*

Let's make another jump in our estimation of your effectiveness as a technology asset manager. Let's guess that your documentation is pretty well managed and you are fairly comfortable with your license counts. (*Okay, it's a mental mirage, but it sounds pretty good, doesn't it?*) You have completed an enterprise-wide review or audit of your systems. You are not under an audit notice, so where is the big savings I keep talking about? Here we go.

Dump the junk

Now that you have a decent image of your systems, software, and related paperwork, how many copyrighted products does your company have present that nobody uses? If you can work with the technicians and users to identify unnecessary and high risk products, you can delete and uninstall them from systems. There will be plenty of these.

Settlement: IL – Higher Education Institute - $95,000

What will your savings be? Start with the savings represented by compliance audit cost avoidance. How many illegal
products did you locate and remove? What would the losses
have been had you been audited? Document the numbers for
your success book. Next, look at the reduced cost of tech support because helping people with these unauthorized products
certainly is not part of ongoing technician responsibilities. The
time techs could save by no longer addressing the unauthorized
products will definitely reflect savings both in lost productivity of individual users and the technicians themselves.

How many copyrighted products did you discover that are
either no longer in use or are underutilized? Removing or reducing the presence of these products will once again cut the
costs of your internal tech support. As well, if any are covered
by ongoing external support or maintenance contracts, you'll
show great savings by eliminating or significantly reducing
the coverage provided under those support contracts.

*Real World – In the Spring 2003 issue of CFO Magazine,
a story by Bob Violino,* **Software Vendors the New IRS?**,
*spotlighted Sanders Morris Harris, an investment bank in Houston.
The organization implemented an asset management tool from
Scalable Software, Inc. that analyzes actual employee use of
hardware and software items. Using the resulting data, Sanders
Morris Harris found savings of $15,000 per month by reducing
the license counts of a single underutilized application. Still think
this process doesn't work?*

Shareware strikes again

It's free. It's easy. Just download and forget. Absolutely.
This is precisely what your users think about shareware. There

is only a single miniscule problem with these beliefs—they're wrong. When you ran that automated audit, you discovered a potential king's ransom in possible shareware licensing issues. These titles appear to be everywhere. Maybe they reproduce on the systems late at night after the last user goes home. Maybe phantom technicians from another dimension slipped them past your firewall. Either way, there is a whole boatload of shareware on your systems. You have just discovered a serious and all but invisible problem shared by nearly every company using technology.

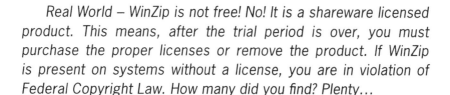

Real World – WinZip is not free! No! It is a shareware licensed product. This means, after the trial period is over, you must purchase the proper licenses or remove the product. If WinZip is present on systems without a license, you are in violation of Federal Copyright Law. How many did you find? Plenty...

Monitor all shareware products. Establish a formal policy or process—a form if necessary—that every user must follow in acquiring and using shareware (or freeware or any other *...ware* product). Include in this process a very clear methodology for removing the products from systems before the trial license concludes. Be sure to document all steps. This shareware management process should be an important element of your license compliance due diligence program.

Real World – An Ohio company undergoing a forced voluntary audit by a major enforcement entity discovered that technicians had neglected to uninstall a time-limited server based evaluation

Settlement: CO – Software Development Co. - $83,963

copy of a major email package. The fine was significant. Ensure that your company uninstalls and carefully documents all evaluation products when the eval period concludes.

Support and maintenance

Now that you have finally collected all of those licenses and legal documents, you can actually read about which products and specific services you should have present in your environment or are entitled to receive. Are you getting the support and maintenance you paid for? Want to bet? Check with the people who actually use that support if you want to review this process. You will nearly always find savings.

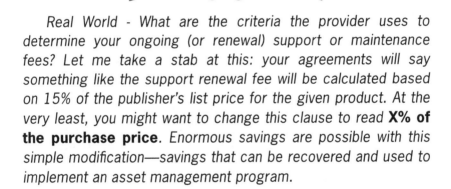

Real World - What are the criteria the provider uses to determine your ongoing (or renewal) support or maintenance fees? Let me take a stab at this: your agreements will say something like the support renewal fee will be calculated based on 15% of the publisher's list price for the given product. At the very least, you might want to change this clause to read **X% of the purchase price***. Enormous savings are possible with this simple modification—savings that can be recovered and used to implement an asset management program.*

Did your acquisitions team buy the gold support level? You know—the most expensive 24x7x365 *right now by golly* service? Do your technicians use even a fraction of this support level? Now that you have the support documents in hand, you can finally check to ensure you are receiving the service levels you are paying for. You can also check with your technical people to see if they actually need this level of support. Want to bet you can cut substantial costs in this arena? Do you doubt my observations? That's okay. Use your new spreadsheet to track actual use of these support levels, then compare the actual use against the contract. Cutting the service by even a single level returns money to the budget. If, after you discover I was right and you feel bad about doubting me, you can buy me a cup of coffee next time we meet.

Real World – After a long-delayed review of support agreements, a small Midwest company discovered that the third party vendor providing support services for Internet and network routers had been inadvertently double-billing the company $10,000 per quarter for nearly two years. Cost recovery exceeded $80,000.

What was the miracle that enabled these potential savings? You probably never had all of your agreements in one place before, did you? Nor had you managed to take the time to read and document the information. Am I right? Now that you have brought everything into a central location you can actually perform these tasks. How much did this process cost? In general, only your leg work in locating and regaining control of documentation.

What do you mean, we bought too much?

I have found, again consistently, that companies are actually more likely to buy too many licenses for a given product, or range of products, than they are to buy too few licenses. Incredibly, the logic is that over-buying will protect the company from non compliance. One company I worked with actually tacked on an additional 15% more license counts than necessary every time they purchased software or operating systems. The justification for this significant amount of over-spending was that the company did not have any solid data showing exactly how many computers it had operating.

For this particular company, the cost of an automated tool — even one that would do nothing more than count the computers on the network and provide basic configuration data — would have been far less than the revenue thrown away on a single enterprise software title acquisition. In this particular case, the company asset manager was actually able to justify buying the discovery tool based on eliminating this purchasing practice.

*Real World – In the same CFO article we just discussed, Quan Ha, of Sony Pictures Digital, reported that his company was able to cancel a proposed $10,000 software purchase. The company's newly purchased configuration discovery tool from Attest Systems, Inc. revealed that Sony Digital **already possessed** the product and had enough unused licenses to cover the purchase.*

What was the miracle that you would use to identify and correct this problem? That simple discovery tool — the tool you most likely didn't have operational prior to now. Also, the tool you put in place just to manage compliance that can now perform additional duties — if you selected the right tool. In Sony Digital's case, the cost of the tool — $12,000 — was almost instantly recovered by the discovery of unused licenses. Where in the technology projects arena could you get this rate of return this quickly? Only in IT asset management.

Settlement: TX – Telecommunications Co. - $30,000

Operating system roll-out

The latest operating system has finally hit the market. Your asset acquisitions team decides to acquire it — because it is a good business case, not Guido's latest addiction fix. Your technicians immediately begin to fan out across the enterprise to determine which computers are capable of using the new system. They are looking for size of the hard drive, the free space available on the hard drive, the RAM on each computer, the number of software applications on each computer that are compatible with the new operating system (and the number of applications that are not compatible), and a multitude of other compatibility issues. The cost of the review is enormous and can occur as frequently as twice in any given twenty month period. How can you avoid these recurring costs?

The discovery tool you acquired to conduct your compliance review should also be capable of discovering all of the information noted above. Instead of technicians performing hands-on checks of systems, the majority of your computers can be audited for hardware by your configuration discovery tool. In addition, the discovery tool should be able to produce reports that document conformance or non conformance with every criteria listed above. Technicians will know precisely what changes each individual computer requires prior to the roll-out. Also, since each computer's needs are clearly documented, technical buyers can now purchase exactly the right products for upgrading the computers that do not comply. Cost savings — ongoing cost savings — are enormous. All because of the compliance audit tool you carefully selected.

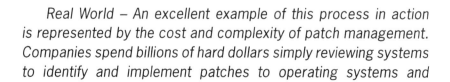

Real World – An excellent example of this process in action is represented by the cost and complexity of patch management. Companies spend billions of hard dollars simply reviewing systems to identify and implement patches to operating systems and

Settlement: CA – Software Development Co. - $33,138

software—including anti-virus updates. An effective configuration discovery tool will reveal in a single sweep of corporate systems the numbers and specific locations of systems that have received a given patch or update, as well as the systems that did not receive the change. Would access to this information represent savings to your company? Or, would you rather continue sending technicians out to personally visit every computer to confirm its status.

The savings you will find in hardware and systems upgrades alone will most likely pay for your new discovery tool. Do the math. Count your computers — no, wait — you can't count your computers because you don't have a discovery tool to perform the count. (*Am I being too cruel here?*)

Another word about patch management

Let's take another look at dumping the junk. Do you keep track of the costs relating to patching and fixing defective software products? Consider the amount of time and effort the enterprise expends every year fixing defects in software. Let's say you purchased a product costing $50 per seat for your four hundred seats — $20,000, right? Within a two year period the company was attacked twelve times by viruses, Trojans, or similar malicious code that took advantage of defective code in the same software. Your cost to apply patches each time averaged $6 per seat — $2,400 times 12 events equals $28,800. Did you just pay an additional (nearly) 1.45 times the value of that software just to repair the defective code, or did I make a mistake on the math?

What would happen if every corporate software consumer kept track of the expenditures for repairing defective code and included those figures in their next negotiation with the software providers? What would happen if you tracked the accumulated costs (directly impacting your business) that are caused by defective software? I know—I'm scaring the daylights out of you, but let's look at this logically. If any other supplier of goods was selling products that contained a volume of major defects approaching, or exceeding, twelve in a two year period, wouldn't that company be expected to compensate consumers? Want to really start pulling your hair? Try totaling up the costs of those same defects over a five year period. Now go to ten years.

Remember UCITA from Chapter 3? Products can be sold containing known defects? How interesting. Could this legislative trend and the growing volume of defective software code be directly linked? What if you factor in the legislative attempts to deny researchers access to the software code along with denying them the ability to publish their findings? If only the copyright holder is legally permitted to conduct defect research and communicate the results—and this same group of copyright holders is working to pass legislation permitting known defects in their products—who is monitoring product quality for the consumer? Something to consider, don't you think?

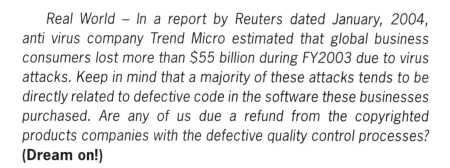

Real World – In a report by Reuters dated January, 2004, anti virus company Trend Micro estimated that global business consumers lost more than $55 billion during FY2003 due to virus attacks. Keep in mind that a majority of these attacks tends to be directly related to defective code in the software these businesses purchased. Are any of us due a refund from the copyrighted products companies with the defective quality control processes? **(Dream on!)**

Settlement: AZ – Advertising Agency - $25,491

According to an SIIA (You remember them from Chapter 2, right?) press release dated 7 June, 2004, the cost of piracy to the software industry reaches around $12 billion annually. The BSA, on the other hand, informs us that its research indicates the global cost of piracy for 2003 touches $29 billion. (*Golly. Who* can *we trust?*) The point that I am trying to make, though, is that, if viruses (or other malicious codes) are taking advantage of defective software and costing consumers over $55 billion in a single year, then perhaps we need to invest a little more time, money, and legislative energy in preventing and controlling defective code than we're pouring into preventing piracy. (*Makes pretty good sense to me. How about you?*)

Proactive opportunities and savings

Okay. We've looked at reactive savings opportunities—those that you can achieve with little or no investment—those you can achieve using only the single configuration discovery tool made necessary by a compliance audit. Until now, you may have had no basic formal process for identifying savings opportunities and recovering—or avoiding—unnecessary spending. Most companies are not aware that many of these savings opportunities exist. Let's decide that you want to *phase in* an enterprise IT asset management program. Based on everything we have discussed, you could easily justify the need, propose the program, identify the necessary tools, and set up the processes with minimal up front investment.

Let's take a look at proactive savings options. These are the ones that *really* pay the bills.

Paper is money

There is huge potential for revenue in your paperwork. Some of it represents cost avoidance—as in the audit scenarios we have discussed. However, a significant portion of revenue recovery will be reflected in potential long term savings and cost reduction opportunities originating from invoice recon-ciliations.

Consider: in many of the scenarios on the previous few pages we looked at cost recovery opportunities that came about simply through a fresh review of contractual agree-ments. These reviews were only made possible because some dedicated asset manager finally managed to collect and orga-nize all of the licenses, agreements, and other documentation covering software assets. Keep in mind that nearly all of these management processes can be applied to virtually all technol-ogy assets — including hardware and services.

Until now, in the hustle and bustle of day-to-day opera-tions, you have had little or no time to review existing docu-ments. Take that time now. Once you have collected the docu-ments — at essentially no cost — you can at last sit down for half an hour or an hour every day and review and summarize each document. If any of your proofs of possession documentation are missing important data, you may now take time to have them corrected. The cost avoidance opportunities, should you be audited, are obvious; if twenty receipts from the same ven-dor have minor errors and you can arrange to have that vendor correct the errors, then those adjusted receipts represent sig-nificant cost avoidance in audit penalties. If, as in the router example mentioned previously, you locate invoices that are duplicated or that cover unnecessary products, the savings are once again obvious.

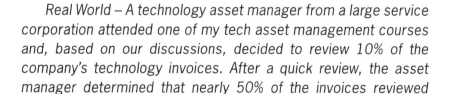

Real World – A technology asset manager from a large service corporation attended one of my tech asset management courses and, based on our discussions, decided to review 10% of the company's technology invoices. After a quick review, the asset manager determined that nearly 50% of the invoices reviewed

---

Settlement: CA – Orthodontist Group - $27,146

contained significant errors that reflected potential for cost recovery. Why wasn't this step taken before? Because it was not a priority and was not an issue on the operational radar screen.

———————⌣———————

Do you remember the example of the support agreement that was governed by an automatic yearly renewal clause that defined the renewal as 15% of the publisher's list price? If you had negotiated that clause to read 15% of the *purchase* price, how much would you save with each renewal? Let's take a look.

If the initial product publisher's list price was $50 per seat in 2000 and you acquired 400 seats, your first year of support would reflect 15% of the $20,000 license fee, or $3,000. Unfortunately, for you—and very conveniently for the copyright holder—during the second half of your first year of possession, the list price of the product went up to $65 per seat. Your cost for the second year of support will now be around $3,900. The third year, the list price rose to $80 per seat and your support renewal cost you $4,800. Do you sense a pattern here? Seems like the cost of support continues to rise in direct proportion to the latest publisher's list price.

Here is the rub: the software industry, as a whole, does not actually publish a formal list price for its products. When a list price is even suggested, it is generally far above the product worth because it is used as an initial quote prior to negotiating reductions. With the exception of very tiny companies, virtually no one should be paying list price for products. The issue here is that since list prices are generally not public information, the publisher can easily quote you *virtually any price* as its current list price.

If you did not negotiate the clause covering the price base of support renewals, your support fees could easily skyrocket simply because the copyright holder had a bad fiscal year. If, on the other hand, you negotiated the cost of ongoing support to reflect 15% of the *actual purchase price*, your support costs will remain constant at $3,000 per year for the length of the contract. That reflects a $900 savings during the second year renewal and another $1,800 savings in the third year. What do you suppose the savings would be over the entire life cycle of this product?

Real World – During a compliance enforcement audit, one of the enforcement entities, quoting the publisher list price, attempted to set the value of a single product license at more than $250. At this level of the negotiations, the enforcement agent was preparing to determine the penalty for each configuration of the unlicensed product—usually a figure of 1.5 to 4 times the publisher list price. If the company being audited had 20 illegal copies of the product, this would have reflected a base penalty of $5,000 for this single product if they were only penalized at the basic list price. The enforcement agent, however, wanted the company to pay 3 times the list price per violation, or $15,000 in penalties.

Personally, I don't know of any company that would be willing to pay $250 per seat for this particular product. In fact, the average corporate consumer usually pays around $45 per seat for this item. That means, in this instance of copyright violation, the actual value of the product misuse would reflect 20 seats times $45 instead of $250 per seat. When you calculate the penalty based on this figure, even at 3 times the per seat fee, the penalty drops from a possible $15,000 to $2,700. Isn't it interesting how a publisher's phantom list price can impact our businesses?

Settlement: CA – Entertainment Ticket Co. - $473,500

Duplication of effort

A few pages back, we discussed the tendency of companies to allow unused licenses to become invisible. Through a lack of tracking processes or a certain level of un-management, we tend to lose track of where everything is and what we own. This habit tends to encourage us to purchase the same products over again or purchase other products that perform the same function. Here is how it often works.

The accounting department purchases a *must have* database product to manage the books and corporate assets. As is usually the case, this program, designed around accounting best practices, is not compatible with your technology asset management applications so you won't be gaining access to the data any time soon—besides, knowledge of corporate finances is way above your pay grade. Shortly thereafter, the legal department acquires another database to use in tracking the status and content of legal documents. This database may actually contain scanned copies of many of the agreements for which you are responsible but you will not be granted access because you are not a *trusted member* of the legal department. Besides, you're one of those techno-dweebs. What on earth would *you* know about contracts and legal documents?

Am I finished, yet? Hardly. Concurrent with the legal department acquisition, the human resources department obtains a new database for tracking employee records. You will not have access to this database, either, because employee records are confidential to everyone but the personnel department, the IRS, junk mail distributors, and spammers. Does this series of scenarios sound familiar? It should. It's definitely the most frequent one of its kind that I encounter.

"So," you say, "what's the problem?" The problem is that the records that technology asset managers need to perform their jobs are being virtually held hostage by other departments. Short of an Act of Congress, you generally cannot gain access to them. Consider these:

Settlement: IL – Technology Consulting Co. - $480,000

- You cannot gain access to the legal documentation.
    - » As a result, you cannot review the original licenses or support documentation,
    - » If you do not know the permissions provided in these permissive documents, you cannot possibly be compliant,
- You cannot gain access to accounting system documentation.
    - » As a result, you have no idea which acquisition documents are being retained,
    - » Nor do you have any control over the document destruction periods,
- You have no access to the human resources database.
    - » You have no formal method of tracking which technology assets each employee is responsible for maintaining or using,
    - » You have no formal method of tracking which employees have been trained on, and agreed to, company anti piracy policies and procedures

Essentially, the technology asset management team is out of the loop and forced to play a constant game of catch up. How is all of this a duplication of effort? What if every one of the previous three departments, plus yours, will be maintaining its own database — a database that may or may not be compatible with the others. Each department will be duplicating a high percentage of input data as it configures and uses its own data. Your support technicians will have to become proficient with four separate database structures and operations procedures. Since the records of each data base are considered top secret by each department, they'll obviously have to be housed on separate servers, right? Unnecessary costs? Absolutely, and the list goes on and on.

Of even more importance, since most advanced databases are quite expensive, you will be paying for four separate systems that are essentially performing the same function. And, since implementation is usually much more expensive than the products themselves, trying to implement four distinct applications when you could implement only one constitutes a rather poor business decision, don't you think? You will also be paying external support and maintenance fees on four systems instead of one or two. If you merged all of these databases into a single enterprise database, the cost savings can become astronomical.

I am well aware that most companies have encountered this problem. I understand that, at very least, the issues of egos and departmental turf will represent significant barriers to accomplishing this project. However, if a given company could realize the cost recovery opportunities of an effective centralized database—again, the savings opportunities are exceptional. Couldn't those same savings be put to use making the wise company more competitive?

Volume purchases

One of the most effective cost savings opportunities that result from gaining full control over your IT asset management environment is your expanded opportunities for taking advantage of volume purchasing offers. In the example above, the company will save a significant amount because it is no longer acquiring four separate databases with each application only representing a few narrowly defined departmental seats. Instead, in the case of the single core database, the entire range of corporate users is calculated as part of the license and the per seat cost will drop dramatically.

I would be willing to bet that your company acquires its anti virus software as a volume purchase asset. If the company is effective, there is only a single brand of anti virus on the

Settlement: WA – Toy Catalog Sales Co - $525,000

systems. Yes, I am aware that some companies utilize more than one anti virus as a checks and balances assurance process. Standardizing the anti virus reduces costs for the original product acquisition, for in-house technical support, for signature updates, and more. Why not use the same common sense for all other IT assets?

Real World – In an article in CIO magazine, January 15, 2005, **Prune IT Systems, Not Budgets**, *Michael Schrage revealed information that confirms some of the unnecessary costs involved in redundant systems. Mr. Schrage commented that General Motors and other companies have discovered that their various departments might be maintaining from six to as many as 12 different databases. The costs of supporting even half this many same-service applications increase dramatically when you consider potential data incompatibilities, support issues, operator skill sets, and the loss of volume purchasing power.*

How many products does your company have that could be consolidated into a single service?

Real World – Sallie Mae eliminated over forty software products that were performing redundant tasks. This streamlining project generated cost savings exceeding $1,000,000.

What? We bought the warranty?

How many times have you encountered a malfunctioning system that was in obvious need of direct technician attention? How many times has a tech worked on a system, spending hours finding and correcting a basic hardware failure? Did you ever follow up on the repairs to see if the system was under warranty? Most companies tend to not track warranties for two simple reasons. First, because no individual person is willing (or permitted) to take control over the paperwork. And second, because, in my experience, the techies are simply too busy to have to deal with the issues.

Wait... You were too busy to determine if a system was under warranty before you broke the seal on the case and voided the warranty? Absolutely. And the reason your techies are too busy to track this process is that the company usually fails to control the documentation detailing which systems are under warranty. If a techie has to spend two or more hours searching for a warranty it is much easier to simply fix the system and move on to the next emergency. After all, the primary job of the techies is to keep the systems operational, right?

Once again, if all you had was a thoroughly organized paper filing system, it would take virtually no time to determine if a given system was under warranty prior to investing scarce time and revenue bringing it back up to speed.

Here is a near reversal of what I just suggested. If you know up front that the company tends to repair first and check paperwork later (if at all), why not simply quit wasting money on warranties? After all, you are aware when you make the purchase that your corporate culture approaches warranties and systems down-time in a specific manner. Why not save the warranty money for another investment?

Settlement: CA – Manufacturing Co. - $33,500

Real World – In a related concept, a company I worked with was acquiring computers with a built in sound card. However, somehow, every system was still being ordered with an add-on synchronization cable for a plug-in sound card. The cables cost $15 each and, when I caught the error, the company had already purchased five or six hundred computers. Lost revenue, approximately $7,500.

I know. It isn't a warranty but it is the same concept: ordering something you have no need to order or that you will not use. How many instances do you have of technicians performing repairs that were actually covered under warranty? You probably didn't know until you regained direct control over your paperwork.

Criteria? What criteria?

I realize that I have already put you on the spot about criteria with my, "Most companies don't have *any* acquisition criteria" lecture. But, this is yet another huge savings opportunity requiring no expenditure on your part. Do you monitor each purchase to determine if you actually receive what you ordered or contracted to receive?

Real World – Remember the company that was paying $3,000 a year support for a product it hadn't used in years? When we called the software publisher to cancel the contract, the representative replied, "We wondered if you guys were going to contact us." It seems that the person they were using to provide the actual

Settlement: CA – Musical Instrument Co. - $90,000

support had retired several years previously. The company manager assured me that, "...we have him on retainer if you had called for help." Not for $3,000 per year, you don't.

⌣

Within the average corporate technology asset management program there is very little follow up of either acquisition criteria or product functionality delivery criteria. But your company is about to be more effective, right? Now that you have all of your paperwork in one place, you can review the deliverables and identify the products and suppliers that are providing the value you purchased.

⌣

Real World – In late 2003 a large multinational corporation in Northeastern Ohio discovered that its Enterprise Resource Planning (ERP) System was in difficulty. Well, I suppose difficulty is a pretty benign word for the impact. Essentially, the problems with the system traced back to interdependent systems, the core ERP implementation, and other related processes. The cost? Nearly $100 million. How would that type of difficulty impact your bottom line? If a product doesn't work correctly, fix it or displace it!

⌣

Start keeping track and documenting results or failures. You are not keeping a hit list here. You are maintaining and tracking control of the quality of projects, products, services, and systems. To perform your job responsibly, you should be capable of historically tracking successes and failures as well as the events that contributed to each. Develop a basic measurement scale so that you can begin quantifying these issues.

Settlement: CA – Graphics Co. - $86,078

The numbers will give you the ability to document precisely how effective any given product or service is when you communicate with management.

Remember that if you don't put a number to it, you cannot defend your results. Have I given you enough to think about? Here are some additional issues to review:

Employee Theft

This one is actually quite simple. If you do not have a detailed and current record of the products you possess, how will you know when software, master media, or hardware grows legs and wanders off? I have actually helped implement multiple IT asset management programs for corporations that originally only wanted the processes in place to curb employee theft of technologies.

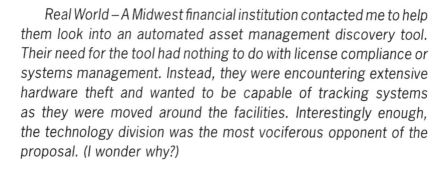

Real World – A Midwest financial institution contacted me to help them look into an automated asset management discovery tool. Their need for the tool had nothing to do with license compliance or systems management. Instead, they were encountering extensive hardware theft and wanted to be capable of tracking systems as they were moved around the facilities. Interestingly enough, the technology division was the most vociferous opponent of the proposal. (I wonder why?)

How much hardware does your company lose every year simply because no one knows precisely where any of it is located, who checked it out, or who used it last?

Settlement: CA – Vocational School District - $50,000

Auto-Renewals

How many of your technology agreements include an auto-renewal clause? Copyright holders love to include this clause because corporate consumers tend to permit auto-renewal contracts to become invisible. The way this process works is that if the provider does not receive a written notice of intent to cancel the contract by a certain date the contract auto-renews itself. Miss that date by a single day and many of the less than sensitive providers will continue sending invoices each year until you hit the target. If your company does not have a very powerful lock on the status of every contract, the chances are very good that you may have auto-renewal contracts that continue to exist even for products you no longer have configured.

How many auto-renewal contracts do you have? At what frequency do they auto-renew? When was the last time you updated either the agreement or the contact information within the agreement? Want to locate some savings without the need to invest money? This is another opportunity.

Software Activation

Here is an interesting concept. The software industry tells us that they must institute software activation because of high piracy rates for their products. While I can understand this reasoning, it is difficult for me to see beyond the emerging custom of implementing activation for copyrighted products, then following up activation with software subscription, rental, leasing, or simply yearly payments.

Over the past several years, we have seem a definite trend toward activation on the parts of several major software publishers. This initial action is usually followed up with a yearly subscription pricing model. The impact that the entire process has on you and your organization is that you will soon be losing the perpetual licensing option. Within a very few years, you will be paying yearly fees on all of your major software and operating systems. Hint: your costs will go up—a lot.

I should note at this point that this subscription based licensing model is one that the mainframe users have been forced to live with for years—and they do *not* like it. Subscription licensing tends to be much more expensive and more open to value-added services and fees. I believe that down the road you will find that many of those same additional services and fees were the ones that came with your perpetual license—way back when.

Real World – Have you noticed how publisher supplied templates have trickled down to practically nothing? Oh, they're still available—all you have to do is visit the publisher web site and register to download them—for free. Let's stop a moment and think patterns, here. First you give it away for free. Then, when everyone depends on the product, you slowly begin to tighten up on its distribution and availability. Once you have determined the potential market for the product, you can begin charging a fee. (Go ahead. Prove me wrong.)

Time Theft

If your employees are cruising the Internet in search of music, games, software, fonts, movies, or any other non-business item, they are essentially stealing time from the company. Confronting them with this precise issue would be pointless—creating a potential altercation coupled with ongoing difficulties in interpersonal relations. However, what if your discovery tool notified you that P2P executable files were beginning to appear on systems? Could you eliminate those files quietly, *"so my fellow employees wouldn't be in trouble?"* Doing so

Settlement: CA – Toy Manufacturer - $55,000

would eliminate the threat of copyright violation; it would enable you to enforce policies in a humane fashion; and your relationships with other personnel might not be damaged.

Consider another example. How much time are personnel at your company spending on IM applications? Does your company regulate these? Does your company forbid their use on corporate computers? If your discovery tool was set to monitor the existence of IM applications, would employees be less likely to install, or misuse one and possibly be less likely to use IM for play time?

Vendor and Product Supplier Management

An incredible number of individuals responsible for acquiring and managing technologies have essentially no in-depth knowledge of vendors and providers. What do you know about each of your vendors? How about each of your suppliers? Do you know their yearly financial cycles? How about their corporate financial year end and other critical dates? Have you developed a matrix of vendors and providers that rates service and products according to your needs criteria? Do you let vendors know, up front, that you have certain expectations in terms of their performance?

Here is an interesting concept. Has anyone mentioned to you that contractual compliance is actually a two way street? Many of you who are reading this material have been audited by the compliance enforcement industry for software license non compliance. You were challenged because you were suspected of breaching the requirements and commitments of the copyright holder's license contract. The copyright holder has every right in the world to monitor that compliance. However, shouldn't it make sense that any contractual agreement between two companies needs to stipulate compliance expectations for *both* parties?

How often do you place *your* compliance expectations for the product, service, or vendor in a license or agreement? You probably do so in nearly all of your consulting agreements, right? Why not your agreements with copyright holders? If you acquire a product with the expectation of it performing a specific service, shouldn't that product's provider be contractually obligated to ensure that its product does, indeed, perform the service for which it was purchased? Why is it that software is one of the only products on the market that does not have to perform the function which it claimed to perform or for which it was purchased?

Could it be that the consumers of technology have been so busy acquiring technology we have permitted sharp practices in contracts and licensing that we would never tolerate in any other acquisition? Could it be time to take a long and very serious look at our contracts and vendor relationships? Can I answer for you? *Yes*, it could be, and is, time!

Real World – I'm fairly certain that you invested pretty good money in this book. You did so because you expected some specific return on your investment. It is my task to ensure that you get your money's worth. Otherwise, my book is a bad investment and I haven't delivered on my commitment. If my product does not provide that positive return on investment, will you buy another one of my books? Probably not.

Then why would a knowledgeable corporate consumer blindly invest tens of thousands (millions?) of dollars in technology products that are defective, do not provide expected value, cost much more than they are worth, and are not warranted to be free of viruses—and many of these copyrighted products are, in fact, not warranted to provide any specific functionality to the consumer?

Settlement: TX – HVAC Co. - $71,173

Remember, every "X" number of dollars you lose on poorly designed technologies represents the full time yearly income of one or more employees. How many jobs are at risk due to your company tech purchasing practices? Expect your vendors and product suppliers to stand beside their products—not hide behind expensive liability litigation. Now, measure their performance and ensure that they do so.

Do you want more?

If you have nothing more than a basic paper filing system of vital documentation—you can...

If your system is limited to filing cabinets, or even boxes of papers, you can still gain control. First, organize the papers according to the suppliers' names followed by individual products. Keep all documentation for a given product together in the same file. Review and summarize all legal agreements.

How much did this cost you? Even the smallest company can perform this simple step. Here are some of the savings you can locate with this simple filing system:

- Centralize IT asset records – cost avoidance and reduction,
- Site licenses linked to the wrong site – potential breach of contract,
- Network licenses without volume control – potential for exceeding license counts – breach,
- Concurrent licenses with incorrect user number settings, or not monitored for precise usage counts – potential breach,
- Missing proofs of purchase – non compliance cost avoidance,
- Incorrect invoices – Direct cost reductions as well a non compliance cost avoidance,

- Duplicate invoices – Significant cost reductions and potential cost recovery,
- Unlicensed products on systems – If you collected all the licenses and have located a product that is present without documentation – non compliance cost avoidance,
- Support agreements
  - » Support not being delivered – cost savings,
  - » Support delivered at lower intensity scale – cost reduction,
  - » Support unnecessary – cost recovery,
- Redundant products – too many products performing the same services – cost reduction (Where have you heard this one?).
- Unused or underutilized products – cost reduction,

Get the picture? You can accomplish all of the cost recovery or savings opportunities we just listed with nothing more than a box of documents. No tools or special programs would be necessary. If your company has nothing in place today, start with this step—collect and read your documentation.

Real World – A Great Lakes company decided to centralize all software-related documentation. Facilities in several states sent their records to the headquarters facility. Pallet after pallet of plastic-wrapped stacks of disorganized documentation soon began to arrive at HQ. The single individual responsible for monitoring software assets could generally expect to invest several hours trying to locate a specific software product record or master media. After we coordinated the centralized documentation, the

---

Settlement: NC – Civil Engineering Co. - $45,000

same individual could access a very simple database, locate the specified product or item, and open the correct file drawer in the secure storage room where the item was stored. This simple process of centralization and organization reduced the time to locate asset materials from several hours to less than two minutes.

Would any of the items we've discussed represent cost savings opportunities for your company? What if the same processes reduced the incidence of lost master media and license documentation by 80%? What if the same processes located dozens of products the company was not even aware that it owned? What if those processes also helped you locate support or maintenance agreements you no longer required, or that you could reduce?

And then there are those piracy and non compliance things...

Are you in control of your costs?

Are you interested in additional savings opportunities? Watch the biztechnet.org web site. We will continue to post cost reduction strategies. Do you have a strategy that works? Let us know & we'll help share it with other companies that need help with their asset management process. Keep in mind that what you share will be repaid by materials shared by others. If we communicate intelligently with one another, *everyone* stands to benefit.

What have we learned, here?

- If you don't already have an automated discovery tool – get one.

- If necessary, use the free tools to conduct a pilot study to establish your baseline.
- Use the baseline statistics to clearly define your needs and potential liabilities.
- Eliminate unused or under-used products.
- Monitor and remove shareware.
- Monitor support and maintenance.
- Do not over-buy—it's not only expensive but it demonstrates lack of tech environment controls.
- In some environments, the unnecessary costs relating to a single operating system roll out could have paid for an automated discovery tool.
- Patch management—adjusting defective software products—is an incredible financial drain on the IT budget.
- Reconcile all invoices for accuracy and follow up with providers.
- Locate and eliminate products that provide redundant services. Narrow them down to one or two.
- Monitor the IT environment to identify potential volume purchase opportunities to reduce costs.
- If you buy warranties, don't fix the systems yourself. If you fix the systems yourself, don't buy the warranties.
- Set effective acquisition and life cycle services expectations criteria for *all* tech purchases, then follow up to ensure they are met.

What questions should you be asking?

1. Where does this company stand on every one of the bullet points just covered? Create a matrix and chart it out.

Settlement: NJ – Architectural Firm - $49,642

2. Which of the listed issues can we rectify without incurring additional costs?

3. Which of the issues are costing us the most?

4. In what order can we address each issue?

5. What is the best guess estimation of cost recovery or savings we could generate by addressing this information?

6. Do we keep a lessons-learned book so we can learn from our mistakes as well as our successes?

Ready to move on?

You'll find even more savings ideas in the next chapter.

Chapter 10

How Can I Improve My IT Investments?

Chapter Goals: Finally, we have to move forward...

Set standards

Manage by exception

Set and manage criteria

Monitor support

Read the contract

Understand disposal

Negotiate Everything

Start - HERE

Industry experts have estimated that you will spend over $6 per software product in ongoing costs for every dollar you spend on the initial product. (And this does not include the huge investment you will make for implementation.) All that extra, mostly unbudgeted, revenue simply because we fail to effectively manage the software assets. Change the pattern — take control of your assets.

Standardize the Environment

Technology environments, by nature of their evolution, tend to be composed of diverse products — both hardware and software — as well as services. We grew fast and deliverables changed even faster. Successive releases of products, even within the same software publishers' product lines, are very frequently incompatible with one another. As consumers, we are facing on a nearly daily basis the need to purchase new hardware or software simply because the latest hardware, operating system, or software will not function correctly with legacy applications or systems.

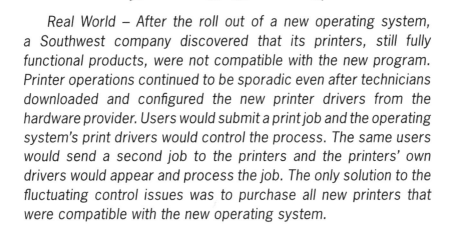

Real World – After the roll out of a new operating system, a Southwest company discovered that its printers, still fully functional products, were not compatible with the new program. Printer operations continued to be sporadic even after technicians downloaded and configured the new printer drivers from the hardware provider. Users would submit a print job and the operating system's print drivers would control the process. The same users would send a second job to the printers and the printers' own drivers would appear and process the job. The only solution to the fluctuating control issues was to purchase all new printers that were compatible with the new operating system.

Once you have conducted an automated review of corporate systems, you will have a detailed overview of brands, product names, versions, and releases that the company possesses. How many products are performing the same services? Could you reduce licenses of a given product (such as a word processing application in use in a single department) and consolidate all licenses into a single product line? If every desktop computer was of the same brand and model, and configured with the same software, wouldn't your acquisition personnel be more capable of accessing better volume purchase options? Even if you only purchase two to four computers at one time, wouldn't this concept still reduce costs?

Settlement: CA – Accounting Firm - $90,000

Consider, for instance, your cost for providing internal technical support. If your technicians were fully trained on a specific but narrow range of standardized corporate hardware and software titles, wouldn't your support costs be reduced? Consider the price, even if only in training time or learning curve, for your technical support personnel (and users) to become thoroughly familiar with multiple products — all of which provide the same functionality. If corporate printers were all standardized, support costs would drop, but so would the costs of consumables such as toner cartridges because, once again, you could purchase in quantities.

What products should you standardize? For now, start with desktops, printers, PDAs, pagers, cell phones, operating systems, and software. You will encounter some pretty stiff opposition to this concept. After all, each individual in the company, especially the executive staff, continues to believe that the new toys are for their enjoyment and status, rather than corporate productivity tools.

Real World – I visited the office of a director of technology support in an East Coast company. The two of us discussed the need to standardize products (in this case, PDAs) across the company. We were both concerned about which brand and model would effectively cover the widest range of actual needs. The director chuckled at my discussion of PDAs and opened a desk drawer to show me over a dozen iPACs. He had already encountered an entire executive staff that absolutely had to have iPACs, only to discover that the average executive was not computer savvy enough to effectively use the product. The costs of supporting this single executive perk nearly broke his support budget. He recalled all the iPACs and purchased $40 basic PDAs for the executives—inexpensive products that accurately reflected the

---

Settlement: CA – Interactive Entertainment Co. - $339,000

actual needs of the executive user: contact list (phone directory), scheduler, expenses, and memo/to do list. His support costs dropped immediately.

There are some users in every corporate environment (we all have them and we all appreciate their perspective) that have pretty much zero technical abilities beyond a basic etch-a-sketch™ skill set. I used the phrase *actual needs* in the example above. Keep in mind that actual needs are most often determined by the individual executives or engineers who must have the most complex—i.e. expensive—toys. The phrase has evolved away from productivity tools to refer, instead, to the latest executive status symbols. Your job as a software asset manager or technology asset manager is to bring the toys in line with the business requirements of the company.

In terms of software toys—how many **special employees** *do you have who absolutely must have the top of the line software packages? These could be the engineers who just have to have four different versions of that expensive CAD program—which means four different licenses on a single system. Or the scenario might include those executives who have to have the most complex (and expensive) professional desktop productivity suites—so they can periodically mis-type a memo. I've seen computers in custodial rooms that contained a full line of high end productivity software—with the custodians practically laughing over the mystery of "Why do we need this thing?"*

Settlement: CA – Health Manufacturing Co. - $130,000

Remember our brief discussion of cultural change management? This is a prime example of where your abilities to initiate and manage change—real human change—will come into play. The better you are at encouraging effective change, the more successful you will be as a technology asset manager.

Once you have standardized your environment—all the same basic hardware and software packages on each desktop—your costs for tracking assets will begin to drop. Remember when you ran your first automated audit? (*I know, you haven't even finished the book yet, let alone run the audit.*) Here is an overview of what happens. In that first audit run you discovered every software application and hardware configuration in the known universe, right? Your users appear to have had it all—way beyond Bogie and McCall. And what percentage of all those products were your fellow employees actually using?

Very few. Your next step is to follow up the first review with a careful process of eliminating unnecessary products. Move through this process slowly, recognizing that many products, though they initially appear to be unused, might only be accessed a few strategic times per year—such as an end of year financial application.

Each time you conduct a systems review, you will cull out more unnecessary products until you have narrowed down the environment to a core of products that serve a direct business purpose. These will be your standards. Once you reach this level of control, your audit tool can be modified to ignore the standard products and only alert you when a standard product is missing or a non standard product has been loaded.

Manage by Exception

You have finally reached the point where your actual software and hardware products, numbers, and versions are reduced to only the most effective business tools. How do you maintain control over the systems and ensure that unauthorized products do not creep in? This is the concept of manage by exception.

In this process you will begin monitoring your systems to ensure that all authorized copyrighted products remain configured, and unmodified, on each system. If an authorized product is not present, you will notice that it has been removed or modified when you review the discovery tool exception report. An effective discovery tool will also help you determine the date and, often, the time the product changed. For example, one of your users tends to download MP3s from his PDA onto his desktop. The exception report will note that music files have appeared on the system where, previously, no music files were located. Your next exception report will alert you to the new files and include the precise path to their location. Now, instead of forcing your way through a voluminous mass of raw data, you have reduced your focus to a narrow range of exceptions—systems changes.

In addition, you should now be capable of using your discovery tool to monitor the hardware itself. If a change has been made to the hardware, you will be alerted by the discovery tool, or you will catch it in your exception reports. For instance, you might be having problems with potentially defective RAM on select systems. Your exception report will locate any changes in RAM and note on the exception report that RAM on specific systems has dropped by 50%.

Essentially, once you have reached a given level of standardization, you will be capable of a much higher level of systems control as well as an enhanced awareness of systems changes. Standardization isn't just a matter of obtaining volume purchase options. It also applies to a full range of life cycle management issues.

Set and Monitor Criteria

Why did you buy this product? Why did you use this vendor? Why obtain this service? We spoke earlier in this text about the necessity of setting product criteria, as well as pro-vider criteria. If you had established clear criteria, how would you track them to determine your return on investment and satisfaction for a given product or service? Your configuration discovery tool will provide a percentage of this information but you still need the original criteria to measure against. Let's predict that you have established your original product crite-ria for software and hardware. Now it's time to follow up and monitor those criteria to evaluate deliverables.

Using the discovery tool, you can identify which products have required patches, or adjustments, across their life cycle or across another time span you might wish to measure. What if, during this time period, you determine that a given product has required abnormally high levels of modification and fo-cused attention by technical personnel? Will you then be able to predict future patch/fix costs for use in guestimating your budget figures? How about gaining the ability to document historic out of scope costs for use in renegotiating more fa-vorable future contractual agreements? Without clear criteria and without a clear view of your environment these costs are virtually invisible. You just keep on going over budget and you can't pin down the ultimate causes of the overruns.

*Set realistic criteria. Use your software asset man-agement tools to monitor deliverables in view of the expected criteria. Modify criteria and renegotiate con-tractual agreements that do not favor your company. After all, you **are** the customer, aren't you?*

Support (and maintenance) - Proven budgetary black hole...

Did you purchase ongoing technical support? Now that you have located your licenses and other agreements, I'll bet you know precisely what support levels apply to each product, right? Could you use this newly discovered (or simply refreshed) information to begin a formal process for tracking actual support use? You should now know the exact intensity of support you have contracted to receive. Next, establish how much of the support your personnel are actually using. If you cannot discover this internally, you have just discovered a serious potential financial problem; there may be no control over the relationship between contracted support levels and utilized support levels.

Okay, so you couldn't locate this information internally. That isn't a big surprise, but it doesn't necessarily mean the data is out of your reach. Try this: contact the provider and have them send you a report of the support your company actually acquired; if possible, also have them include when the support was requested and who requested it. If the supplier will not send you a report documenting support use, you might want to consider a new support resource. Let's pretend that you have your support summary in hand and we'll run through a savings opportunity scenario.

If you are paying $10,000 per year to support a given product and your technicians called in a total of two support requests, shouldn't you be seriously concerned that you're paying $5,000 per support contact? This cost per contact can be an indication that the original support criteria might have been incorrectly determined. What if, at your next renewal, you renegotiated this support contract to reflect a per contact fee of $500 for support calls? Based on your historic use, your future support fees could easily be reduced by 80%. Did you just save the company some pretty impressive money?

What if the support agreement we just reviewed was for a three year contract? At $10,000 per year, your company will pay out $30,000 in support fees over the life of the contract. If your agreement was based on the number of actual contacts, at $500 per contact, you would have spent approximately $3,000 for support of the same product—a savings of 90% for six contacts based on the two contacts per year mentioned previously.

Consider taking another step in this scenario. What if you modified the next support agreement to reflect a support fee of $500 *per incident*? A per incident agreement is even more economical for the consumer than a per contact agreement. Here's why. Let's say you have a $500 per contact agreement for router support. One of your routers decides to take a digital vacation and technicians require four calls to external support to correct the problem. In a per contact agreement, the cost of this single event was $500 times 4 contacts—or $2,000. If, on the other hand, you had negotiated a per incident support agreement, this single event would constitute one incident. Your total cost under the per incident agreement would have been only $500—a savings of $1500. This is a great example of how a trained technology asset manager can save a company significant dollars.

Remember the example of warranties? Companies don't track warranties so they tend to represent lost revenue. In this case, you can use your newly reorganized documentation coupled with your discovery tool to identify changes in systems under warranty. Remember, simply cracking the seal on a systems case can void the warranty. If a technician opens the case to modify the system, you'll know because the exception report will note the changes. If you have negotiated an agreement that your company performs the actual warranty work then reports it for re-imbursement, you will now have clear documentation not only of the repair but also of the initial failure that made the repair necessary.

How does this relate to criteria? Once again, thanks to your newly organized documentation and discovery tool, you will have solid documentation for repair trends on specific corporate systems. If you begin now to track these over time, the next time you set criteria for systems acquisitions you will be

Settlement: TX – Engineering Firm - $100,000

capable of more accurately determining the brand and model system that requires the least service. Your new criteria can now be based on statistical strategic information rather than Guido's opinion.

Set your criteria using strategic information. Evaluate products and services to assure that they meet criteria throughout their life cycles. Periodically review criteria and, if necessary, modify them to ensure that they remain valid.

Manage Vendor Deliverables

If you are not already managing vendors, it is time you started to do so. I constantly encounter companies that are dissatisfied with their vendors or product providers. Why, in this incredibly competitive world, would you remain with a vendor that provided goods or services that were not delivering a satisfactory return on your investment?

Wait. Let me guess. You do not monitor vendor service levels because your CEO plays golf with some of your vendor CEOs? Am I close? How about this one: because we have always done business with them? Want one more? How about: they're the biggest name company providing the product? Is there anything in those three statements that even implies the quality of the product or service? We've discussed criteria ad nauseum but here it is again. If you do not establish deliverable criteria expectations for vendors, you will not be capable of measuring their performance. If you do not monitor the degree to which a vendor conforms to a certain standard of service or quality, how will you know when you are getting your money's worth?

Real World – If you know that a specific vendor habitually produces invoices with numerous errors, would you continue

Settlement: TX – Computer Training Co. - $66,387

*working with the vendor? Would you search for displacement products? Would you dedicate an employee to closely monitor every invoice the vendor submits? Would you do **anything** proactive?*

When I mention this interesting little habit in a training seminar nearly half of the attendees present will correctly identify the vendor without my having to even ask who it is. Do you work with a vendor like this? Want to bet money on it? (Because you are probably *already* betting, and losing, money on it.)

Read Every Contract

I have yet to see a technology-related contractual agreement that did not contain significant traps for the consumer. I always hope that the trend isn't a matter of sharp practices on the part of suppliers but is, instead, a reflection of how the legal profession has impacted our potential business relationships. As Jimmy Buffit says, *"Fins to the left. Fins to the right and you're the only bait in town."* People always seem to be looking over their shoulders at the next potential litigation event. Unfortunately, the average corporate technology consumer is not in this group.

How many of your software contracts have you read? No, wait. I mean *really* read? Let me guess. None. You aren't alone. Somehow, while we fully intend to read these documents, we just never quite get around to doing so. "So what?" you say. "After all, it's just software. And, besides, this vendor won't sue me. We're friends." Dream on. Let's take a look at what thrilling twists of plot we miss when we fail to read the contract.

Example License Clause: *Licensor warrants for a period of one year from the Acceptance Date that the Programs, unless modified by Licensee, will perform the functions described* *in the Documentation provided by Licensor when operated on the Designated System.*

Problem? What does this clause tell you? First of all, the product is warranted for one year from the acceptance date. Did you define an acceptance dating process in the agreement? Did you include an acceptance testing and evaluation process in the agreement? I think I can answer this for you: no. The reason I know is because this clause came from a selection of shrink wrap licenses — the ones you can't negotiate.

Solution? We already discussed not buying shrink wrap. In case you didn't already get the message — don't buy shrink wrap products for your company. However, this same clause will very frequently show up buried in many other licenses — even those you negotiate. Why? Because consumers do not read their licenses and the clause slips by without being challenged. Since you did not set a testing process or date of acceptance, the vendor will determine it for you. Their interpretation will usually be the date you paid for or received the product. Either way, those dates may be a long way from the date you actually install the software only to discover that it doesn't perform the functions you expected.

In addition, you will find that the acceptance date noted in this clause will be the one that controls your technical support. Most suppliers are quite aware that products may not be brought into immediate use by the consumer. Using this arbitrary acceptance date can, and will, represent significant reduction in the actual useful life cycle of the *included* support. You could very easily be paying support fees on a product that is sitting on a shelf awaiting implementation simply because you did not clarify and control the acceptance date.

This product is warranted to perform the functions as described in the documentation provided when operated on the

---

Settlement: CA – Television Production Co. - $40,000

designated system. Did I miss the part about the product functioning according to the buyer's—your—criteria? When you purchase a product, you expect that product to provide some clearly defined business service—your acquisition criteria. When did the buyer lose control over the required functionality? Of course, if you haven't clearly defined the criteria you expect, the provider will define it for you.

And this thing about the designated system? What happens if the computer using this particular product dies? Can you simply relocate the product onto a replacement system? Maybe you can, but probably you cannot. After all—remember the tendency to interpret the letter of the agreement rather than the spirit? The agreement *does* clearly state *designated* system. Maybe you can get written permission from the provider to relocate the product. Of course, it'll take a while and the system will be unusable until permission is granted. Then again, maybe the provider will just let the problem pass—at least until you are audited for non compliance.

Am I acting paranoid again? Absolutely. My task with this content is to alert you to the possibilities of negative scenarios, not paint a pretty picture of loving business relationships with vendors who never sue their customers. While we all hope for great win/win vendor relations, the realities of our world necessitate that we take responsibility to protect our companies (and ourselves) from the potential problems we might have to face after the money changes hands. Remember the *right to audit* clause?

Let's take a look at one more invisible element of a fairly standard license clause. You're going to love this one.

Example License Clause: (The copyright holder and its representatives will) *...provide the Product and support services (if any) AS IS AND WITH ALL FAULTS, and hereby disclaim all other warranties and conditions, either express, implied or statutory, including, but not limited to, any (if any) implied* *warranties, duties or conditions of merchantability, of fitness for a particular purpose, of reliability or availability, of accuracy..., of results, of workmanlike effort, of lack of viruses, and of lack of negligence, all with regard to the Product...*

Problems? The product and services are provided *as is and with all faults*? You work in, or own, a business, right? Are the products and services your company produces covered by a clause such as this? I rather doubt it. This clause scares me to death — and it should scare you, too. You are paying big money for products that the producer tells you up front could easily be defective. Not only could the products be defective but the producer of the product will not be responsible for the defects, or the lack of fitness for a particular use, or the product reliability, or the accuracy or completeness of support, or the quality of workmanship, or the presence of viruses, or...the list goes on.

Read your agreements before you permit yourself or your company to be legally bound by them. Read the agreements and be certain they are acceptable *before* you hand over the money. Read the agreements and do not buy the product if you cannot negotiate a mutually beneficial agreement with the provider.

Create a cheat sheet of contract clauses for use in negotiations. Build two lists. The first is a list of clauses you will accept in contracts, licenses, and agreements. The second list is composed of clauses you will not accept. Prioritize both lists according the most important to the least important clause. Keep the lists up to date with constant reviews of old and new clauses. Use the lists in negotiations to build

Settlement: CA – Internet Co. - $33,000

> agreements that represent your interests as well as those of the provider.

Understand & Control Disposal

How many computers has your company disposed of over the past ten years? Who took them away? Where did the individual items go? If asked, could you prove that your systems were disposed of according to federal guidelines?

Wait. Am I suggesting that there are federal guidelines for disposing of computers? Well... Yes, and no. Up until recently, asset management personnel didn't consider the potential for technologies to have a negative impact on our environment. Unused hardware simply went into the dumpster or out to the curb for pickup. Unfortunately, all of this hardware, in the form of circuit boards, cathode ray tubes, batteries, and etc. has begun to show up in land fills and other not-so-legal dumping grounds. Also, unfortunately, this same hardware is simply *loaded* with toxic chemicals (Pick one, *any* one). Finally, just to keep us all in panic mode, the Environmental Protection Agency (EPA) is permitted to fine us up to $10,000 per toxic chemical if hardware that is disposed of illegally can be traced back to our companies.

> In 1999, experts from Carnegie Mellon estimated that as much as 70% of all no longer useful computer products were squirreled away in attics, closets, and other storage locations.

Somebody finally discovered the impact that we were beginning to have on our environment and, once again, the rules have changed. I think, though, that we can all get behind this particular requirement. After all, it's our drinking water that's in danger of being polluted, right?

Settlement: CA – Glazing Contractor - $25,000

What you will need to do is ensure that you carefully track the disposal process for every potentially toxic item. Don't panic on me. This isn't as difficult as it first appears. The most effective way to address this problem is to ensure that you retain a qualified disposal service. (*Do not even* think *of calling Vinnie!*) There are multiple options for disposal services. Some will charge you to haul materials away. Some will pay you because they can recycle the systems or recover the precious metals. (*Let's see. Which one should you hire? Good thinking!*)

The key is that you need to ensure that the disposal company is approved for disposing of toxic materials. Then you will have to keep very clear records of the materials the company picks up. Include serial numbers wherever possible and ensure that the authorized company agent signs off on specific lists of products they collect. Also, and check with your legal people on this, ensure that you have a clear document, signed by the disposal company, that transfers all responsibility for disposal to that company.

Real World – In California, the e-Waste Recycling Act (of 2003) tacks on a $6-$10 disposal fee to the initial cost of any cathode ray based (tube) product. In Boston, MA, landfill operators can be fined up to $25,000 for accepting televisions, computer monitors, or other cathode tube products. (In 1992, the EPA banned cathode ray tubes entirely from all landfills.)

How does this effect your business? The hardware industries are pushing hard to pass legislation that places the responsibility— thus, the cost—for disposal on the consumer. Once again, we are confronted with an industry that creates toxic materials and, through extensive lobbying, wants the public (that means you) to pay to clean up the mess.

Settlement: CA – Online Entertainment Co. - $70,000

You might be wise to monitor legislation addressing disposal of toxic substances—computer circuit boards, batteries, monitors, cell phones, toner cartridges, and etc—to ensure that your needs are represented in the eventual laws.

What toxic chemicals or ferrous metals are hiding inside our tech toys? The chemicals include, but are not limited to, lead (as much as 5-8 pounds), mercury, lithium, cadmium, and PCBs. Metals include, but aren't limited to, gold, platinum, silver, copper, and steel.

There is a good chance that you are sitting here becoming upset because you donate systems to charities or those in need. If that's the case, relax. Some of the more effective disposal companies will actually provide you with a donation program where-in they issue a charity of your choice vouchers toward purchasing a new or used system — based on the materials you turn in for disposal. This is actually a good idea because it lightens the load on your favorite cause. They no longer have to force old systems to work. Instead, they collect the vouchers until they have enough — then they acquire a new and reliable system. An additional plus is that, check with your CPA, you could easily get the deduction for the donation.

Constantly Update Disaster Recovery!

Toward the end of Chapter 7, I discussed the critical nature of disaster recovery in terms of licenses and documentation. I won't repeat it now, but it is critical that you keep in mind:

- All documentation — originals or the copies — must be duplicated at your off site disaster recovery facility.

Settlement: CA – Environmental Planning Co. - $120,000

> » The off site copies will permit you to prove that you actually owned valid product after the disaster obliterates your on site originals.

- At least once a quarter, you should include copies of your raw discovery tool reports in the materials maintained off site.

> » This will enable you to recover every computing device to reflect its precise configuration prior to the disaster event.

- Or you could enjoy truly valuable quality time, not to mention money, arguing with the copyright holders and insurance companies after the event.

Negotiate Everything

This is the big one—negotiating. Actually, negotiating isn't the big one; as technology consumers, our *failure* to negotiate is the big one.

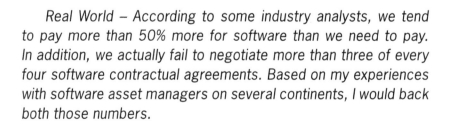

Real World – According to some industry analysts, we tend to pay more than 50% more for software than we need to pay. In addition, we actually fail to negotiate more than three of every four software contractual agreements. Based on my experiences with software asset managers on several continents, I would back both those numbers.

Why would we fail to negotiate? One reason is that many IT providers, and I'm certain that they do not do this on purpose, intimidate consumers with their rigid prices and subtle verbal cues. Time and again, in negotiations sessions, I have

---

Settlement: CA – Manufacturing Co. - $80,000

heard vendors make the, "That's our price" comment — without the strongly implied, *"Take it or leave it,"* tacked on at the end. Many consumers, hungry for their over-due techno-drug fix, immediately panic and pay the fee (ransom?). After all, if you don't pay, they'll take their bright, shiny, new, state-of-the-art toys and go play in someone else's sandbox, right? Wouldn't you just love to tell them to go ahead and leave?

That's exactly the way I often feel. As soon as some suppliers know that you are 100% dependent on their products, the price goes up, the service goes down; quality begins to suffer, and the demands escalate. Are you the customer? Is this your money that you are spending? Try pointing out the door to these hard nosed negotiators a couple times and see what changes take place in your relationship.

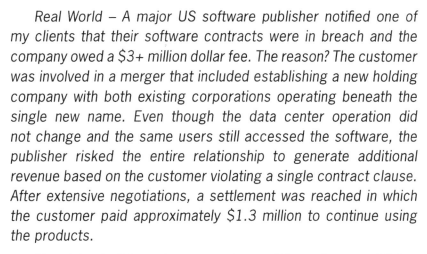

Real World – A major US software publisher notified one of my clients that their software contracts were in breach and the company owed a $3+ million dollar fee. The reason? The customer was involved in a merger that included establishing a new holding company with both existing corporations operating beneath the single new name. Even though the data center operation did not change and the same users still accessed the software, the publisher risked the entire relationship to generate additional revenue based on the customer violating a single contract clause. After extensive negotiations, a settlement was reached in which the customer paid approximately $1.3 million to continue using the products.

My advice to this customer was to send the software publisher away. We even located displacement products for the software in question for the initial cost of $90,000. The customer went ahead and paid the additional millions, citing the justification that changing products would disrupt business operations.

Settlement: CA – Manufacturing Co. - $63,000

Wouldn't it be nice to have this kind of spare change laying around the office? (For more information regarding how this type of practice can impact your company, take a look at the article discussing Stiffing & Sharp Practices on the biztechnet.org web site.)

"We're too small to negotiate." I have certainly encountered this one frequently enough. Too small is a single computer—and even that can be parleyed into reduced prices if you are stubborn enough. The point is, as soon as you reveal your absolute need to acquire their product, you are doomed to pay their prices. Then, once you pay the initial amount, you will probably find yourself continuing the trend with every subsequent purchase.

Real World – You can purchase two- or three-user business packages for a fraction of the total price of three single licenses—if you know where and when to look for the deals. You can also purchase preconfigured systems and simply standardize on the products already installed. Be careful, though. Remember the hard disk loaders and our failure to acquire or retain accurate receipts? If you know how to use upgrades, go ahead and buy them—again, carefully. Instead of buying a professional office suite for your single computer company simply purchase a compatible word processing application that includes a spreadsheet function.

Here is an easy cost reduction option: track the dates that your providers end their fiscal year. Time your acquisitions to occur several months prior to these

Settlement: CA – Disability Benefits Co. - $160,000

dates and close the deal the day before year end. Care to wager on your chances of obtaining some pretty interesting discounts?

"We're the industry standard." This third reason for failing to negotiate never ceases to amaze me. Who made this particular company or product the industry standard? Are they the only viable game in town? If so, they can be the industry standard. Otherwise, any product or service has plenty of competitive products or services from which you can choose—if you understand how to choose.

For every negotiation you must have at least one BATNA, Best Alternative to a Negotiated Agreement. If you have an alternative product or service to the one being negotiated, the provider loses significant power over your buying decision. If you do not have an alternative product, one your company is willing to commit to, you will lose every negotiation.

"I don't know how to negotiate." This is most often the core of our problems. The people who purchase technologies are frequently either not experienced technicians or not experienced negotiators. Do your purchasing people have a clear understanding of the unique requirements of technology acquisitions? Do they understand the precise way the products and services are actually being used on the front line? Do they work closely with the asset manager and technology personnel to identify criteria and ensure that the proper controls and guidelines are negotiated into every agreement?

Settlement: TX – Engineering Firm - $43,250

Real World – In the "price of support" auto-renewals example in the previous chapter, was the contract correctly negotiated? Remember, if the license stated renewals were priced at 15% of the publisher's list price, your company wound up paying twice as much for the support. If the license agreement clause read 15% of the purchase price, your company saved considerable revenue.

In general, only an experienced negotiator with knowledge of technology life cycle utilization — or direct input from technology asset management experts — could have caught the potential difference. Are you a trained negotiator? How much training have you had? Do you know the key license and agreement terms and conditions? When you enter a negotiations session, are you thoroughly prepared?

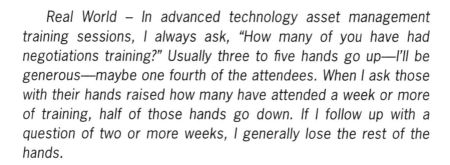

Real World – In advanced technology asset management training sessions, I always ask, "How many of you have had negotiations training?" Usually three to five hands go up—I'll be generous—maybe one fourth of the attendees. When I ask those with their hands raised how many have attended a week or more of training, half of those hands go down. If I follow up with a question of two or more weeks, I generally lose the rest of the hands.

In general, as corporate consumers, we are not training our technology asset managers — that would be, you — to negotiate.

Settlement: TX – Manufacturing & Engineering Co - $100,000

When you walk into a negotiation session with the average technology product representative or sales person, you will be sitting across the table from someone with *months* of negotiations training. Coupled with all of that time learning negotiation techniques, the average rep also invests a significant amount of their professional time conducting actual negotiations. Open the door to any negotiations session and watch the process.

There you sit, the technology consumer, the person with money to spend on technology products and services, the one with virtually no negotiations training, and the one who negotiates around ten total hours per year. You are *not* going to win. (If you want to change this trend and take more control, look at the *Real World Negotiations Series* on the biztechnet. org web site.)

Mergers & Acquisitions

Consider how often companies buy other companies, merge into new entities, and sell their corporation to another. Software license compliance and technologies inventories represent significant, and hidden costs of M&A activities. The most frequent approach to an M&A assurance audit happens when technicians from one company review systems of another to check to see if both companies' environments will be compatible.

If you are, or might be, involved in an M&A process, it is your responsibility to conduct a compliance audit on the company being absorbed or sold. If this audit is performed prior to the transfer of ownership negotiations, the costs to set problems straight can become part of the acquisition fees. If this pre-acquisition audit has not been conducted, you could find a very unpleasant compliance confrontation in your future.

Real World – A Chicago company acquired another organization. The acquisition was announced publicly and, shortly there-after, the company was contacted by a copyright enforcement entity. It seems that the company that was acquired was not compliant with its software licenses. The settlement for the incorrectly licensed software—not applicable to the acquisition costs because that transaction had already been concluded—exceeded $200,000. (Don't forget to multiply by 3 to 6 to estimate actual event impact.)

Is a merger or acquisition in your future? If you are selling your company, you can increase the value by conducting and certifying your compliance as part of the selling fee. If you are acquiring a company, you should conduct your own compliance audit of the company to ensure no unpleasant surprises show up later on. In addition, it is important to note that an effective discovery tool will also identify and document the presence — or absence — of hardware and much of its internal components.

Real World – During discussions with a financial institution about the value of a discovery tool, an executive mentioned that the institution had accepted a company's stock of notebook computers as a loan guarantee. The lending institution had no automated evidence confirming the borrower even possessed the notebooks in question.

Settlement: FL – Payphone Service Co. - $123,500

A simple controlled discovery tool run of the borrower's environment would have documented the precise number of notebook computers as well as their actual configuration.

Consider Open Source Products

No. I mean *seriously* consider using open source products. What is open source, anyway? Basically, the concept and definitions of open source have evolved quite a bit over the past few years. One of the easiest ways to illustrate open source is to explain its opposite — proprietary software.

Proprietary software is a product, or range of products, that are wholly owned by the copyright holder. These applications distinguish themselves because licensees (that's you and me) are provided with the program — not the source code on which the program is based. In this case, control over the source code translates into full control over the product. Essentially, only developers authorized by the copyright holder can gain access to, and modify, the source code — therefore only a limited scope of personnel have the ability to enhance the given program. Another interesting aspect of proprietary code is that, theoretically, only the copyright holder is generally permitted to investigate and modify the code for defects.

Real World – Two of the (in my opinion relatively lame) reasons the proprietary software industry cites for not using open source are that a.) the code is not warranted to be free of defects, and b.) the code is not warranted to be free of viruses. Guess what? Neither are most proprietary products. At least, with open source, you can do something if the product is defective. With proprietary products you have to assume that the copyright holder will act responsibly and adjust the product, because you certainly can't do anything to help yourself.

Settlement: MN – Commercial Printing Co. - $260,000

Products based on open source code are different than proprietary products. With open source, you control the code so you can generally modify or enhance it as necessary, and the changed application is yours for no charge. Any changes you might want made to proprietary code will not only involve substantial fees from the copyright holder but, once those changes are made, (at your expense) they quite frequently become the property of the original copyright holder—meaning you'll get to pay for them again at some later time.

Is there more? Oh, yes. However, this is not the forum for a diatribe on open source. Consider this, though: many open source products are free, or nearly free, to acquire and use. In general terms they are every bit as secure and dependable as proprietary products (*actually, in my experience more so*). In addition, open source represents a sort of cooperative ongoing project. This means that companies and people just like you are constantly digging into the source code to enhance it and make it more valuable as well as developing—and sharing—additional necessary features. A significant key to using open source products is this: *you are in control of the product*—not some software publisher. I shouldn't have to mention how important it is to gain and maintain control of your environment—this should be an absolute priority.

An example of potential value in open source is represented by the desktop productivity product Open Office. This product could very easily replace the major professional office suites currently in use in virtually every small to medium sized company. And the cost? Let's see... Nothing. Yep, it's a free open source product. Take a look at the following excerpt from the Open Office license on my computer:

2.1 Initial Writer Grant (of license)

Writer...grants You a world-wide, royalty-free, non-exclusive license to use, reproduce, prepare Modifications of, compile, publicly perform, publicly display, demonstrate, market, disclose and distribute the Documentation in any form, on any

---

Settlement: KS – Software Development Co. - $263,423

media, or via any Electronic Distribution Mechanism...and to sublicense the foregoing rights to third parties... (Thanks to: openoffice.org)

If you can find rights like these in any proprietary product, I'd be amazed. Besides, why, oh why, would you pay up to $300 per computer for a product when you can get essentially the same functionality at no cost—not to mention at no risk for piracy litigation. Want to cut one to six copyrighted products from your environment? This is only one of many options for doing so.

> *If your company has the attitude that "we can only use this single proprietary product so we can remain compatible with other companies" you may have addiction issues. Or maybe you just enjoy spending more and being subject to random piracy audits.*

For detailed information on open source, look at: www.opensource.org.

Upgrade those OEM Licenses?

Do not even *think* of applying an upgrade license to an Original Equipment Manufacturer (OEM) licensed product. In general, the OEM license is between you and the hardware manufacturer that built your system. In other words, if Dell™ built your systems, the operating system and software that company placed on the systems is actually licensed by Dell—not, for instance, by Microsoft™. Since this license is not with the copyright holder, very few upgrade options are applicable. Essentially, and most frequently, if you want to move up from an

OEM licensed product, you have to purchase an entirely new fully licensed product to qualify. As usual, read the original OEM—as well as—the new license.

Yes, you can be in violation if you upgrade a product that doesn't qualify. Remember, the kid behind the counter at the local office supply store has no clue. In fact, I have found multiple qualified resellers that don't have much of a clue, either. After all, their primary job is to sell the product. Although the number of resellers who might make this mistake is in the minority, *you* will still be the one named in the piracy suit.

Put your systems to sleep!

Do your systems operate in the green? Not long ago, I heard a statistic claiming that as few as one third of all corporate computers are actually being utilized during any given business operations hour. (I'm still looking for a source to validate this stat.) If this is true, what would happen if you set every desktop computer to "go to sleep" after ten minutes idle time?

According to the EPA, you could save as much as $100 per year on your power bills per system. Would this represent a reasonable ROI on a very simple modification on your technical and cultural environment?

To calculate this for yourself, locate your power provider cost per kilowatt hour and total up the number of KWH used by a "standard" computer in a single business day. Multiply the figures together, then multiply the resulting total by your company's total number of operational days per year. The final figure will be the cost of that single computer (don't forget the monitor). Now multiply this figure by the total number of computers your company owns. Interesting concept?

And it will cost you essentially nothing to implement this cost saving option.

Professional Networking

We spend so much time re-inventing the tech asset management wheel that I'm often amazed we accomplish anything efficiently. For some odd reason corporations are so wrapped up in their ultra secret internal societies that they frequently refuse to communicate with other corporations. The technology industries have managed to utilize this isolationist attitude to divide us and conquer us. It never ceases to amaze me how often software and technology asset managers are quite frankly afraid to speak out. The reasons? Their company will not permit them to network with other asset managers — or, if they are permitted, they're not allowed to discuss their negotiations, licensing, asset management techniques, or anything else for that matter. Others are actually afraid to speak out because a given software publisher, enforcement group, or some industry *force* will take it personally and... And what? (*I never get an answer. Just a fearful look.*)

So, let's see. Picture an entire globe covered by corporate technology consumers purchasing more than $59 billion in software in a single year. If we interpret the statistics another way, these same companies are investing as much as 60% of their yearly IT budgets in software or related products and services. (Source: BSA and IDC Global Piracy Report) Here is my point: together, the corporate technology consumers represent a formidable force for global change — but not while we refuse to work together to effect that change. If you are thinking that I'm being unrealistic, (*I have been accused of being a convicted altruist.*) then keep in mind that the technology industry players spend significant time and money working together to develop more sophisticated methods of dipping their collective fingers into our respective pocketbooks. Basically, as long as the majority of companies insist on playing the "Lone Tech Consumer Ranger," global changes will be done to us — not by us.

Want to improve the industry? Then, network and communicate with one another in a meaningful way. Work together to develop strategies for countering the license tactics, piracy auditing tactics, product feature bloat, price gouging, and all the other issues we tend to whine about over by the espresso machine.

Not long ago, I was invited to a conference of software publishers. The theme? Licensing strategies. (*These people have to be nuts to invite me to this particular conference...*) Unfortunately, I couldn't go—which probably saved me from spending a day or two in the conference host city jail for instigating a public disruption. Even more unfortunately, I have yet to be invited—or been permitted to attend (because I'm not a customer)—many other conferences that purport to represent the global software or technology consumer. As long as we prevent one another from effective networking to enact changes, we will remain the victims of our own isolation.

What have we learned today?

- Setting standards for hardware, software, support, and services will significantly reduce life cycle costs.

- Once you have completed your automated audit and set standards for hardware and software, you can cut costs through managing assets by exception—if it is there and should be there, ignore it—if it is there and should not be there, highlight & remove it—if it is there, should be there, but has been modified, check it out.

- Set and manage life cycle criteria for every operational IT asset. Ensure that you get your money's worth or find another product or service that will provide it to you.

- Few companies invest any significant time in seriously reading the contracts that accompany tech products. Start doing so.

- Negotiate everything. Let me put this a different way— *negotiate everything*.

Settlement: CA – Engineering Firm - $134,000

Questions you could be asking.

1. What systems and software standards do we have in place?

2. What standards are in use by effective members of our industry?

3. How can we transform our operations to include the bullet points above in the day-to-day operation?

4. Who monitors our IT-related contractual obligations?

5. Who negotiates agreements and what criteria do they follow?

6. Which software products (or operating systems) in my environment could be converted to open source? How much could I save the company by doing so?

7. Are you "putting your systems to sleep?"

Are we finished? How much did you save, today? Do me a favor: how did the suggestions in this book impact you or your business? Email me a note with the details.

Want to save more? Please look over the conclusion and summary on the following pages. You'll be glad you did.

Author's Conclusion

So, there you have it. In the pages between my introduction and this conclusion you have been exposed to a wide range of frequently hidden software and copyright piracy issues and methodologies. You should have located savings opportunities that potentially reflect cost reductions of at least 5%-10% of your technology budget. Some of the savings will be for cost avoidance. Some will be for reduced operations costs. If I have been unclear, if you have additional questions, or if you have comments about the content, feel free to send me an email at pirates@biztechnet.org. Also, if you noticed a subject or issue that I may have left out or explained incorrectly, let me know and I'll review, then modify the next release of *Modern Pirates*.

For now, here is a quick review of some of the strategic information you should come away with after reading *Pirates*

- Make yourself and your organization clearly aware that the average company loses significantly more revenue through non-management of technology assets than it will ever lose through non compliance or piracy litigation.

- Executive management: wake up, learn about the risks you are taking, and provide genuine leadership and open support for your software and technology asset managers. Please do not use these people as scapegoats. Remember SOX: do you want to look good?

- Appoint, train, and *enable* qualified professionals to manage software and technology assets throughout their life cycles. Then listen to, and act upon, their recommendations.

341

- Acquire technology products based on your actual needs criteria—not sales hype. If products do not meet criteria, do not accept them.

- Do not buy shrink wrapped copyrighted products for your business. The licenses are in no way favorable to the consumer and the prices are never acceptable.

- Do not accept click wrap licenses for the same reasons.

- *Never* accept a legal agreement that you cannot negotiate. Ensure that your negotiation teams are fully trained and qualified to negotiate realistic technology agreements.

- Always consider including mutually beneficial alternative dispute resolution clauses in every technology agreement.

- Conduct an intelligent review of your criteria in terms of potential products then seriously consider acquiring and using open source products whenever possible.

- Do not be afraid to *displace* existing products or services if they do not meet your expectations or your budget.

- Monitor enforcement industry practices and consider boycotting products from copyright holders that regularly sue their customers for non compliance. This is particularly true if the copyright holder will not permit you to negotiate mutually favorable license (or agreement) terms and conditions.

- Demand that governments take action to regulate the enforcement industry and require *every* enforcement entity to formally report its activities. (Take a look at the footers of this book for a non threatening way to report activities.)

- Always check and verify receipts, proofs of purchase, and documents of authenticity. Be absolutely certain that all details are present, and accurate. Be certain you actually *receive* all documentation.

- Ensure that purchases are made through qualified resellers. Then monitor those resellers to confirm that your licenses and documentation were actually registered with the copyright holders.

- Ensure that license-related documents are properly filed and secured.

- Ensure that copies of all license-related documentation and configuration reports are deployed to your off site disaster recovery facility.

- Do not dispose of software license- and purchase-related documentation without a careful review of the environment to ensure they are no longer required.

- Read and summarize every single copyrighted product license agreement. Become clearly aware of your utilization requirements. (*Read this one twice. It's* that *important.*)

- Track the movement of licensed products across the enterprise and across their entire life cycles. Know precisely where every licensed product is located at all times.

- Create, publicize, and *enforce* effective technology policies. Ensure that policies explain not only what must be done but why it must be done. Review policies regularly and keep them up to date.

- Prepare a formal strategic compliance audit reaction process to use in countering an audit threat. Ensure that all management personnel are made aware of, and follow, the process.

- Acquire and implement an effective configuration discovery tool — one that meets *your* unique corporate criteria. Then ensure that the tool is actually used.

- Monitor local, national, and international legislation activities and *speak out* against legislation that favors the rights of the technology producers at the expense of the consumer. (Remember, if you don't do anything about what's being done in legislation, you will eventually find that what is being done is being done to you!)

- Demand that government entities base legislation on research conducted by industry neutral organizations that have no financial or operational links to special interest software or hardware corporations.

- Create, and maintain, a thorough lessons learned book to track your successes and failures.

- Develop a very clear understanding of your corporate culture and the individual personalities that make it up. Be certain all activities and projects take cultural needs into consideration.

- Network honestly and frequently with other asset management professionals.

The savings you realize from following these bullet points, alone, will easily justify the cost of this book. I wish you luck in managing your technology assets. If you need advice or assistance, our web site (biztechnet.org) is only a click away.

Software & Technology License Agreements

Now, please take a quick look at the following pages to catch a glimpse of the next book in the Real World Knowledge Series. *License Agreements* covers critical knowledge that you will require to review, understand, and negotiate beneficial software licenses, and other agreements.

Coming Soon!

Software & Technology License Agreements

Book Two of the Real World Knowledge Series

By Alan L. Plastow

Introduction excerpt:

What knowledge, training and perspectives should you acquire to review, understand, and negotiate beneficial software licenses and other technology agreements? In a series of surveys conducted over a three year period and involving hundreds of front line professionals, I have determined that a majority of software and technology asset managers does not have clear knowledge of the impact of specific terms and conditions on the corporation. Nor do many of the corporations represented by these beleaguered personnel fully comprehend the cumulative effects of ineffectively negotiated agreements on the life cycles of software and hardware assets.

It is extremely difficult to negotiate favorable agreements when one party in the negotiation process doesn't have the same level of strategic knowledge or sophistication as their counterpart. The technology industry, and software publishers in particular, invest enormous time and money in developing favorable (to them) template licenses and agreements. In addition, these same companies ensure that their sales and negotiation personnel have been provided with exhaustive formal training in tactical negotiations as well as being backstopped by an extensive support network of strategic data and content area experts. Add to this the fact that most technology sales personnel conduct negotiations for a living—nearly every day—negotiation after negotiation and it is little wonder that their at-the-table experience levels are enormous.

What does your company have to counter these forces? Most frequently, no person or group of people, in the average corporate consumer organization can come close to this level of sophistication. (Obvious question: who's going to win?) *License Agreements* provides the average software and technology asset manager, as well as other concerned business professionals, with knowledge and tactics necessary to negotiate more effectively.

Below are several excerpts from *License Agreements* that are virtually guaranteed to save your company significant revenue and executive heartache. Please keep in mind that I am not a lawyer. I am not providing you with legal advice. The focus of this text is to attempt to explain, in the language of real human beings, some major contractual terms and conditions and the ways in which they will impact your company. Always review any legal document with qualified legal professionals before signing. (*Oh, and of great importance, you can move significantly closer to the head of the license knowledge class simply by actually* reading *the documents before agreeing to them. Most businesses don't.*)

License Terms and Conditions Examples:

Clause

"State of Governing Law"

This clause is included in virtually every technology agreement. In its simplest intent, the state of governing law clause provides the litigation and legislative framework for the agreement. Under what specific laws will this agreement be regulated?

Impact

If the state mentioned in this clause is Maryland or Virginia, then your company will be bound by the laws of one of these states. Since both of them are states where the Uniform Computer Information Transaction Act (UCITA) has been passed into law, you will most probably be bound by its terms. (*More on this in the upcoming book.*)

Also, if the state of governing law is a state where a Super Digital Millennium Copyright Act is valid, you could find yourself in significant difficulties simply for using a virtual private network, a security firewall, or any device or service that allows you to transmit or receive anonymously over the Internet.

Counter

Do not permit the state of governing law to be Maryland or Virginia, or any state where legislation (such as SDMCA) has been enacted that is exclusively favorable to your counterpart's industry. (*More on this in the upcoming book.*)

Clause

"Right to Audit"

The right to audit clause signifies your willingness to permit the copyright holder, or its representative, to audit your company for compliance.

Impact

You need to be aware that, with this clause in your license, your company can, and will, be audited by the copyright holder or its representatives to ensure ongoing compliance with license terms and conditions. As noted in *Modern Pirates*, this is one process that can cost you significant unbudgeted revenue along with public damage to your corporate credibility.

Counter

You actually have three choices with this clause. First, you can ignore it and hope that no compliance-related problems arise. (After reading *Modern Pirates*, you should know that this option is pure fantasy.)

Second, you can eliminate the phrase "or its representatives" from the clause. If written correctly, this should have the effect of taking the independent membership compliance enforcement companies out of the equation. Removing this phrase, alone, could cut your audit risk by as much as 60%.

Third, you can eliminate this entire clause. The copyright holder (or its representatives) would then not be permitted to audit you for compliance. To gain this option, you might want to establish a voluntary audit reporting and reconciliation process in its place. This process would permit your company to conduct its own periodic audits and report the findings in a non-confrontational manner. It also might include the option of reconciling license short-falls should they occur and be voluntarily reported. (*More on this in the upcoming book.*)

Clause

"Alternative Dispute Resolution"

An alternative dispute resolution (ADR) clause will provide mutually agreeable options for settling any disagreements between the contractual parties that stop short of litigation. Options include, but may not be limited to, mediation, arbitration, binding arbitration, and mediation followed by arbitration.

Impact

The most significant impact of this particular clause is that it seems to be conspicuously absent from the majority of technology agreements. Without an ADR clause, the parties in the agreement, you and the provider of goods or services, will generally find yourselves confronting one another across the litigation table should you have a disagreement.

Counter

Ensure that every agreement has a mutually beneficial clause that clearly spells out the steps to be taken in the event of a disagreement between parties. (*More on this in the upcoming book.*)

Want to change your industry?

How many terms and conditions are included in the average technology agreement? What do they mean? Should you negotiate modifications or eliminate them? How can you stop the current trend of technology agreements favoring only the producer of the goods? How can you modify agreements to provide mutual comfort and value to the parties involved?

Look for and read—

Software & Technology License Agreements
Book Two of the Real World Knowledge Series
By Alan L. Plastow